CONFESSION AND RESISTANCE

CONFESSION AND RESISTANCE

Defining the Self
in Late Medieval England

KATHERINE C. LITTLE

University of Notre Dame Press
Notre Dame, Indiana

Manufactured in the United States of America

Library of Congress Cataloging-in-Publication Data

Little, Katherine C., 1969–
Confession and resistance : defining the self in late medieval England /
Katherine C. Little.
    p.   cm.
Includes bibliographical references and index.
ISBN-13: 978-0-268-03376-7 (pbk. : alk. paper)
ISBN-10: 0-268-03376-5 (pbk. : alk. paper)
1. English poetry—Middle English, 1100–1500—History and criticism. 2. Chaucer,
Geoffrey, d. 1400. Parson's tale. 3. Gower, John, 1325?–1408. Confessio amantis.
4. Hoccleve, Thomas, 1370?–1450? De regimine principum. 5. Self in literature.
6. Confession in literature. 7. Confession—History of doctrines—Middle Ages,
600–1500. 8. Lollards. 9. Wycliffe, John, d. 1384—Influence. 10. Christianity
and literature—England—History—To 1500.   I. Title.
PR311.L58   2006
820.9'353—dc22

                                                              2006003886

∞ *This book is printed on acid-free paper.*

CONTENTS

ACKNOWLEDGMENTS

I have benefited from the advice and encouragement of many while writing this book, and it is a pleasure to thank them here. First and foremost I would like to thank David Aers for his unflagging generosity in overseeing this project when it began as a dissertation and his helpfulness as I revised it. I consider myself fortunate not only to have been his student but now to count him as a friend. Thanks also to the other members of my committee, Sarah Beckwith, Leigh DeNeef, and Stanley Fish, who helped to guide this project with helpful advice and good humor. I am deeply grateful to the following friends for discussing my ideas with me: Dorrie Armstrong, Eva Badowska, Jennnifer Bosson, Andrew Cole, Kate Crassons, Heather Hirschfeld, Ethan Knapp, Jennifer Snead (for reading and rereading), Erin Sullivan, and Christina Campbell Zausner. Thanks also to colleagues and students first at Vassar College and now at Fordham University, particularly Mary Erler and Jocelyn Wogan-Browne. I received research assistance from Vassar College, Fordham University, and the Huntington Library, for which I am grateful. At the University of Notre Dame Press, Barbara Hanrahan, Rebecca DeBoer, and the copy editor Elisabeth Magnus were a great help throughout, as were the readers for the press, all of whom I thank. Thanks to my family, especially my mother, Mary Ann Beverly, for their support. Finally, thanks to Paul Neimann for last-minute and miraculous assistance.

Earlier versions of chapter 1 and 3 appeared as "Catechesis and Castigation: Sin in the Wycliffite Sermon Cycle," *Traditio* 54 (1999): 213–44, and "Chaucer's Parson and the Specter of Wycliffism," *Studies in the Age of Chaucer* 23 (2001): 225–53, respectively, and I gratefully acknowledge permission to reprint them here.

Introduction

Since the publication of Anne Hudson's *The Premature Reformation* in 1988, scholars have rediscovered the writings of the Lollards (or Wycliffites), the late medieval English followers of John Wyclif.[1] This renewed interest has generated a complex description of the Wycliffite heresy, from their views on images, the Eucharist, and the disendowment of the clergy to their participation in a more widespread anticlericalism, in calls for the translation of the Bible into English, and in the "laicization" of English religious writing.[2] But disagreement about the significance of the Wycliffites and their impact on the culture of late medieval England remains: Were they a marginal group or more representative of late-fourteenth- and early-fifteenth-century religious, political, and intellectual concerns?[3]

This book argues that the Wycliffites and the controversy they engendered in the medieval period should be understood in terms of the history and the sources of the self.[4] That is, Wycliffite writings challenge orthodoxy not only in terms of doctrine (their position on the Eucharist, for example) but also by reforming the language given to church members to understand and speak about themselves; throughout their writings, the Lollards demonstrate a concern with both the language and the practices through which the self is shaped and encouraged. In this attention to self-formation (what we might also call subjectivity), Wycliffite reform sets aside the traditional cultivation of interiority concentrated on the confessional and provides alternative models of Christian identity based on Scripture. A study of the particular modes of Wycliffite resistance is therefore also a study of the history of medieval selfhood and cannot fully be grasped by enumerating the doctrinal positions taken by the Wycliffites.

My claim for the relevance of the Wycliffites to the study of subjectivity may come as something of a surprise because their surviving works seem to offer little attention to individuals, whether as characters in narratives or in terms of the revelation of an inner life. Their writings are largely collective and anonymous, consisting of biblical exegesis and translation, polemical treatises against the established church (and its sacraments, perceived riches, corruption, and so on), and sermons (which combine exegesis and polemic).[5] There are several accounts by Lollards that could be described as autobiographical (notably *The Testimony of William Thorpe* and "The Trial of Richard Wyche"), but these make up a very small percentage of the surviving texts. As a result, Wycliffite writings have not been considered fertile ground for discussions of subjectivity.[6] But as their massive sermon cycle, the *English Wycliffite Sermons*, and their numerous devotional treatises suggest, the Wycliffites were very much concerned with shaping Christian identity through instruction (in scriptural texts, exegesis, and the requirements of belief). Indeed, it is this sustained attention to pastoral instruction that makes the Wycliffites central to the history of the self.

The Wycliffites' interest in pastoral instruction is a reforming one, and two aspects of that reform will be the focus of this study. Perhaps the most definitive is the Lollard insistence on the Bible—their attempt to replace the authority of the established church with the authority of Scripture.[7] Such a change would radically affect the language of lay instruction by abandoning the church's traditional pastoral instruction: the extremely detailed and extensive language of sin, contrition, and many of the requirements of belief as well as the brief illustrative stories (the exempla) with which late medieval preachers peppered their sermons. Consider, for example, a Wycliffite sermon writer: "[T]his swerd failith now in prechynge of Goddis lawe, for prelatis han scaberkis withoute swerdis, and othere haue swerdis of leed, bi whiche thei tellen worldli wordis with fablis and gabbyngis on God" (The sword of the Holy Ghost fails now in the preaching of God's law because prelates have scabbards without swords and others have swords of lead, by which they tell worldly words with fables and lies about God).[8] In this passage, the writer redefines lay instruction by challenging the language traditionally provided to the laity, categorizing it as "worldli wordis" and lies, and by offering an alternative, "Goddis lawe" (the Bible). To reform the language of lay instruction is to reform the self-understanding that language makes possible: the identity based on the traditional teaching and practices of the church (here described as fables and lies) would give way to an identity based on biblical models of resistance.

Second, the Lollards attempted to reform traditional pastoral instruction by rejecting auricular confession: "[S]chrift of mouthe is not nedeful to helthe of soule" (A spoken confession is not necessary to the health of the soul).[9] Confession to a priest (schrift) had been required of all church members annually since the Fourth Lateran Council of 1215, and a great quantity of pastoral instruction was devoted to its efficacy and necessity in the form of sermons, handbooks for priests and laity, devotional treatises, and plays.[10] These texts reveal that the established church had cultivated a version of interiority based on the confessional: the self-examination of sins. In rejecting "schrift," the Wycliffites also rejected the traditional model of interiority.

As their reformed instruction suggests, Lollards belong not only to the history of dissent (through which they have long been understood) but to the history of the self. This book argues that their writings offer, therefore, an opportunity to investigate a particular moment in that history—a moment in which traditional models are disrupted and alternatives proposed.

But Lollards are not the only ones disrupting/ proposing alternatives

Traditional Discourses and the Self

The history of the medieval self (and, indeed, the modern self) is bound up with the history of auricular confession. This special relationship between confession and the self (as subject) is perhaps most famously articulated in Michel Foucault's *History of Sexuality:*

> The confession is a ritual of discourse in which the speaking subject is also the subject of the statement; it is also a ritual that unfolds within a power relationship, for one does not confess without the presence (or virtual presence) of a partner who is not simply the interlocutor but the authority who requires the confession, prescribes and appreciates it, and intervenes in order to judge, punish, forgive, console, and reconcile; a ritual in which the truth is corroborated by the obstacles and resistances it has had to surmount in order to be formulated; and finally, a ritual in which the expression alone, independently of its external consequences, produces intrinsic modifications in the person who articulates it: it exonerates, redeems, and purifies him; it unburdens him of his wrongs, liberates him, and promises him salvation.[11]

In this passage, Foucault identifies the way in which the practice of confession *produces* the subject by providing him or her with a particular language (the first-person speech of the confessional) in a particular power relationship (between priest and penitent). Although Foucault is primarily interested in the power of the confessor, I would like to draw attention to the power of language, the way in which the penitent's speech changes him or her.[12] From Foucault's perspective, the subject is formed in the confessional through those "intrinsic modifications." What is most groundbreaking about Foucault's account is its argument that the importance of auricular confession lies precisely in this production of subjects, in its "technology of the self," and not, as previously understood, in its theological nature.[13]

Although Foucault's version of confession provides a useful (and certainly influential) insight into medieval auricular confession, it elides both the resources within traditional discourses of auricular confession and the possibilities for resistance. For example, Foucault writes, "The Middle Ages had organized around the theme of the flesh and the practice of penance a discourse that was markedly unitary. In the course of recent centuries, this relative uniformity was broken apart, scattered, and multiplied in an explosion of distinctive discursivities."[14] Although Foucault's "unitary" vision of the medieval period has been criticized by medievalists, accounts of medieval selfhood remain much indebted to a Foucauldian approach to confession, arguing for its primacy in the study of the self.[15]

Foucault's account does underline the role of language in producing the self as subject, a view at the basis of modern theories of subjectivity.[16] To read the self in this way is to understand it as subject to the possibilities and limitations inherent in the language into which one is born; one does not preexist that language and shape it to reflect oneself.[17] This is the approach offered in Emile Benveniste's foundational essay "Subjectivity in Language," in which he writes:

> Language is accordingly the possibility of subjectivity because it always contains the linguistic forms appropriate to the expression of subjectivity, and discourse provokes the emergence of subjectivity because it consists of discrete instances. In some way language puts forth "empty" forms which each speaker, in the exercise of discourse, appropriates to himself and which he relates to his "person," at the same time defining himself as *I* and a partner as *you*. The instance of discourse is thus constitutive of all the coordinates that

define the subject and of which we have briefly pointed out only the most obvious.[18]

As this passage suggests, the speaker becomes a subject only in inserting him- or herself into a preexisting language by appropriating the "empty forms" (here the pronoun *I*), just as Foucault's penitent takes on the "I," becomes the "subject of the statement." In this way, Benveniste opens up what Foucault has restricted to the confessional—the possibility for subjectivity in all forms of language.[19]

Benveniste's version of subjectivity provides a broader approach, one that fits both the practice of confession and the discourses of lay instruction that were generated around it. From this perspective, auricular confession offers a language (of instruction) through which we might approach medieval self-formation and the kinds of selves this language made possible. To investigate confession primarily as instruction is, of course, to set aside its sacramental aspect (as well as minimize its Foucauldian aspect, a subject to which I will return below); confession was, after all, an essential component to the sacrament of penance.[20] Yet it is important to note that confession was importantly like preaching, a means to instruct the laity in the requirements of belief.[21] That confession was understood as instruction is apparent in the official documents circulated in England to educate the laity in the wake of the Fourth Lateran Council: Archbishop Pecham's Lambeth Constitutions in 1281 and Archbishop Thoresby's instructional program (1357), which circulated in both Latin and English versions and is known as the *Lay Folks' Catechism*.[22] All of these detail the requirements of Christian belief and the strategy for making these requirements known to the people—preaching and confession. For example, the English version states:

And he comandes and biddes in al that he may,
That all that haues kepyng or cure undir him
Enioygne thair parochiens and thair sugettes,
That thai here and lere this ilk sex things,
And oft sithes reherce tham til that thei kun thaime,

. . . .

And that parsons and vikers and al paroche prestes
Enquere diligently of thair sugettes, in the lentyn tyme,
When thai come to shrift, whethir thai kun this sex things.

[And the archbishop commands and requests in all that he may
that all those who have spiritual oversight enjoin their parishioners
and their subjects to hear and learn these same six things and to
rehearse them until they know them. . . . And that parsons and
vicars and all parish priests inquire diligently of their subjects at
Lent, when they come to confession, whether they know these six
things.][23]

The parishioners are supposed to hear and learn the requirements of the
faith from preaching and must then repeat them individually in confession,
which seems to be understood here as something of a test. Similarly, the
large numbers of texts for pastoral instruction consistently offer both preaching and confession as two sides of the same coin for instructing the laity.[24]
Consider, for example, the author of the early-fourteenth-century *Oculis
Sacerdotis,* William of Pagula, who writes: "But if the priest, on account of
the shortness of time and the multitude of penitents, cannot explain such
matters to each one individually, then he ought to preach them publicly at
the beginning of Lent."[25]

As the *Lay Folks' Catechism* and the *Oculis Sacerdotis* make evident, the
Fourth Lateran Council generated a veritable industry of texts for lay instruction. Leonard Boyle notes, "Within fifty years of the council there was
a profusion of episcopal or synodal constitutions all over Europe and a remarkable array of manuals of confession, *summae* of moral teaching, expositions of the Ten Commandments, compendia of vices and virtues, collections
of sermons and sermon exempla, and general manuals of the pastoral care, in
Latin and in various vernaculars."[26] The sheer number of texts concerned
with pastoral instruction suggests that this council, and the resulting attempts to instruct the laity, must be viewed as foundational for the identity
of the laity and the church. By imagining what the laity did not know (but
should) and the clergy's duties in teaching them, these writings articulated
an identity that was both a reflection of what existed and a goal to be
sought.[27] This identity was constituted out of elements that preaching and
confession were to communicate: the knowledge of oneself (as either lay or
cleric) in relation to a larger community (whether of the entire church or just
the local parish), in relation to history (conveyed in teachings from the Bible
and the traditions of the church), and finally, in relation to one's own interior (the self-examination of sins and virtues).

Lay instruction provides a number of different discourses for shaping the self, and it is worth emphasizing their possibilities instead of the uniformity or homogeneity that Foucault found or that scholars of "traditional religion" continue to find.[28] The most familiar is the pastoral language that the church desired to communicate to its members.[29] The *Lay Folks' Catechism,* for example, outlines the following requirements of belief: the fourteen articles of faith, the commandments, the sacraments, the works of mercy, the chief virtues, and the chief vices.[30] These texts insist upon the relevance of this knowledge in shaping the lives of their listeners/readers: "al creatures that loues god almighten / Awe to knawe and to kun, and lede thaire lyue aftir" (all creatures who love God almighty / Ought to know and to understand, and to lead their lives following him).[31] In addition, these texts provide detailed demonstrations of how the laity will go about shaping themselves, or "leading their lives," according to this knowledge. As stated in the *Fasciculus Morum,* an early-fourteenth-century handbook for preaching and confession, "Circa autem detractionem est sciendum quod ille detractor dici potest qui alieno crimine delectatur aut continue bonum in malum convertens" (About backbiting we must know that we can call "backbiter" a person who takes pleasure in someone else's sin and constantly turns good into evil).[32] This passage and many others like it demonstrate the way in which this pastoral language functions in the process of subject formation, providing pronouns for the reader/listener to inhabit (the "empty forms" that Benveniste describes). This is true for an individual reader of this text, who might ask him- or herself, "Do I take pleasure in others' sins? Am I, therefore, a backbiter?" or for the penitent whom the priest asks, "Do you take pleasure in others' sins?" In either case, the subject is produced in relation to the language offered by the priest (or this text) as he or she "appropriates" the identity to him- or herself and defines the self in relation to "backbiting."[33]

The author does not end his discussion of backbiting (or any other sin) with this exposition; he continues with a story, of which I cite only the beginning: "Unde narratur de quodam detractore qui . . . simulavit se velle confiteri set non fecit et mortuus est" (A story is told about a backbiter who . . . pretended that he wanted to confess, but he did not do so and died).[34] This passage reveals another discourse that the *Fasciculus Morum* shares with many other late medieval sermons and confessional handbooks: narrative. It is worth emphasizing that knowledge of such narratives is never explicitly defined as a requirement of the faith (like knowledge of the sins and virtues or works of mercy), but narratives are, nevertheless, offered for a similar purpose: to shape listeners/readers. Robert Mannyng's *Handlyng Synne* (another early-fourteenth-century text) uses a story to illustrate the command to confess only about oneself:[35]

> Do nat as the pharysu
> Preyde god agens hys pru.
> He yede to the cherche wyth a man
> That men calle a publykan.
> A publykan ys yn oure sawe,
> A synful man out of the lawe.
>
> . . . .
>
> Thys pharysu bygan to preye
> And seyde as a shrewe shuld seye,
> "Lord, thanked mote thou be
> Y am nat as y outher se,
> Coueytous ne lecherous of flessh,
> And nat as he thys publikan ys.
> Eury woke y faste twys
> And gyue my tythes of ryche prys."
> Loke how he made hys auauntement
> Of that gode that god had hym sent,
>
> . . . .
>
> Bysyde stode the publykan
> And knegh hemself a wykked man,
> And durst nat loke to god vpward,
> But knokked on hys brest ful hard,
> And seyde wyth hert ful dredfully,
> "Lord, thou haue on me mercy."
> The publykan had moche thank;
> The pharysu before god he stank.

———————

[Do not do as the Pharisee, who prayed to God to his disadvantage. He went to the church with a man whom men call a publican. A publican is, in our language, a sinful man, outside the law. . . . This

Pharisee began to pray and said as a wretch would say, "Lord, I thank you that I am not as others I see: covetous nor lecherous, and not as this publican is. Every week I fast twice and give my tithes of great value." Look how he bragged of the goods God had sent him. . . . Beside him stood the publican, and knew himself a wicked man and dared not to look upward to God but knocked on his breast hard and said fearfully with a full heart, "Lord, have mercy on me." The publican received much grace. The Pharisee stank to God.] [36]

The narrative of the publican and the Pharisee provides models for speaking about and understanding the self, an "I" to imitate (the publican) and an "I" to avoid (the Pharisee). As such, the story can be understood as a kind of metacommentary on the way the self emerges in language: each character's function in the narrative is quite simply to speak. The story also offers Benveniste's "empty forms" such that the listener may inhabit the "me" of the publican's speech (or that of the Pharisee). In this way, the story imagines speaking about the self as a negotiation of various subject positions (the publican or Pharisee), as the writer encourages the "thou" to become the right kind of "I." In addition, the absence of the priest, the "I" that only speaks offhandedly (as "y have herd") but is implicit throughout in relation to the "thou," demonstrates the sophistication of this text because the priest conceals his own authority by imagining confession as a purely spontaneous form of speaking about the self (for both the publican and the Pharisee). In sum, this passage highlights dramatically the efficacy of understanding selves in terms of subjects, in the possibilities that Benveniste describes, at their entrance into a language that preexists them. Indeed, the confession is here not a particularly Foucauldian one, "the obligatory and exhaustive expression of an individual secret," because the publican speaks only what he and everyone else already know, nor can it be understood as the assertion of some stable identity that preexists speaking.[37]

Although the penitential handbooks, like sermons, are clearly interested in generating and investigating subject formation through narrative as much as through pastoral language, scholars have largely neglected this process. Instead, most scholarship on this topic has separated out narrative as the concern of the laity, setting aside the complicated relationship between these different strands (subjectivity, narrative, pastoral language) that both the *Fasciculus Morum* and *Handlyng Synne* demonstrate.[38] To be sure, the use of narratives is not ubiquitous in lay instruction. There are Latin and vernacular handbooks for preaching and confession that neglect them entirely: the Latin *Summae* of Raymond of Pennaforte and Thomas of Chobham and the English *Book of Vices and Virtues* or *Ayenbite of Inwit*, to name a few.[39] Nevertheless, vernacular works often share an interest in including narrative in homiletic materials. Even those texts that criticize storytelling acknowledge that there are stories appropriate for instruction, such as stories about the Virgin Mary or Jesus' parables. The author of the *Cursor Mundi* notes that "Men yernen iestis for to here / And romaunce rede in dyuerse manere" (Men yearn to hear jests and to read a variety of romances), but

> Of suchon [the Virgin] shulde ye matere take
> Ye crafty that con rymes make
> Of hir to make bothe gest and songe
> And preise hir swete son.

> [You should take your material from the Virgin, those of you who are skilled at making rhymes, and make both stories and songs about her and praise her sweet son.][40]

As these texts suggest, one cannot ever reduce either the instruction of the church to purely doctrinal matters or the stories to some entertainment value that exists separately from them, precisely because much of church doctrine grows out of narrative.[41] What, after all, are the gospels besides narrative?

The centrality of narratives to lay instruction should point to another relationship between language and the self in the medieval period, another model for recapturing the variability of self-formation that Benveniste describes. The possibilities have been elegantly theorized by Alasdair MacIntyre:

> [M]an is in his actions and practice, as well as in his fictions, essentially a story-telling animal. He is not essentially, but becomes through his history, a teller of stories that aspire to truth. But the key question for men is not about their own authorship; I can only answer the question "What am I to do?" if I can answer the prior

question "Of what story or stories do I find myself a part?" We en-
ter human society, that is, with one or more imputed characters—
roles into which we have been drafted—and we have to learn what
they are in order to be able to understand how others respond to us
and how our responses to them are apt to be construed. It is through
hearing stories about wicked stepmothers, lost children, good but
misguided kings, wolves that suckle twin boys, youngest sons who
receive no inheritance but must make their own way in the world
and eldest sons who waste their inheritance on riotous living and go
into exile to live with the swine, that children learn or mislearn
both what a child and what a parent is, what the cast of characters
may be in the drama into which they have been born and what the
ways of the world are.[42]

In its question "Of what stories am I a part?" this passage demonstrates the
fundamental significance of narrative to selfhood/subjectivity. This significance should come as no surprise (least of all to literary critics); Fredric
Jameson describes narrative as "the central function or *instance* of the human
mind."[43] But it is still worth emphasizing that narrative as MacIntyre describes it is a resource for the self/subject both variable and rich. The "we" in
this passage may encounter only certain stories, but the variety of stories and
the variety of responses to those stories are a striking contrast to the agony
of subject formation in the Foucauldian confession: "[O]ne confesses one's
crimes, one's sins, one's thoughts and desires, one's illnesses and troubles;
one goes about telling, with the greatest precision, whatever is most difficult
to tell. . . . When it is not spontaneous or dictated by some internal imperative, the confession is wrung from a person by violence or threat; it is driven
from its hiding place in the soul, or extracted from the body."[44] Foucault's
work makes quite apparent that the subject is produced in relation to power,
in a process that not only can be violent and invasive but leaves no choice to
the speaker. In emphasizing the relationship between auricular and criminal
confessions, Foucault underlines the inquisitorial aspects of confession instead of the more subtle forms of coercion that occur in the story of the publican and the Pharisee cited above. In addition, Foucault's monolithic view
of confession obscures the differences between the discourses available to
both priest and penitent as well as the possibilities for resistance inherent in
choosing another story.

Although I have been using the terms *subject* and *subjectivity* to explain medieval pastoral instruction, it seems that these terms cannot be separated from a number of Foucauldian associations that make them problematic for the discussion of the medieval self, particularly in the discussion of confession. For this reason, I would like to propose the term *self-definition* as an alternative for what the investigation of lay instruction might tell us about the medieval self. This term responds to both of the concerns with subjectivity that I have indicated above—the variability of discourses for speaking about and shaping the self and the possibility of choice and resistance. I believe that this term is, therefore, more inclusive in that it allows for definitions one is forced to accept as well as those that one chooses. After all, one can be defined by force as a heretic, a married man, or a sinner, just as one can be "individualized by power."[45] One can also choose to define oneself voluntarily, as a younger son, or a king, or even a sinner. In other words, *self-definition* recovers, as *subject formation* does not, that being a self is a constant negotiation between the historical forces that shape the self and the choices that one makes.[46]

Wycliffites and the Reform of Pastoral Instruction

Thus far this introduction has been concerned with examining the ways in which traditional discourses provide resources for shaping the self through the languages and practices of pastoral instruction. And paramount here has been my desire to return choice and possibility to the discussion of lay instruction and the selves it shaped.[47] My interest in choice has to do with the particular situation of lay instruction at this time; as scholars have long noted, late-fourteenth- and early-fifteenth-century England witnessed increasing lay interest in devotional materials and therefore the potential for disruption as the laity took over the languages and practices that had hitherto belonged to the clergy.[48] It is this potentially disruptive call for lay (and vernacular) education that characterizes the Wycliffite heresy. In this way the Wycliffites may be understood as an extreme example of the more general questionings and appropriations of this period, in which "the literate laity were taking the clergy's words out of their mouths."[49] A Wycliffite sermon writer makes use of the liberating metaphor of Holy Writ as pasture in order to promise access to what has been fenced off from the laity:

[T]hey seyn that thei ben herbyrys bettur than comun pastur, for eerbys of vertew that growen in hem;—certes, makyng of eerberys in a comun pasture wolde destruye the pasture and lyfe of the comunys, bothe for dychyng and heggyng and deluyng of turuys. And yif we marke alle syche eerberys in Englond that be plantyd of newe in comune Cristis religioun, as thei spuylen the remenaunt of temporal goodys, so (that is more duyl) thei spuylen hem of vertewes: for alle cristen men schulden ben of o wille, and variaunce in syche sectis makyth variaunce in wille, and gendreth discensioun and enuye among men.

[The orders say that they are gardens and better than common pasture because of the plants of virtue that grow in them. Certainly the making of gardens in a common pasture would destroy the pasture and life of the commons because of the ditching and hedging and digging of earth. And if we look at all such gardens in England that are newly planted in Christ's common religion, we see that they rob the rest of temporal goods just as they rob them of virtues (and that is more distressing): for all Christian men should be of one will, and variance in such sects makes a variance in will and engenders dissension and envy among men.][50]

Lollard instruction offers itself as a disruption of the traditional languages of self-definition: a tearing down of those hedges that have transformed common pasture into private gardens. Indeed, the writer sees himself as metaphorically altering the landscape within which the laity live and the landscape that gives them their identity and, in this way, demonstrates the possibility of resistance to tradition and of alternative models.

In the chapters that follow, I shall investigate the Wycliffite reform of lay instruction, focusing on its consequences for self-definition. In the first two chapters I argue that Lollard texts, the *English Wycliffite Sermons* and *The Testimony of William Thorpe*, reveal a crisis in traditional religious language and its capacity to shape subjects and represent the interior. These texts offer, therefore, a series of redefinitions—of the language of sin, of the function of narratives in instruction (as discussed in chap. 1), and of the language and practice of confession (as discussed in chap. 2). These redefinitions necessarily disrupt traditional discourses of self-definition by separating out discursive strands that had been previously linked: narratives and pastoral language (such as sin, contrition, and confession).

Once Wycliffism is understood as a disruption in the languages and practices of self-definition, its impact on contemporary writers can be more clearly evaluated. The second part of this study, chapters 3 and 4, will investigate the effect of this disruption on three texts that draw on and respond to these traditional languages: Chaucer's *Parson's Tale,* Gower's *Confessio Amantis,* and Hoccleve's *Regiment of Princes.* While each of these texts invokes traditional language (particularly confession) and must, therefore, be understood as orthodox, each writes a concern with Wycliffism into that exploration, demonstrating that the traditional language of self-definition is under threat. In addition, the texts replicate to varying degrees the divisions that the Lollards have initiated between the different discourses of lay instruction, in this way demonstrating evidence of a historical shift in thinking about the resources of confessional discourse in particular. Indeed, one can map the texts onto a pre-Wycliffite to post-Wycliffite spectrum, with Chaucer's and Gower's texts demonstrating the capacity of the traditional languages of confession, despite the threat of the Wycliffites, and Hoccleve's text exploring (and even appropriating) the Wycliffite view of confession, despite its overt hostility to Wycliffism.

As indicated in the trajectory of this argument, the Wycliffite disruption can be understood largely, although not exclusively, in terms of debates around confession as a means of self-definition. This focus should come as no surprise because this practice was so central to the identity of the laity and their self-definition as Christians, but it has two important consequences for how scholars understand the practice of confession in late medieval England. The first is quite simply that we should not accept the link between the medieval practice of auricular confession and speech about the self (the popular definition of confession) as historically uncomplicated.[51] The second consequence is for the Foucauldian history of the subject that has been written around the practice of confession—a history of continuity between the medieval and the modern confessing subject.[52] I would like to suggest that this continuity is more a product of our own desires to see it than a reflection of the texts' own continuous engagement with confession as a language particularly suited to speaking about the self. In arguing for this revision, I do not intend to separate the medieval self once again from the modern (or early modern) self as alien and "other." Rather, I am offering my own form of resistance to what I see as a dangerous consequence of prioritizing the confessing self—the perpetuation of precisely the "antinomies" between self and other and individual and society that Benveniste discards in his theory of subjectivity: "And so the old antinomies of 'I' and 'the other,' of the individual and society, fall."[53] After all, the study of confession consistently sets the self against the other (whether that other is the priest, the discourses of the church, or another authority figure), as if this were the only process of self-definition worth examining or, perhaps, the only process of self-definition at all. While this perspective on confession is important, it limits self-definition to a series of conflicts between the interior and exterior, self and other, individual and society, instead of emphasizing the variability and multiplicity of empty forms that Benveniste describes.[54] Our preference for the conflict between self and other, individual and society, runs the risk of inscribing the limitations of our own ideology of selfhood upon the medieval texts that we read without recognizing that we might one day see differently. This book offers, I hope, a necessary corrective.

Chapter One

NARRATIVES AND SELF-DEFINITION

[W]ho schulde now knowe emperours, wonder of philosofres, oþer folwe þe
apostles, but hir noble dedes and hir wonder werkes were i-write in stories
and so i-kept in mynde? . . . For storie is wytnesse of tyme, mynde of lyf,
messager of eldnesse.

Ranulph Higden, *Polychronicon*[1]

So John Trevisa, translating a work of history in late-fourteenth-century
England, introduces readers to his text by praising the usefulness of narratives. For Trevisa (following his source), narratives are necessary not only for
passing on knowledge of the past, of "emperours" and "philosofres," but also
for providing readers with models to imitate, the "noble dedes" of apostles.
Trevisa describes a similar mirroring function for both text and readers: just
as the texts reflect the actions they report, so do readers hold these actions in
mind as idealized reflections of their own (future) actions. Although brief,
Trevisa's comment draws attention to the relationship between the stories
that are "i-kept in mynde" and the selves that readers (and listeners) construct in relation to them. This link between narrative and self-definition is
taken up in rather a different manner by a Wycliffite writer contemporary
with Trevisa, who writes,

> To som men it plesuþ for to telle þe talus þat þei fynden in
> seyntus lyuys, or wiþowton holy writ. And suche þingus plesuþ
> ofte more þe puple. But we holden þis maner good, to leue such
> wordis, and tristen in God, and telle surly his lawe, and specially

his gospel; for we trowen þat þei camen of Crist, and so God seiþ hem alle. And þes wordis, siþ þei ben Godus, schulden be takon as byleue; and more wolon þei qwikene men þan oþur wordis þat men knowe not.[2]

While this writer is also interested in "wordis" that "qwikene" men, he indicates an important distinction between the stories that Trevisa has grouped together. For this writer, there are two kinds of narratives: the tales "wiþowton holy writ" that "som men" use, and the law, especially the gospel, that "we" (the Wycliffites) use. Although the Wycliffites use the term *lawe* rather than *tales* or *stories*, they are indeed referring to narratives they embrace, "his gospel." For the Wycliffites, the dichotomy between the two kinds of narratives (*talus* vs. *gospel*) is a guide for reformed instruction; it determines what kinds of stories should be "kept in mind."[3] At first glance, this passage seems to be rather straightforward in its desire for a kind of generic classification that would separate fables from more appropriate moral teaching and in this sense seems to echo Chaucer's Parson's distaste for "fables and swich wrecchednesse."[4] Yet the last line conveys an understanding of texts that has more to do with the reader's understanding than with the text's genre or provenance: "oþur wordis þat men knowe not." This line surprises because the writer has just defined what these "oþur wordis" are— that is, the tales—and any reader of Wycliffite polemic cannot help but have a clear idea of their hatred for both the exempla and the more sensationalistic hagiographies that they describe as the lies and trifles used in contemporary preaching.[5] For this reason, *knowe* should not be taken as meaning "be familiar with" (in this particular instance) but rather the reader's experience of the text that Trevisa describes as "kept in mind." From this perspective one can read the distinction between tales and Holy Writ as having as much to do with the mirroring function of these narratives, their influence on the readers, as with their relation to God's authorship.[6] In this way, Wycliffite reformed instruction goes beyond scriptural fundamentalism, the insistence on the biblical text and the biblical text only. It is always aware of the motives for and uses of interpretation, the reader's response to the narrative. Indeed, as much as the Wycliffites might insist upon the existence of God's word outside the context of its readers, they are also profoundly aware of its importance in a process of self-definition.[7] In their attempt to reform how the words will be "takon" as much as the "byleue" itself, the Wycliffites necessarily alter the language provided to the laity to narrate themselves, the words that "qwikene men."

To argue that the Wycliffites should be understood as participating in a debate over self-definition may come as something of a surprise, and not only because their texts make use of a generalizing language, "trewe men" to describe themselves and "sects" to describe others, that seems to preclude any discussion of individual selves.[8] But more importantly in the history of Wycliffite scholarship, Wycliffites have been understood as traditional reformers, distinguished from their contemporaries only by the insistence and the extremity of their views.[9] For example, a recent scholar of the *English Wycliffite Sermons (EWS)*, H. Leith Spencer, describes Wycliffism as "radical conservatism" that "produced sermons which are in many respects highly traditional."[10] If we continue to read Wycliffite texts from this perspective, then we approach them with the assumption that Wycliffites' lay instruction shares the same understanding of selfhood as that of their orthodox contemporaries. Such an approach to Wycliffism seems to me, however, to misunderstand the relationship between the languages (or discourses) one uses and the subject positions that are made available through those languages.[11] Wycliffites did, in fact, change the language of lay instruction in their texts, as I shall demonstrate below, and therefore changed the selves that that language made possible.

This change can be understood only in the context of the traditional discourses of lay instruction, disseminated primarily through vernacular sermons. I have chosen vernacular sermons to illustrate this dialogue between Wycliffism and orthodoxy for two reasons. First, both Wycliffite and orthodox writers agreed on the importance of lay instruction through preaching. One can certainly argue that the Wycliffite movement was possible only because of the popularity of vernacular preaching in England, particularly that of the friars who preceded them. Second, a more practical reason, enough vernacular sermons survive to draw a comparison between the two groups.[12] This chapter shall therefore begin by outlining the relationship between narrative and self-definition in the instruction offered by the established church; I shall then argue that the Wycliffites challenged this traditional relationship, thus calling into question the selves shaped and encouraged by orthodoxy.

Traditional Approaches

In the medieval church, lay instruction was particularly tied to narratives. A glance at vernacular sermons will reveal a variety of narratives about sin, redemption, conversion, damnation, salvation, or persecution. To be sure, Christianity, then as now, is a religion based in narrative—the stories of the Hebrew Bible and those of Jesus' life (as well as in the interpretations of those stories).[13] Nevertheless, the narratives that informed medieval preaching also included a wide range of what we would now describe as extrabiblical—the exempla and saints' lives that were a staple of medieval preaching.[14] These narratives were used not only to justify the practices of the church but also to encourage identification and action on the part of the listeners; in this way, they provided the laity with a language to describe and to understand themselves as Christians, sinners, participants in the practices of the church. The sermon's (ideal) relationship to its listener is made clear in John Bromyard's early-fourteenth-century encyclopedia for preachers, *Summa Praedicantium,* in which he writes, "As the mummer when describing or mocking anyone recites intimate details about him, as the doctor gives his specific prescriptions, so let the preacher deliver a detailed account of the sinner's state and its dangers, with special reproofs."[15] Bromyard's words make clear the importance of listeners' recognition of themselves in the narratives used in lay instruction, or, to use a more psychoanalytically inflected term, their identification with the traits or the character described by the priest. This mirroring function suggests one of the ways in which these narratives participated in the process of self-definition.[16] Another is that the narratives were used as links by which the *pastoralia* and church requirements, such as annual confession or almsgiving, were tied to (or even provided a structure for) the individual's own narrative of his or her life and experiences. In this way, they demonstrate the ideological working of narratives; the capacity of a narrative to "hail" a person, to bring him or her under the authority of the established church.[17] I shall distinguish these two forms of recognition, although they are importantly interdependent, as the psychological (when listeners are encouraged to see themselves in relation to the details of the story) and the ideological (when listeners are encouraged to see themselves in relation to the practices of the church).

This encouraged identification (because, of course, we can never know whether the audiences did, in fact, identify as the writers imagined they would) worked largely through the figural interpretations to which all narratives were subjected in medieval exegesis.[18] And it is perhaps best exemplified in the narratives of Christ's healing. Consider, for example, two stories used in Lenten sermons in the late fourteenth century: the Canaanite woman who begs Christ to heal her possessed daughter (Matt. 15:21–28) and Christ's healing of the deaf, dumb, and blind man who is possessed by demons (Luke 11:14–28).[19] Each provides a character at the center of this narrative, mother or deaf man, with whom the audience is meant to identify. For the writer of a Lenten sermon in the *Middle English Sermons (MES)*, the Canaanite woman "is vndirstonde [as] euery synnefull creature resonable preyinge to God for is dowthure, þat is, for is owne sowle, dede in synnes" (66). Mirk claims that "[t]hys woman and hur doghtyr bytokenyth a man þat haþe hys concyens trauelyng wyth þe fende of dedly synne"(*Festial*, 95). In addition, both authors address listeners as "ȝe" or "we" and command them to think about their relationship to the characters in the narrative: "Loke now to þis man" (*MES*, 145), "Take ensampull" (*MES*, 152), and "[t]akyng also ensampull" (*Festial*, 95). It is worth noting the way in which these interpretations thematize subjectivity by relying on personal pronouns and direct addresses.[20] In other words, these are never abstract discussions of sins and sinners, as may sometimes be found in penitential manuals, such as the *Summae* of Raymond of Pennaforte or Thomas of Chobham; these sermons insist on the individual listener as the center of the interpretation.[21]

This identification, then, offers a psychological insight to its listeners based on the details of the narrative: sin is an affliction that can be identified and then healed. In both narratives, the demons that possess the characters—the daughter of the Canaanite woman and the deaf and dumb man—represent sin. For the daughter, the demon is "þe fende of dedly synne," and for the deaf-mute, the demons are the sinful "oþes," "wordys," and "þoghtys" that prevent him from speaking. The sermon writer may use this opportunity to describe the seven sins in detail, as is apparent in the *MES* (sermon 12), in order to facilitate their identification or to reinforce sin as a state to which all listeners are subject: for example, "Is not he blynde þat may lett to do ill and ȝitt doþ itt?" (*MES*, 147). Finally, the equation of sin with demons allows the listener to see sin as both a part of and separate from the self.[22] In this way, the narratives reinforce sinfulness as a temporary state that can be changed through the proper actions.

Second, listeners' identification with the characters positions them in a narrative with a known outcome, an outcome known in both earthly terms (the practices of the church) and heavenly terms (salvation). In other words, identification with the character in the narrative should lead listeners to follow the practices of the church, and this is the ideological component of these narratives.[23] For example, one author places listeners and himself in the action of the narrative: "lat vs crie with þis womman, of whom þis gospell spekeþ of, havynge in vs stedefast beleue in God; and latt vs sey þe wordes þat she seid, 'Haue mercy on me'" (*MES*, 145), in order to read this appeal as a confession: "But God, þat delivered þis vommans douȝter fro þe fende þat turmented hure . . . ȝeve vs grace so for to beleue and so to repente and shryue vs" (*MES*, 145–46). Here the Jesus of the biblical narrative figures the priest and confessor in the listener's narrative of future actions. Similarly, for Mirk, the woman represents anyone who "may no way be holpen, but ȝyf he goo to God and holy chyrch, and opynly schryue hym to þe prest" (*Festial*, 95). Mirk turns the desperation of the Canaanite woman to his advantage; just as she must humble herself to Jesus (who seems to scorn her), the penitent must humble herself in appealing to the priest in recognition that this action is the only one that will cure her. Like the healing of the Canaanite woman, the healing of the deaf-mute is also appropriated to encourage the sinful listener to confess. The author of a sermon for the second Sunday in Lent writes that "[f]or as often as God enspireþ a synneful mans herte to do good and to repent hym for is synne and to com to amendement þorowe shrift of mouthe, so ofton he casteþ þe fende oute of man" (*MES*, 143). This passage connects God's action in healing the man to the practice required of the penitent. The casting out of sin is read in both narratives as a vomiting up of demons, a purgation that again reminds the listener of his or her Lenten obligations, the physical purging of fasting.

The persuasiveness of this traditional approach can be attributed to the authors' sensitivity to the narrative. In both narratives, the authors retain the detail about the character that makes this character significant: the Canaanite woman approaches Jesus and begs for his attention; the demon in the mute man prevents him from speaking. The authors use these details to match a very real situation in the life of listeners—not having approached the church, not having confessed.

Despite the writers' respect for the affective power of these narratives, it should be noted that they exert a strong interpretive control over them;

clearly the writers are concerned that listeners' identifications keep them within the practices of the church. This interpretive control and its limits are most apparent in the figure of Jesus. On the one hand, the interpretations appropriate Jesus into the narrative trajectory of individual sinners (that of sin and redemption) despite the writers' acknowledgment, at the same time, that he is very much different in kind from the Canaanite woman and the deaf-mute man. For example, the story of Jesus' temptation is offered for the listeners' identification in the same manner described above. There is the psychological identification, in which listeners are encouraged to see themselves in Jesus' resistance to sin: the devil "ys most bysy forto make yche man to gylt yn þes þre synnes most þes fourty dayes" (*Festial*, 83). These sins are then named and described for the listener: gluttony, pride, and avarice. And there is the ideological identification, in that Jesus fasts as those during Lent must: "Crist ȝaue vs ensampull for to faste, for first he fastid hym-selfe" (*MES*, 141), "schouyng to vs and all cristen men and pepull þe uertu and þe mede þat comyth of fastyng" (*Festial*, 82). In this way, Jesus' story becomes that of self-examination (discovering sin) and penance (the fasting), the same story offered to the listeners. This interpretation is perhaps clearest at the end of a sermon in the *MES:*

> Now, sirs, itt is full necessari þat we take hede to oure-selfe inspeciall þis holytyme, for þe fende þat tempted oure Lord will not lett to tempte vs to breke þis holy faste to gloteny and lechery, and to suche oþur vices, for he wates well in þis holy tyme þat we be aboute to amende vs of all oure ewill lyvynge þat we haue done here-before. And þer-for when þat he tempteþ vs to do ill, take we ensampull of oure Lorde, and lattes vs answere as he dud, and sey, 'Goy, þou fende, for man lyueþ not only in brede, but in iche word þat commeþ fro þe mouþ of God. þer-fore goy þou, Sathanas; I will not breke my fast, ne I will no þinge do as þou tempteþ me to do; but I will do almes dede for to amende my misdedis. (142)

Here the author translates Jesus' words to Satan seamlessly into orthodox concerns for a late-fourteenth-century penitent. And, in so doing, the author has completely disguised his act of translation: he does not gesture to his own control of the narrative by invoking figuration (as he has done elsewhere); rather, he offers the practices of the church as a natural consequence of identifying with Jesus.

Of course, this interpretive approach runs into trouble with Jesus' actions in other narratives that cannot be so easily appropriated for the story of the individual sinner in relation to the church—Jesus' teaching, miracle working, and preaching. When telling these narratives, Mirk and the sermon writers of the *MES* seem to be particularly concerned to limit the listeners' identification within the practices of the church. For example, in the narratives of the loaves and fishes, the authors draw attention to the figural meaning of loaves and the fishes (rather than Christ's action in multiplying them or preaching to the people) in order to reinforce the practices required of the laity. For the author of the *MES,* Christ is a model for material giving, alms, despite the author's reference to the loaves and fishes as "goostely fode" (151). Similarly, Mirk allegorizes the loaves and fishes as lay actions: the loaves are contrition, shrift, dread of sinning again, and perseverance; the two fishes are orisons and alms (*Festial,* 103).[24] Once again, the emphasis here is on Christ's "almsgiving," and almsgiving is, of course, the only action in this narrative allowed to the laity.[25]

The mode of interpretation as recognition, however limited that recognition might be, explains the presence of exempla in these sermons. Exempla have an interpretive function in relation to the scriptural narrative—to reinforce literally what has been read figurally; in the exempla, therefore, confession to a priest is described as such and not as the casting out of demons. This function seems to me to be essential to understanding why the exempla are there in the first place and why the Lollards are so set against them. Exempla capture listeners' recognitions within the practices of the church, and their function in sermons is, therefore, far more identifiably ideological than the biblical narratives, which always carry the potential of encouraging an inappropriate identification, such as with Jesus' preaching instead of his almsgiving. This ideological aspect has been extensively discussed by Larry Scanlon in *Narrative, Authority, and Power,* in which he defines the exemplum as encoding a certain view of power; it is "a narrative enactment of cultural authority" that "assumes a process of identification on the part of its audience."[26] As such, exempla offer characters who, unlike those in the Bible, must be driven to approach God through the church, usually through miracles of some kind. The Lenten miracles, for example, all follow the same formula: a person either sinful or devout refuses, entirely or in part, to obey a practice such as confession, almsgiving, or fasting; this refusal results in some kind of revelation of either an angelic or a demonic nature; and the character ends up forgiven or damned. The plot line of the narratives and even the narratives themselves repeat across different settings and sermons and sermon cycles. For example, both Mirk and the author(s) of the *MES* use the narrative of an otherwise devout woman who cannot confess one shameful sin.[27] In the midst of her despair, Jesus appears to her and sticks her hand in one of his wounds. She cannot wash off the blood until she has confessed the sin. This narrative can function at many different levels: to warn the listener that even the most devout person is subject to sin; to establish that Jesus is allied with the practices of the church (in the face of Lollard criticism, this might be important); to underline the necessity of confession; and to reveal Jesus' great mercy.[28]

As the exposition of both the scriptural narratives and the exempla makes clear, the story of the individual sinner and his or her redemption or damnation exerts a kind of ideological and psychological control on the narratives of church members. To be sure, this control may seem rather obvious given that readers today still express their desire to identify with the characters in narratives, but we should be aware that this narrative strategy has consequences beyond the individual reader's identification.[29] If this is the mode for addressing sin in the established church, then what are the possibilities for reform allowed by this strategy—not only the reform of the individual (his or her reintegration into the community of the saved) but, more importantly, the reform of the community, possibly even of the penitential system itself? To answer this question, I would like to turn to *Piers Plowman,* a text that is consistently concerned with exploring the limitations of traditional discourses, such as preaching and confession, to imagine or enact reform.[30] Because this poem is, of course, a poem and not a sermon, it provides precisely the kind of self-reflexivity about the language of preaching that is so lacking in the orthodox sermons themselves.[31] Moreover, the particular status of *Piers Plowman*—as both deeply committed to traditional discourses and deeply critical of them—makes it a compelling bridge between orthodox and Wycliffite texts, as I shall demonstrate here.[32] My discussion will necessarily be brief, focusing on passus 5 of the B-text, which details the confession of the seven Sins upon hearing Reason's sermon.[33] Although scholars have noted the central paradox of the Sins' confessing, the questions raised by this particular episode for the reformist potential of this work have not been extensively discussed.[34] One might begin by noting that this episode describes reform through the traditional penitential process—

the story of the individual sinner.[35] That this is a moment of reform for the community as well as the individual cannot be doubted. As John Burrow writes, "What Langland has in mind here is not a total apocalyptic transformation of society. . . . He means rather to show the kind of change, or conversion, that can be expected of people here, now, and in England. His problem was to find some form of action which would represent such a change."[36] Indeed, at first glance, this episode seems an endorsement of the identificatory process of the individual sinner familiar from the orthodox sermons discussed above. After all, the Sins appear to define themselves successfully as sins. For example, and one could choose any passage at random, Sloth's speech reveals the sins of the clergy that are common to estates satire:

> I haue be preest and person passynge þritty wynter,
> Yet kan I neyþer solue ne synge ne seintes lyues rede;
> But I kan fynden in a feld or in a furlang an hare
> Bettre þan in *Beatus vir* or in *Beati omnes*
> Construe clausemele and kenne it to my parisshens.[37]

Sloth's language reveals a process of recognition—he has recognized himself in the portrait of sin detailed by a preacher in just the way Bromyard has described (although, of course, these details do not appear in Reason's sermon earlier in the passus) or in a penitential handbook. Langland emphasizes that this is indeed recognition by having the Sin himself acknowledge his sinfulness. Although the Sins' speeches are indebted to the language of sermons that describe them, they are presented as self-examination. In this way, the speeches demonstrate the success of the church's psychology of sin; that language has been appropriated by the penitent for his or her self-definition.

Nevertheless, this recognition seems somewhat overdetermined because the listener is a mirror image of the conventional teaching: of course Sloth can recognize himself as Sloth, but will a human penitent also see him- or herself in the confessional discourses of the church? Langland sets this question aside in this particular sequence and only returns to the problem of individual recognition later in the poem, in the confession of Hawkin the Active Man in passus 13 and 14. Certainly Hawkin's confession emphasizes not so much the details of the sins, although it also relies on traditional accounts of the seven capital sins, as the process of recognition itself for everyone involved. This emphasis is clear in the way in which both Hawkin and the dreamer "take heed" (13.315, 318); in the dreamer's watching, "waitede wisloker" (13.342); and in perceiving, "Pacience parceyved" (13.354). In this second sequence, confession is the process by which one becomes aware of one's sins and sorrows for them, and although this process is certainly meant to reform the penitent (Hawkin wishes that he had never been born at the end of passus 14), that reform does not include the social world that he inhabits. Indeed, the dreamer awakes before a contrite (and absolved) Hawkin returns to the community.

This brief comparison of the earlier and later confessional sequences should suggest the oddity of the reform that Langland has imagined in having the Sins themselves confess, as opposed to a kind of Everyman figure, as Hawkin might be taken to be.[38] After all, these penitents are not penitents but abstractions characterizing the entire community. In "substituting" these abstractions for individual penitents, Langland seems to suggest that it is the community in its entirety that needs to be reformed and not just the individuals, that perhaps the sinfulness of the community is greater than the sum of its individual parts.[39] Moreover, in having abstractions confess, Langland highlights a particular problem with this mode of reform—where will the desire for reform come from? On the one hand, the sequence preserves the traditional view—that the desire comes from the penitent him- or herself. On the other hand, one might note that here that penitent is not really a penitent at all but an abstract and collective representative of the sinfulness of a number of people. Even this choice can be viewed from two different perspectives: the Sins represent the interior state of the community (thus reconfirming that it is the interior that produces the desire for reform), or the Sins represent standardized teaching on the Sins and remain, therefore, collective. These ambiguities suggest two possibilities at once—reform comes from every individual's desire to reform, and reform comes from outside the individual (in the castigation of sinfulness in the sermons and satires from which the Sins are drawn).

I have attempted to demonstrate here that Langland's portrait of confession underlines the magnitude of the task of reform as well as "some misgivings" about it.[40] If this episode were merely polemic against the sins of the community, a typical satire, we would understand the need for reform but not the how of it. Instead, Langland dramatizes the assumption behind contemporary sermons and other satires, that reform depends on every individual recognizing himself as a sinner and repenting within the practices of the established church.[41] In this way, Langland's use of the satirical traditions shows what he shares with them, a belief that society must be reformed, and what he does not, "misgivings" about the practices available for that reform at this moment.[42] Although the poem certainly imagines a reform for the duration of passus 5, as everyone sets out on a pilgrimage to "Truthe," we know that this reform cannot be sufficient—perhaps one must start over entirely. Indeed, even at this point the tenuousness of this hope for reform is made clear in the deferred absolution of Covetousness, which cannot take place until he restores all that he has taken by cheating (5.270–71).

My discussion of reform has thus far concentrated on that of the community because that is what Langland emphasizes in this part of the poem. But one cannot forget that the story of the individual sinner was also a story about the individual's healing, the casting out of the demons. While the self-definition of the Sins in Langland's text is largely successful, if tautological, there is one important moment when it seems to fail in its capacity to address and to heal an interior state. This takes place in Envy's confession, as seems fitting, since envy is the sin that is most characteristically internal. He is introduced as "Enuye wiþ heuy herte" (5.75) and says,

> "I myȝte noȝt ete many yeres as a man ouȝte
> For enuye and yuel wil is yuel to defie.
> May no sugre ne swete þyng aswage my swellyng
> Ne no Diapenidion dryue it fro myn herte,
> Ne neiþer shrifte ne shame, but whoso shrape my mawe?"
> "ȝis! redily," quod Repentaunce and radde hym to goode:
> "Sorwe for synne is sauacion of soules."
> "I am sory." quod enuye, "I am but selde ooþer."
>
> (5.122–28)

> ["For many years I might not eat as a man ought
> For envy and ill will are hard to digest.
> Is there any sugar or sweet thing to assuage my swelling
> Or any *diapenidion* that will drive it from my heart,
> Or any shrift or shame, unless I have my stomach scraped?"

"Yes, readily," said Repentance, directing him to live better;
"Sorrow for sins is salvation for souls."
"I am sorry," said Envy. "I'm seldom anything else."][43]

I have included the translation from Donaldson's version because this passage is fraught with double negatives that make it unclear to what extent Envy is questioning the existence of a solution to his problem. This confusion certainly adds to the passage's emphasis on the difficulty of casting out sin, of making the internal external in confession. It seems (because of the "but" at line 125) that Envy is setting shrift and shame at odds with another solution, the scraping of his stomach. This expression certainly locates the sin very clearly inside his body, but it is also an odd confusion of the figurative and the literal: a figural character insists on the materiality of his sin— that it can be cast out only by scraping his stomach. And, even odder, this formulation separates confession (shrift) from its figurative equivalent in contemporary sermons, the scraping of purgation. Finally, the passage seems to indicate that Repentance is a bad listener, or at least is unable to provide Envy with the means to understand what he must do to be healed. The conventional phrase about sorrow allows Envy to continue describing his sin rather than to move on to contrition for it, and, indeed, there is no real end to his confession.[44] Indeed, Envy's final confessional words, that he will amend if he may, underline the uncertainty of his future amendment, an uncertainty intensified by the absence of any discussion of satisfaction for his sins.

Langland's text demonstrates, in the small episode that I have chosen, an anxiety that the traditional means for reform, here penance, may not be entirely adequate to the task. Moreover, the text reveals what is to blame: the identificatory processes through which the laity are instructed in the requirements of the faith. Like Langland, the Wycliffites see the traditional approaches as blameworthy, but unlike Langland they imagine a new relationship between narrative and self-definition to reform the community.

Wycliffite Interpretation

The Wycliffite approach to narrative and self-definition is best exemplified in the late-fourteenth-century *EWS* because these sermons contain the most extensive exposition of biblical narratives in the vernacular.[45] Using the familiar structure of traditional sermons, the biblical passages provided by the Sarum missal, and often the familiar allegorical interpretations of biblical narratives, the sermons disrupt the identificatory processes of traditional exegesis and therefore set aside individual sin to focus on institutional sin, particularly that generated by the practices of the established church.[46] The shift ultimately displaces the individual from the focus of the sermons; the individual's sins and the individual's actions in avoiding or succumbing to that sin no longer affect his or her salvation. In addition, in rejecting the identification and discussion of individual sin, the Wycliffite sermons draw attention to the potential inadequacies of this traditional language to narrate the interior. It is a paradox of these sermons that their attack on the sins of the established church should disrupt the very mechanisms for talking about sin, although it is perhaps appropriate that a cycle that has as its purpose an attack on the established church would be so concerned with institutions and groups rather than the individual.

The most obvious shift in the use of narrative is the reliance on Scripture alone to educate the laity: no exempla or pastoral formulas are included in the sermons.[47] One might ask, then, What are the consequences of this shift for the ideological and psychological uses of narrative so central to lay instruction? At the most basic level, the Wycliffite sermons seem to reject self-definition entirely. They do not address the reader directly—as "you" or "we"—but rely on the third person, "men seyin." Moreover, they do not encourage the listeners' recognition by introducing them into the narrative or directing them to "take ensampull" from it. This apparent abandonment of the listener as an individual is made all the more noticeable in the absence of the pastoral requirements—the detailing of the Ten Commandments, the seven works of mercy, and so on.

Upon closer inspection, it seems that the sermons are nevertheless quite interested in the relationship between narrative and self-definition, particularly in rewriting and redefining the traditional approach, described here as encouraged identification. This project of redefinition is most apparent in the sermons' approach to sin. There is no systematic articulation of the sins either in a list or in the context of a biblical narrative, even though the narratives consistently refer to sin as a concept. Perhaps most importantly, the sermons separate the sins from the scriptural narratives with which they are associated in the interpretations of the established church. The best evidence for this claim is that the sermons on the Sunday Gospels (set 1), which draw their pericopes from Jesus' parables and actions, rarely refer to specific sins.[48] When they do, they avoid associating particular sins with particular characters in the sermons.[49] To be sure, many of the afflicted characters whom Jesus heals are read as representatives of sinful men, as they are in orthodox sermons. For example, the deaf and dumb man healed by Christ is described as mankind: "Iesu took mankynde þat þus was seek, not in eche persone but singulerly in one" (12/46–47). Although this figuration, like that of the traditional sermons, could be used to encourage identification, the writer does not say more than "And so may men see how myche þei ben to blame þat been dowmbe and deef in þis maner of worchyng" (12/63–65). In addition, and more importantly, when the sermon writers do discuss sins as more than abstractions—in terms of the contemporary world rather than "mankynde" in general—they begin to change the concept of sin. In doing so, the Wycliffites depart from the interpretive traditions of the established church, in which the figuration of sin is used to produce both psychological and ideological recognition. In the Wycliffite program, sin is no longer figured as an individual, and therefore psychological, characteristic, such as an abbess's ribaldry, a chapman's despair, or a knight's greed, but as a characteristic of the two churches, the saved and the damned, or real institutions, such as fraternal orders. As such, it is no longer understood as an affliction shared by everyone in the Christian community.[50] In thus redefining sin, the Wycliffites allow listeners to reject the ideology of the individual sinner, to separate themselves from the practices of the church.[51]

The new view of sin is apparent in the exposition of the parable of the bridal feast at which a guest is thrown into outer darkness (Matt. 22:1–14). This parable is traditionally interpreted to explain the relationship between the church and salvation, and in this respect, the Wycliffite writer is quite traditional.[52] Moreover, the Wycliffite writer and his contemporary, the author of the sermon in the *MES,* agree on the figuration of the servants sent out to invite the guests: saints, apostles, and priests. However, the authors' application of these figures to the audience differs markedly. Using the same method as in the Lenten sermons discussed above, the author of the *MES* encourages listeners' recognition of themselves in the narrative: "He [God] send oþur messangers to bid men come to heven, as doctours and prechors of þe word of God, as þei do now daye by daye, but ȝe sett not by hem þe more harme is. Som goyn to *youre* citte, þat is, to *youre* vnclene felischippe as to þe taueron and to oþur vnhoneste place; som to *youre* vnthrifty marchandize" (18, my emphasis).[53] The warnings are addressed to individual listeners—to ensure that "þou haue oon þe leveree of clennes" and, more importantly, to think of the day when we must give account of how "we haue spende þe vij verkes of mercy" (*MES*, 18). With his repetition of the word *your*, the author insists that each listener understand the story's relevance to his or her own life. It is the listener who has been invited to the feast by "prechors" (including the one speaking at this very moment), and it is the listener's own life that is characterized by sin: "vnclene felischippe" and "vnthrifty marchandize." Drawing on the traditional interpretive mode, the writer emphasizes listeners' psychological and ideological recognition. By placing listeners within the story, the author has given them a language to describe both their present state of sin and their future story of salvation or damnation, ultimately reinforcing the requirements listeners must follow to consider themselves members of the church and part of this story: they must become clean of sin (through confession and fasting), and they must know the seven works of mercy (bodily and spiritual).

The Wycliffite version of this parable abandons the traditional mode of recognition, transferring whatever identificatory potential he sees in the narrative to the institution and away from the individual's psychology and the practices he or she must perform. For the Wycliffite writer, the parable offers a language to describe the state of the church (not the state of the individual) at the moment he is writing: "[N]ow in þese laste dayes God bad his seruauntis clepe men, boþe good and euele, into þe chyrche" (20/59–60). This emphasis on the institution is also evident in the figuration: "þer ben here two manerys of chirches: holy chirche or chirche of God; þat on no maner may be dampned; and þe chirche of þe feend, þat for a tyme is good and lasteþ not" (20/66–69). This reading has important consequences for the interpretation of the man cast into outer darkness, whose status as the individual damned soul is neglected in favor of "þes þat wolde not last in grace," who cannot answer God "how þei entredon into þe chirche" (20/71–72, 76–77). There is no "you" who must decide what to do to be saved. For this writer, then, the danger is not that the sinners do not recognize themselves in relation to the messengers who appeal to them (the "prechors" and "doctours" in the sermon above) but that they do not recognize the institution to which they belong. In fact, the sermon shows that the identificatory process is far more complicated than described in the previous sermon: in the

Wycliffite version the damned appear to belong to the right institution because they "profi3tede to Cristes chirche" and are called "frend" by Christ (20/74, 75). But instead they are traitors to Christ's church and "more to be dampnyd þan men þat neuere entreden þus" (20/78–79). What is striking in this view of the damned is that their damnation does not result from their individual actions or thoughts, the "vnclene felischippe" and "vnthrifty marchandize" described in the contemporary sermon discussed above. Here sin has nothing to do with the individual's psychology but is a characteristic of his or her institutional allegiance. In this way, the Wycliffite sermon not only denies the common identification with the individual sinner but offers a commentary on the traditional interpretive mode—that the recognition encouraged by the established church may be, in fact, a misrecognition.

In disrupting the traditional relationship between sin and the individual, the Wycliffites generate a new understanding of reform, one that is no longer reliant on the individual's self-examination, repentance, and reintegration into the church. In this way, the Wycliffites respond to the problem Langland reveals in his procession of confessing sins: How can the reform of individuals be translated into the reform of institutions, such as the clergy? This shift is apparent in the Wycliffite expositions of biblical passages that are traditionally interpreted as authorizing self-examination, the process that the sinful must undergo before they can be reconciled again to the church, such as the sermon on the passage *Estote misericordes* (Luke 6:36–42). Before discussing the Wycliffite version, I offer this passage from the *Glossa Ordinaria* to demonstrate the centrality of self-examination to the reform of church members in traditional thinking:[54]

> Vere peccans peccantem castigare non valet, quia qui superbia vel odio vel alio vicio praeuenti . . . hi tales amant magis vituperare et condemnare, quam corrigere et emendare.

> [Truly, a sinner is not worthy to castigate a sinner, because those prevented by pride or hate or another vice . . . prefer to scorn and condemn rather than correct and emend.]

> Si quem vis reprehendere, primum vide si similis ei sis, quod si es: pariter ingemisce, et noli eum tibi obtemperare: sed pariter conari

mone. Quod si non es similis, tamen quia olim fuisti, vel esse potuisti, condescende, et non ex odio sed misericordia argue. Raro ergo
non sine magna necessitate sunt obiurgationes adhibendae.

[If you wish to reprehend someone, first see if you are like him. If
you are, groan equally (with him) and do not desire him to obey
you, but warn (him) to try equally (with you). If you are not like
him, nevertheless because you once were, or could have been,
humble yourself, and rebuke him not out of hate but out of mercy.
Rarely, therefore, and not without great necessity are rebukes to be
applied.]

Hi enim odio vel liuore omnia accusare suscipiunt, et volunt videri con-
sultores, sine exemplo suae emendationis. Sed prius debent auferre tra-
bem invidiae, vel maliciae, vel simulationis de occulto sui cordis, vt vale-
ant eiicere festucam irae vel alicuius liuoris culpae de oculo fratris.

[Indeed, these people undertake to make all their accusations with
hatred or envy and want to be seen as advisors, without the example
of their emendations. But sooner should they take out the beam of
envy, or malice, or pretense, from its hidden place in their hearts, so
that they are strong enough to eject the rod of anger or the fault of
any spite from their brother's eye.][55]

What is, of course, most obvious in this discussion is its focus on sight,
a focus that underlines the importance of recognition in the traditional in-
terpretative approach. Here that recognition is directed toward the self in a
process of self-examination and not toward figures in a narrative (although,
clearly, the possibility for identification with accuser and accused is implicit
within this exposition) or toward the practices of the church. Nevertheless,
like those other encouraged recognitions, it affirms the centrality of the individual sinner, the self for whom recognition is a necessary mode of being
in the church. This self does not, of course, exist in isolation. Rather, self-
examination requires one to look at oneself in relation to another, the sinner

in whom one sees oneself reflected or who needs to be redeemed. It is in this relationship, between brothers or between accusers and accused, that the language of sin operates. In other words, these recognitions are possible only because the language of sin ensures that the experiences and motivations of accuser and accused are read as similar; as if to illustrate this shared language, the writer even details some of the possible sins that might motivate the accuser to accuse: pride, envy, hate. Finally, in establishing a relationship between sight and sin, asserting the perceptive qualities that characterize this language, the author claims that the language of sin allows one to discover what is hidden in the heart, thus making it as obvious (visible) to oneself as the rod in someone else's eye.

Finally, one might note that this passage is certainly concerned with reform, but a reform that directs the gaze away from the other toward the self. From this perspective, the other (the one who was originally seen as other because sinful and qualitatively different) becomes a mirror for the self. In this way, the passage allows a reformation of self via the other but does not allow the reformation of the other. In fact, it does not allow the other to remain other because it extends the similarity between the two even into the hypothetical, *vel esse potuisti* (if you could have been similar).

In contrast, the Wycliffite sermon on this passage not only rejects the process of recognition that leads to self-examination but allows for reform of the other. Sin characterizes the other; sin can, therefore, be seen without invoking a shared relationship. To be sure, the sermon begins by referring to what seems to be self-examination: "Furst schulde a man haue mercy of hymself, and mercy of his moder þat is holy cherche, and þan hath he mercy of al þe ende of his kyn" (4/29–31). But the sermon quickly moves on to condemn the accusers in this world (the lords and prelates) as lacking mercy, and mercy here is read not as the capacity for self-examination (as in the passage above) but as another kind of accusation. Indeed, the writer closes the sermon with a firm separation between the accuser and accused, even between both of these positions and the "we" that is describing them: "Here may we see þat sugetys schylden blame prelatys whan þey sen opynly greet defawtys in hem, as defawte of Godus lawe in kepyng and techyng; for þis is a beem by þe whyche þe fend byndeþ his hows" (4/86–89). Although this passage also relies on vision, there are no obstacles to this vision, as the word *opynly* makes clear. In addition, this gaze does not use the other as a mirror to facilitate recognition of the self. Indeed, there is nothing in this passage about looking into one's heart; rather, this accusing eye is looking outward and is not at all encumbered by its own sin. Even the beam that is supposed to be in the eye of the accuser appears only in that of the accused.

While sin is still the motive for reform, the approach to it has changed radically. Perhaps most obviously, the language of sin does not facilitate self-examination here because the writer does not allow it to characterize the accuser as well as the accused. For the Wycliffite, those who correct and those who sin stand on opposite sides of a divide; there is no language, such as the seven capital sins, that would provide a common ground out of which to build mercy. This divide is most clearly seen in that those who are offered mercy, the Pharisees, and those who offer it, the accusers, are never reconciled. On one side of the divide are the clerks, who are called Pharisees. They are characterized by their sin, in this case the lack of mercy: "Þe leste mercy of men ys among clerkys, þat wolen not ȝyue goodus of grace but ȝif þei sullen hem. And þerfore þis sinne is heresye byfor God, þe moste and þe fyrste þat partiþ men fro God" (4/19–22). On the other is the author, who is merciful according to his own definition (the correction of faults). The irreconcilable nature of these two positions is furthered in the discussion of sin: the sins of the clerks derive not from faults within but from their position in the church. For example, the sermon does not blame priests for lechery, gluttony, or covetousness, sins satirized in late medieval ecclesiastical satires. Rather, it attacks all clerics for selling the "goodus of grace." In short, priestly sin is in corruption of the office, not in corruption of the individual—the sins he might share with his audience. Indeed, blaming a priest for individual corruption, such as indulging in expensive tastes, would conjure up very different associations in the minds of the audience, who might also desire to indulge themselves, than blaming a priest for selling grace. In addition, the passage about blaming sin, quoted above, quite forcefully makes the sins of the accused prelates dependent on their position within the established church, whereas the listeners, the "sugetys," do not share this powerful position and thus do not share this sin of not "kepyng and techyng" God's law. As a result, the sermons reject the process of self-examination that should lead to individual reform.

The changes to the modes of recognition so central to the teaching of the established church necessarily have an effect on the story of the individual sinner. As noted above, the narrative of the individual sinner who miraculously changes his ways appears not only in the "fictional" tales labeled

"Narracio" in Mirk's *Festial* but repeatedly in the "holy writ" to which the Wycliffite sermon cycle so self-consciously restricts itself. Yet the sermons systematically redirect the focus of these narratives away from the individual sinner, even though the affective power of these narratives is a powerful tool in traditional homiletics. Instead, the Wycliffites transfer the language of sin from the listeners to the institutions in order to emphasize structural sin, to claim that institutions create sin in as powerful and significant ways as an individual's choice to commit adultery or kill a friend. This claim is apparent in the exposition of those narratives in which Jesus heals the afflicted—for example, the Canaanite woman and the deaf-mute man (discussed above in their traditional mode); these narratives are reread to shift attention away from the internal possession, and its association with sin, and toward the external circumstances that enable that possession. Certainly, the writers of the other sermon cycles might be in agreement that sin comes from the outside and that one is possessed by it. Nevertheless, here the emphasis is on examining the external circumstances that enable sin, whereas the other sermon cycles focus on what to do once it has arrived inside.

The Wycliffite sermons begin their exposition of these narratives in a manner very similar to the *Festial* and the *MES;* in all sermons the characters are offered as figures for the listener's identification: "þis paynym womman is þe substaunce of mannys sowle" (41/64–65). The deaf-mute man is read as the church (42/2), which in a traditional sermon would suggest that he is an Everyman. However, in both sermons the author soon shifts the focus away from the affliction and the healing; indeed, in the sermon on the Canaanite woman, he does not even tell us about her daughter, who is a central part of the interpretation in the orthodox sermons. Although the figuration does not depart from the traditional view—a sinful person can be healed by Christ—in neither sermon does the author use the narrative to describe the audience, their sins, and their future actions (the "Take ensampull" of the orthodox sermons); there is no listener addressed, no "you" through whom the writer connects these figures to the life of the audience and their concerns for salvation.[56] Indeed, the writer loses the details of the narrative: the trajectory in which the Canaanite woman approaches Jesus and begs him to heal her possessed daughter or in which Jesus casts the demons out of the man. More importantly, the interpretations change the status of listeners from participants in their own salvation to witnesses to the struggle between the two churches. Compare the address to listeners in "lat vs crie with þis womman . . . 'Haue mercy on me'" (*MES*, 145) to "[a]nd sone aftyr þes lyf schal come þe day of doom; but byfore, ȝif God wole, þe chirche schal be mendyt" (42/109–11). In this way, a narrative about the struggle with demons inside is absorbed in a larger struggle over the fate of "Cristis lawe" to such an extent that the character in the biblical narrative loses her specificity and therefore her power as a potential point of identification for listeners. And, in this case, that loss of specificity is marked by the introduction of the group, "men seyin," to replace the "vs" that might look to this narrative for a personal model.[57]

In addition to disrupting what I have described as psychological recognition, the Wycliffite sermons change the ideological focus of the narrative. The interpretations offered here do not lead listeners to see the relevance of church practices to their lives; rather, the figuration of the passage leads to an indictment of those very practices. The Wycliffites were, of course, well aware of the traditional interpretations of these passages. Their expositions must, then, be seen as responses to the ideological work performed by the expositions of the established church. For example, in the sermon on the Canaanite woman, the writer uses the terms gained from his figural interpretation, namely heathen and soul, to discuss problems that lie outside the individual: the appearance of the Antichrist.[58] In his interpretation, the conversion of this soul can go both ways:

> And þus by gretnesse of feiþ enformed wiþ charyte ben syche
> sowles maade hool, and turnede vnto Godis children. And, riȝt as
> in Cristis tyme and aftyr by hise apostles he turnede manye heþene
> men to Cristis religioun, so now in tyme of anticrist ben cristene
> men made heþene and reuerse Cristis lawe, his lore and his werkis.
> As now men seyin þat þei schulden by lore of þer feiþ werren vpon
> cristene men, and turnen hem to þe pope, and sle þer persones, þer
> wyues and þer children, and reuen hem þeir goodis. (41/82–90)

For this writer, Christ's action in healing the woman figures conversion instead of confession, and this change allows him to attack the practices of the established church, including confession. Christ's healing becomes the original conversion, the original practices of the church, that have been reversed "now in tyme of anticrist." By repeating the word *turn* in reference to the pope, the writer separates the identification of church and Christ that operates in traditional expositions of this passage. Moreover, since conversion and confession are typically quite closely linked, the "turning" the writer describes could also be the practice of auricular confession. In this way, confession is one of the wrong kinds of conversion that reverses Christ's "lawe." Whereas Christ once freed "heþene men" of demons by turning them to "Cristis religioun," now the process is reversed so that "cristene men [are] made heþene" and, presumably, become hosts to demons once again. The demons who possess the woman become identifiable, then, not only as particular sins but also as particular people: the priests who have possessed the people and made them sin by encouraging them to kill people and steal from them. Interestingly enough, this passage is particularly concerned with the political implications of the laity's identification with church practices. Their acceptance of themselves as church members, their turn to the pope, has particular political consequences, participation in the Despenser Crusade, that are completely obscured in the contemporary sermons collected in the *MES* and *Festial*.[59]

The desire to see sin as produced by the church rather than alleviated by it puts a certain pressure on the exposition of passages, as can be seen in the narrative of the deaf-mute man. Here the writer is interested in the demons, and the writer singles out Jesus' statement on the "malis of þe feend" for discussion (a part of the passage that does not receive attention in the other sermons): "*Whan an vnclene spiri3t is went owt from a man, he wandreþ by drye places and sekiþ hym reste, and whan he fyndeþ noon, he seiþ to hymself 'I schal turnen a3en to þat hows þat I cam offe.' And whan he comeþ to that hows, he fyndeþ hit ydel*" (42/75–79). In this passage, the demons are moving around outside people; the focus has shifted from the interior from which they must be cast out to the exterior from which they threaten. Once the demons are separated, so to speak, from the man and his infirmity, they become a general and undifferentiated category for sin: at once both the sign of sin's existence and the cause of that sin. The demons both inhabit priests because the priests are "ydel fro kepyng of Godis lawe, and ocupyed wiþ mannys lawe þat sownede vnto coueytise" (42/90–92) and cause sin because they "made hem worste men" (42/97–98). In this way, the author describes a world characterized by sin in which the individual has no power to effect change: "And roote of þis malice is coueytyse of prestys, and leuyng of

Godis lawe and hy3yng of mannys lawe; by þis is þe comunte of þe puple maad pore and swept as þe pawment from hulyng of stree, and cooldid in charyte" (42/103–6). The bleakness of this portrait is apparent not only in its circularity—the root of the malice (its cause) and the malice itself are the same, the priests' covetousness—but also in its indefinition—the "þis" that impoverishes the people but is never clearly defined.

Identifying with Christ

As demonstrated above, the Wycliffite sermons often direct our attention away from the traditional practices of identifying sin in ourselves, the narrative trajectory of the individual sinner. Yet the sermons do offer identificatory possibilities in the figure of Christ, and this identification defines the listener in terms of resistance instead of sin. It should not surprise readers that Christ is invoked throughout the sermons in terms of an identificatory approach, as this was also the case in orthodox sermons. What is more surprising is his singularity; there are no exempla of other virtuous men and women or stories of saints (outside the very brief number of saints' day sermons). As the sole point of identification for the laity, the figure of Jesus provides a rare glimpse into the possibilities for Wycliffite self-definition. In the sermon for the first Sunday in Lent on the Devil's temptation of Christ (Matt. 4:1–11), Christ spends forty days in the desert, during which the Devil tempts him to turn stones into bread, to reveal his divine powers, and finally, to worship the Devil in order to gain earthly goods. As noted above, this narrative is traditionally interpreted to encourage listeners to identify their own sins, gluttony, pride, and covetousness, and to describe the penitential acts, fasting and almsgiving, that will address those sins.[60] In contrast, the Wycliffite writer uses this sermon to provide a new identification around resistance. Indeed, the sermon writer makes his interest in the listeners' identification clear, as he had not done in the exposition of the narratives of the Canaanite woman and the deaf-mute man, when he begins the sermon: "Þis gospel telluþ how Crist was temptyd þre tymes of þe feend, and how he ouercam þe feend to techen vs how we schulden doo" (40/1–2). The emphasis on "us" places the listeners of the sermon in relation to the narrative. Although these opening words might remind one of the identification encouraged in the orthodox sermons, "how we schulden doo" does not refer to fasting or to resisting the sins that the established church found in this narrative. Indeed, it mentions only two of the sins, "pruyde and glo-trye" (40/24), and sets these aside in order to detail the institutional sins that should be resisted.[61]

These institutional sins are temptations to misread "godis lawe" and "hooly writ" and "lore," and, as such, they are temptations both inside and outside the narrative. Sin is therefore not an interpretive category that al-lows listeners to apply the action within the narrative—what Satan or Christ does or does not do—to their own lives; rather, it refers to interpretation itself. This shift is apparent in the writer's discussion, after the first two temptations, of what it is to tempt God. He writes, "hit is seyd comunly þat eche man temptuþ God þat chesuþ þe worse weye" (40/86–87) and then fur-ther defines this temptation: "whoeuere entreþ a new religioun þat was not furst ordeyned of Crist, he temptuþ God and synneþ greetly" (40/92–94). Moreover, to resist these temptations, as Christ has done, does not require participation in a practice, fasting or confession; rather, one must resist iden-tifiable institutions: the established church and the religious orders. At this point in the sermon, the writer has invoked the traditional approach, identi-fication, only to set it aside. We still have not learned what we should do; we have only learned of the sins that face us, the institutional sins that are de-tailed throughout the cycle.

It is only in the account of the third temptation, the sin that is not named, that the writer returns to the identificatory mode: "And here men marken how þat Crist was pacient in two temptyngus byfore, but in þe þridde he myȝte not suffre þat ne he spak scharply to þe feend. And in þis ben we tawte to suffre meekely owre owne wrong, but aȝen wrong of God we schulden ben woode to venghen hit, for þus dyden Crist and Moyses and oþre men þat suweden hem" (40/110–16). In this passage, the author sets the listener within the narrative, as the orthodox writers do far more frequently, in order to tell us what to do—to take action. This passage provides a new form of self-examination; "owre owne wrong," and "wrong of God" make up the sin categories, instead of the capital sins that inform the orthodox ser-mons. And it provides a new course of action: suffering and vengeance, in contrast to confession and fasting.[62] In this way, the writer has turned our attention away from resisting our own impulses (pride, gluttony, and covet-ousness) to resisting institutional temptations to misinterpret.[63]

If, as I have been arguing, the Wycliffites are concerned to redefine the self by offering listeners an identification with Jesus' resistance, as detailed above, instead of an identification with individual sinners, then, one might ask, what kind of narrative trajectory do they provide? That of the individual sinner is clear: acknowledgment of guilt and submission to the practices of the church. For this traditional approach the two forms of recognition fit together logically—if one accepts the category of sin, then one must also accept the means for alleviating it. By redefining sin as institutional, the Wycliffites have disrupted the traditional identificatory process through which narrative helps define the self. Indeed, the Wycliffite view of sin is characterized by a peculiar kind of stasis, as demonstrated in the passage on self-examination above.[64] Nevertheless, the Wycliffites do offer their listeners a kind of narrative trajectory through which one might know oneself as a part of the "trewe" (Wycliffite) church, and that is one of persecution:

> Crist bydduþ his seruauntis *to ioye þat day in þer herte, and schewen a glad contynaunce* to men that ben abowte hem, *for certys her mede is myche in þe blysse of heuene.* And þis word cownforteþ symple men þat ben clepude heretykys, and enemyes to þe chyrche, for þei tellon Godis lawe; for þei ben somownede and reproueded monye weyes, and aftur put in prisoun, and brende or kyllude, as worse than theues. And maistres of þis purseewyng ben preestis, more and lasse, and most pryue frerys. (65/102–10)

Here the writer offers an identification with Christ's followers through the term *symple men,* which is a kind of code word for fellow Wycliffites.[65] This identification offers a trajectory of parallel action, apparent in the sentence's list of "and's": ostracism, telling God's law, being summoned and proved, and imprisonment, burning, and death. The movement of the sentence suggests that telling God's law (the defining aspect of Wycliffite identity as indicated both here and in expositions of Jesus' life) logically leads to persecution.[66] In this way, persecution gives sufferers a way to know themselves in relation to fellow church members, an "us" similar to that of sinners who beg for mercy in the traditional sermons: "Crist ordeynede peynes and hate of þe world and pursewyng to men þat he most louede, to techon *vs* þat comen after hem. And þus signes of pacience and pursewyng in þis eurþe schulde be tokne of Godus loue and not signes of anticrist" (51/101–4, my emphasis). Of course, being called a heretic and being persecuted are not a result of the individual's choice in quite the same way that the Canaanite woman's approach to Jesus is a result of hers. In this way, the authors claim that virtues (as well as sins) are institutionally generated and maintained.[67]

Wycliffite Instruction and Interiority

The narrative of the individual sinner describes not only the individual's actions in relation to the church but also the psychological work of self-examination and healing, the casting out of demons. The identification that the Wycliffite sermons offer in Jesus certainly provides a narrative trajectory for the individual in relation to the church but not for the individual in relation to his interior. Indeed, the exposition of narratives about Jesus seems to set aside the interior entirely. One could attribute this absence to the Wycliffite rejection of auricular confession, which structures the exposition of that movement from interior to exterior in the casting out of demons, and, indeed, this rejection is certainly central to Wycliffite reform, as I shall discuss in the following chapter. Yet the Wycliffites did not reject confession as such, only confession to a priest; one might, then, retain the story of the casting out of demons (one could even retain the seven capital sins) without necessarily invoking the priest. The Wycliffites do not, as indicated above, and in this way they suggest the inadequacy of traditional discourses for discovering the interior, for describing the movement from inner to outer. This inadequacy was, of course, also suggested in *Piers Plowman,* as the dead end in Envy's speech.

The most obvious indication of this perceived inadequacy is the absence of the pastoral formulas as they were developed in vernacular instruction: the seven sins, the virtues, the works of mercy.[68] Certainly, these pastoral formulas offered a language for self-examination, as is apparent in any number of vernacular sermons contemporary with the English Wycliffite cycle. For example, the orthodox sermon on the bridal garment (discussed above) uses the seven works of mercy. The absence of these formulas in the Wycliffite cycle points to the Wycliffites' understanding that exterior signs do not necessarily provide a means through which one might approach or discuss the interior. In this way, Wycliffite interiority resists exploration; it is described as a hiddenness: "And so ys eche man þat is born of þis Spiryȝt vnknowon to oþre by manye hydde resownes; and so eche man ys somwhat knowon and somwhat vnknown for wysdam of þis Spiryȝt" (54/52–55). For this writer, the reasons for salvation or damnation can at best be only partially known. If we read these "hidden reasons" as sins or virtues (the reasons for salvation or damnation), then their very hiddenness prevents us from finding them so easily in the figuration of biblical narratives: that is, interior sins cannot be figured as the demons to be cast out because the possession of the deaf-mute man and the woman's daughter were clearly visible to all. The unknowing that characterizes the Wycliffite view of sin must be contrasted with the categories that the established church applies to sin. Although traditional sermons sometimes also imagine the interior as hidden or difficult to know, they devote far more attention to describing and cataloguing sins and beliefs than they do to such observations about the hiddenness of the interior.[69]

In addition to rejecting the sin categories, the Wycliffites reject the definitions of the established church that accompany sin in traditional teaching: "hit is not nedful heere to wyte which is deedly synne and to wyte which is venyal; but eche synne schulde a man fle, lest hit bee deedly to hym" (24/75–77). This sentiment is striking when read next to the writings of orthodox theologians who made the distinction between mortal and venial sins an important aspect of pastoral care. For example, Mirk's *Instructions for Parish Priests* separates his discussion of sin into the seven sins, described as mortal, and the sins of the five senses, which are venial.[70] In contrast to Mirk, the Wycliffite writer refuses entirely to define the sins. His statement reveals both a desire to communicate subtler points of sin to his audience and the inadequacy of typical instruction on the sins and their categories. As he states, the categories of venial and "deedly" (mortal) do not take into account that the danger of sins might in fact be unknown to anyone but God.[71] The Wycliffite rejection of these categories can be read as a rejection of the certainty of the established church, whose categorization reflects both knowledge of and the ability to control sin.

Perhaps as a result of their resistance to established definitions, the Wycliffites are particularly interested in hidden sins. For example, the exposition of the palsied man healed by Christ begins by emphasizing the scribes' sin: *"And whanne Crist saw here þowtes wiþynne, he seyde wharto þei þowten þus euyle in þer hertys* and by þis word he tawte hem þat he was God, for only God may þis wyse wyte what a man þenkuþ wiþynne" (19/8–11). The writer's interest in what is taking place within the scribes is apparent from his interpolation; the italics translate the biblical text, to which he has added the word "wiþynne" to emphasize that the thoughts take place within. And he continues this interest in what one might call interior sin when he figures the palsied man's affliction as disbelief ("[s]chakyng in þe palesye is vnstablenes of byleue" [19/30–31]).[72] This focus on sin does not lead this writer to rail against the sins of the clergy, figured here as the scribes, as in many of the other Wycliffite sermons about sin. Rather, it leads him to discuss what must be done with such an internal sin. Can it be forgiven within the traditional practices of the church—that is, by absolution? At first, the writer states that the church's mechanism of forgiveness does not address a central problem, who might be injured by the sin: "Soþ hit is þat men may here for3yue trespaas doon to hem, and remytte mannys iniurye as myche as in hem is, but not remytten vttyrly synne doon a3enys God" (19/54–57). But the writer ends the sermon in doubt: "[3]if any man wyle telle moore pleynly þis sentence by Godis lawe, I wole mekely assente þerto, 3if þei grounden þat þei seyn" (19/76–78), as if to indicate that the story of the palsied man's forgiveness has brought up the limitations of this program of reform.

As this exposition makes clear, the attention to the hidden sins underlines the difficulty of the Wycliffite educational program. How will the inside become known? How will the demons be cast out? The Wycliffite writer confronts this question by attacking the very trajectory for sin described by the established church. In discussing the hemorrhaging woman that Christ heals (Matt. 9:18–22), the writer agrees with conventional interpretations that her affliction represents sin, but he rejects the traditional means by which that affliction will be healed: "But man may spendon al þat he haþ abowten oþur fysisyens and geten hym absolucion,—3ee after þe day of doom,—and manye indulgenses wiþ lettres of fraternyte, þat heeton hym to come to heuene as sone as he is deed; and 3et may þe fluxe of blood renne wiþ al þis, and he may be deppere in synne wiþ alle þese dispenses" (24/43–49). Although this affliction is, of course, healed in the narrative, the writer imagines that it may not be in the lives of listeners unless they ask Christ for grace. But, as the traditional interpretations make clear, asking for grace (in the narrative) is read as submitting to the practices of the church. What does asking for grace mean in this new context? The writer does not answer this question; instead, he uses this occasion to develop his theory of sin, rejecting the view he ascribes to some men, that there is no sin if no act has been committed: "Here men dowten comunly whanne men synnen deedly wiþynne in þer sowle and don none euel dedys wiþowten in þer body þat anoyen men" (24/67–69). In my reading, this is a question that other sermons in the vernacular just have not considered, and it is perhaps also a question that the formula of the seven capital sins does not allow them to consider. The writer ends the sermon with this distinction between interior and exterior sin:

> By þis may me[n] see somwhat how þei schulden answere to þe dowtis þat ben made and to oþre also. For we schulden byleue þat men may be dampnyde for synne in here sowle, ʒif þei worche not owhtward, for original synne and actual also. And þus may men be sauyd for þowtis in þer herte, al ʒif þei do not owtward meritorie werkys. And þus may men don harm to oþre by þowtis of herte, and profiʒten also to hem ʒif þei ben fer from hem; and sych spiritual harmyng or profiʒt is myche moore þan bodily profiʒt. (24/96–104)

This discussion of sin is concerned not so much with naming the sins as with establishing where they are, a concern apparent in the language of "in here sowle" and "in þer herte" and "owtward." Sin and good deeds can occur in both the interior thoughts and the exterior actions of the individual. Where they are seems to be of utmost importance; the interior good deeds and sins seem to be of more importance than those that are seen: "sych spiritual harmyng or profiʒt is myche moore þan bodily profiʒt." Although the interior sins are more important, this writer does not seem to think they should stay in the interior, because the individual will be damned for those sins unless they are discovered, in their "worche . . . owhtward." The process by which these sins might work their way outward is not, however, discussed because the writer has already rejected the practices provided by the established church.

These sins and works remain undisclosed, unreachable through the languages and practices inherited from the established church. In this way, the writer's discussion of sin uncovers a realm of anxiety about sin that has perhaps been masked by the endless categorizing and defining of the sins in the sermons of the established church. And that anxiety is that these sins might not be able to be described at all because they do not fit into the categories used by medieval sermon writers. Unspoken, they remain inside the penitent. In this way, the sermons gesture toward the individual's conscience as a place that is as important for the discussion of sin and good works as the church outside it, but the sermons finally draw back from discussing the conscience, from providing a narrative for making that interior known. It remains unknowable except to God and therefore indescribable in the language that the established church has provided and enforced.

This unknowability of the interior sins and virtues contrasts strongly with the knowability of the institutional sins that threaten the individual from all sides—the fabling of the friars, the covetousness of the priests, and the papacy's lust for power. In the Wycliffites' world, the correction of sin has less to do with self-examination than with examining one's allegiance to the church. Knowing oneself as a member (and the consequences of membership: persecution) replaces the religious practices, particularly confession, urged upon members of the established church in other sermons. For Wycliffites, then, individuals must still interpret and shape themselves in relation to narratives, but the narratives have changed radically—from those that offer an identity in terms of exculpation and reintegration to those that offer an identity in terms of persecution and resistance.

Chapter Two

CONFESSION AND THE SPEAKING SUBJECT

One of the defining characteristics of Lollardy is the rejection of auricular confession: "schrift of mouþe is not nedeful to helþe of soule, but only sorowe of hert doþ awey euery synne."[1] The reason for this rejection is quite simple: only contrition ("sorowe of hert") can absolve sin, not the priest. Confession to a priest is, therefore, unnecessary. This view is elaborated and repeated throughout Wycliffite writings: "þi confessour can nouȝt wyte wheþer þou be bound or soyled, but bi supposynge þat he haþ of þi trewe speche, ffor þer is no more heresie þan man to bileve þat he is assoyled ȝif he ȝeve hym moneye, or ȝif he leye his hond on þin heed, and seie þat he assoylliþ þee. Ffor þou moste by sorowe of herte make aseeþ to God, and ellis God assoyliþ þee noȝt, and þanne assoyliþ noȝt þi viker."[2] While this passage is overtly concerned with the priest's actions in absolving, it also identifies a concern with the penitent's speech, what the priest can conjecture (suppose) from "trewe speche." It is this interest in the relationship between confessional practice (the actions of the priest) and speaking that is a striking element of Wycliffite writings on confession. For this reason their attack on confession and absolution should be understood not only as an attack on one

49

of the practices central to the established church but as an attempt to reform
the discourses that are produced in confession (here the "trewe speche").
When viewed from this perspective, the Wycliffite polemic against confession reveals a debate about the self in relation to the discourses of the church,
particularly the possibilities and limitations of these discourses for the way
in which the laity can speak about themselves and their interiors. This debate was all the more contentious because of the increasing number of participants; as pastoral and devotional writings were translated into English,
the lines between clerical and lay discourses began to be blurred. For this
reason, the Wycliffites must be seen as part of a larger, vernacular, laicizing
movement in late medieval England and therefore lend insight into the
process by which the language in the penitential tradition was made available to the laity.[3] In this chapter I shall first demonstrate how the translation
of penitential manuals for a non-Latinate audience, an audience that presumably includes some laity, entails a shift in attention from the clerical to
the lay role in the penitential process. Then I shall argue that this shift generates a new, Wycliffite understanding of confession, one more concerned
with the relationship between speaking and the interior than with the categories that name and define this interior. It is this new understanding that
informs orthodox responses to Wycliffism.

Confessional Speech in the Established Church

Although debates over confession were long-standing, the Wycliffites
shifted attention from the role of the priest and contrition to the language
and actions of the penitent.[4] The possibilities for such a shift are apparent
from the very origin of the pastoral mandate on confession. Take, for example, the wording of the Twenty-first Decree of Lateran IV (1215), which
required annual auricular confession for the first time:

> Omnis utriusque sexus fidelis, postquam ad annos discretionis per-
> venerit, omnia sua solus peccata confiteatur fideliter, saltem semel
> in anno proprio sacerdoti. . . . Sacerdos autem sit discretus et cau-
> tus, ut more periti medici superinfundat vinum et oleum vulneribus
> sauciati, dilligenter inquirens et peccatoris circumstantias et pecca-

ti, per quas prudenter intelligat, quale illi consilium debeat exhibere et cuiusmodi remedium adhibere.

[All the faithful of either sex, after they have reached the age of discernment, should individually confess all their sins in a faithful manner to their own priests at least once a year. . . . The priest shall be discerning and prudent, so that like a skilled doctor he may pour wine and oil over the wounds of the injured one. Let him carefully inquire about the circumstances of both the sinner and the sin, so that he may prudently discern what sort of advice he ought to give and what remedy to apply.][5]

On the one hand, this passage emphasizes the priest's power, focusing on his role in the process rather than the penitent's. He is the one with the special skill, here compared to that of doctor looking at wounds, and he is the one who speaks, inquiring about the circumstances. On the other hand, this passage raises an important question about the laity's role in confession: Are they merely passive recipients of the priest's attention? While this decree seems to assert that the laity's role here will be unproblematic (they are imagined as responding to the priest exactly as he requires), the passage also reveals an uncertainty about the participation and self-knowledge of the penitent. For example, the same word, *discern (discretionis/discretus)*, links the penitent and the priest, a link suggesting that confession is based as much on the layperson's ability to "discern" his or her sins as the priest's. But the process of discernment raises some questions. In figuring the penitent as wounded, the passage suggests that the penitent's sins are readily apparent, enough so that the priest may, metaphorically, pour wine and oil over them. In other words, the passage imagines that verbal and physical manifestations of sin are the same. Despite this assumption, the passage does give the priest directions on ascertaining these wounds—to inquire about the circumstances—and, in this way, suggests that the wounds of sin may not be so readily apparent either to the priest or to the penitent.

This passage cannot, of course, be understood apart from the immense amount of literature produced to popularize the decree.[6] And indeed, penitential handbooks and sermons preached about confession reveal that getting the laity to speak about their interior wounds was not exactly as simple as it is made out to be. The instruction, particularly in the vernacular, that arises and circulates after Lateran IV is very much concerned with finding a language and system of knowledge for making the priest's discernment possible. Any investigation of a penitential manual will reveal that the priest gives penitents a very specific language to discuss their identity.[7] This language is established and regularized in the penitential manuals that began circulating in the thirteenth century and were recopied (often with modifications) and translated into the vernacular throughout the late Middle Ages. For example, in the thirteenth-century penitential of Thomas of Chobham, the author writes:

> Circa primum attendum est quod non debet sacerdos statim ex abrupto dicere penitenti: dic peccata tua, sed debet prius multipliciter eum instruere, et multa ab eo inquirere ut devotius et melius confiteatur.

> [Concerning the first (how a priest should hear confession) it must be considered that the priest should not immediately and abruptly say to the penitent: tell me your sins, but rather he should first instruct him in various ways and earnestly inquire about him so that he may confess more devoutly and better].[8]

Here Chobham's priest guides the penitent through a series of questions based on traditional pastoral teaching: the Decalogue, the Pater Noster, the Beatitudes, the gifts of the Holy Spirit, and, most extensively, the vices.[9] These questions standardize the categories of sins and beliefs, and the success of these categories was such that the same ones appear in much later works, such as John Mirk's late-fourteenth- or early-fifteenth-century *Instructions for Parish Priests*.[10] In this text, Mirk follows the same structure outlined in Chobham's manual: he first asks the penitent whether he knows the Pater, Ave, and Creed; then he questions him according to both the Decalogue and the seven "dedly synnes."[11] The continuity in these structures for thinking about sin suggests that in the penitentials "such lists [of sin] both reflect and determine attitudes toward sin."[12] As is clear from the use of the *pastoralia* (the Pater Noster, Ave, Decalogue, etc.), confessional practice encourages speaking according to formulas.[13] One should note that these formulas are not intended to be merely abstract; they are consistently related to the penitent in a process of definition. For example—and one could choose many such from both Latin and vernacular manuals—the author of the *Boke of Penance* writes, "pride is a luste if I ne sal leye. / his awen state þat man walde hey."[14]

I do not mean to suggest that the standardization of this language, such as the seven sins, leads to a standardization of every penitent's identity. Rather, we should think of the sins, as well as the other pastoral formulas, as a capacious psychological language given to penitents by the priest to think about their identity, identity understood both as an inner self and as a self in relation to the larger Christian community.[15] Indeed, the theorization of sins in relation to what people feel and do and say provides a theory of human behavior, even if it is a rather pessimistic one, organized as it is around error.[16] As Thomas Tentler writes, "The examination of conscience, interrogations, general confession, forms of etiquette, and the like, were all designed to get at sin. In different ways they encouraged the penitent to think about his sins, identify them, classify them, and tell them. By these means sacramental confession inculcated an attitude toward sin and the self."[17] Despite this focus on sin, one must not forget that penitents are also asked to describe their belief (the basic requirements listed above) and who they are (in terms of marital status and occupation).

Although the penitentials are very much interested in theorizing all the possible actions and emotions in terms of sins, they are not interested in the relationship between this psychology and the language through which it must be mediated. Instead, they seem to suggest that the work (and therefore potential difficulty) facing the confessional self can (and even will) be found in the priest's (or even penitent's) activity of identifying and naming behaviors as sins, not in the act of speaking itself. In other words, once the priest has asked his questions, both sins and contrition will be easily discerned by the priest. For example, Chobham writes,

Et sicut medicus corporalis multa signa et indicia inquirit de morbo patientis utrum possit curari vel non, ita medicus spiritualis per multa signa debet considerare circa penitentem si vere peniteat vel

non, veluti si gemat, si ploret, si erubescat, et cetera talia faciat. Vel
si rideat vel se peccasse neget vel peccata sua defendat et similia.

[And just as a doctor of the body inquires of the patient's disease
through many signs and indications whether it can be cured or not,
thus the doctor of the spirit should consider by means of many signs
concerning the penitent if he might be truly penitent or not, for
example if he should sigh, if he should cry, if he should blush, and
should do other such things. Either if he should laugh or deny that
he had sinned or should defend his sins and similar things.][18]

Here we see the focus on the priest's power of discerning. The passage even
picks up the language of the Twenty-first Decree about the doctor-patient
relationship of priest and penitent as it encourages the priest to apply the
knowledge about sin, collected in this manual, to the signs he sees in front of
him about the penitent's interior state. Moreover, like the writers of the
Twenty-first Decree, Chobham sees a direct correlation between physical
signs (blushing and crying) and verbal signs (denying and defending). In
this way, Chobham educates the priest to "read" the penitent's interior state
and, in doing so, to impose *(iniungere)* a language on the penitent's actions
and thoughts even as he imposes acts of penance. And he does this through
the questions he asks about the kinds of sin, the circumstances, the penitent's occupation and marital status, and so on.

One might then say that handbooks' concern with the priest's discernment motivates a particular understanding of interiority: these handbooks
are concerned with understanding the penitent's interior using the language
of sin and contrition rather than with investigating how an interior might
be made accessible or inaccessible through the language used to describe it.
This emphasis makes perfectly good sense from the priest's point of view
because the priest is interested in his ability to discern the degree of sin and
contrition rather than in penitents' ability to voice their sin and contrition.
Once the focus of pastoral instruction shifts to include more laity as readers,
the emphasis in confession also shifts: from a focus on discerning (the naming and identifying associated with the priest's role) to speaking. A language
developed for discerning the interior (from the priest's perspective) would
necessarily have quite different problems and potentialities associated with

it than a language developed for speaking about the interior, quite apart from the power relations involved (to which I will return below when I address the Wycliffite views of confession). Of course, this argument works only if we assume that lay-oriented handbooks consistently support the priest's role in confession as separate from that of the penitent instead of serving as replacements for confession, in which case the penitent would merely occupy both positions at once—discerning and speaking. But I think it is fair to say that the vernacular handbooks do describe themselves as aids to confession rather than replacements. In addition, they omit a great amount of the material that goes with the role of discerning, such as material on the attributes of the person, found in Thomas of Chobham's *Summa*, or on contrition, found in Raymond of Pennaforte's *Summa* or the *Fasciculus Morum*. Instead, they focus their energies on detailing the sins themselves.

The shift in interest is most obvious in the content of vernacular handbooks, which are far less interested in theorizing the stages of penance and the problems associated with these stages than in laying out what the penitent must do. A brief comparison with a Latin manual that is somewhat contemporary in date and nationality with the vernacular handbooks that I am using will make this difference clear: the writer of the *Fasciculus Morum* (c. 1300) organizes his entire handbook around the seven sins and includes his discussion of the stages of confession in the sin of sloth. Clearly, readers of this handbook are intended to see it as a guide to understanding penance as a system rather than as a guide to the stages they, personally, are meant to follow. As might be expected, the *Fasciculus Morum* gives very little attention to the details of penitents' speech: "Est ergo confessio secundum Raymundum 'coram sacerdote legittima peccatorum declaracio" (According to Raymundus, confession is the genuine showing of one's sins before a priest).[19] One can compare the extensive discussion of the good effects of confession, which occupies seventy lines, with the brief discussion of how it is done: "Augustinus: 'O inquit, breve verbum 'peccavi,' quod portas paradisi aperit.' Exemplum de David, Magdalena, et sancto latrone, et huiusmodi." (Augustine says: "O short word 'I have sinned,' which opens the doors of paradise!" We find this exemplified in David, Magdalene, the Good Thief, and others.)[20]

In contrast, the vernacular treatises, such as *Jacob's Well* (c. 1400–25) and the *Boke of Penance* (late fourteenth century), detail what is expected of penitents themselves and in this way draw attention to how penitents will confess, will become speaking subjects. Like the Latin manuals that they translate, the vernacular manuals do not imagine any problems with representing the interior in language. This transparency of verbal and physical manifestations is made clear in that the word *declaracio,* used in the *Fasciculus Morum,* is consistently translated as "showing" in the vernacular texts rather than as "declaring" or "claiming," verbs that would emphasize the role of speech in this act. For example, *Jacob's Well* describes the penitential process as scooping out the corrupt water of the well. Casting out the bad water is the speech act of confession: "þe deppere it be in sorwe of herte, & þe holere it be in purpos to leue þi synne, þe more largely & clerly it castyth out of þi soule, wyth schryfte, þi cursed synne."[21] The language to describe that interior space, the pit, is that of the seven capital sins, and the writer prefaces his account of them with this statement: "I haue schewyd ȝou how ȝe schul scopyn out of ȝoure pyt, þat is, of ȝour body, þe corrupt watyr of þe grete curs. Now schal I telle ȝow what stynkyng wose is in ȝoure pyt, nedefull to be fermyd out."[22] In this way, the writer details the function of this language of sin in the penitential system: to describe the interior, the corrupt water in the pit, so that it can be scooped out "to receyue watyr of contricyoun in-to þin herte."[23] Interestingly enough, the writer describes contrition as another kind of water, in contrast to the water of sin. Although this figure makes sense in terms of the tears that go with contrition, it renders the relationship between contrition and the interior somewhat problematic. In other words, sorrowing is not read as scooping, despite the parallel of remorse as a kind of interior digging. Here contrition comes from the outside as water. In this way, the contrition does not belong to the interior (the heart); rather, the interior is imagined as an emptiness that can be filled with corrupt water, the sin, or good water, contrition.

Similarly, in the *Boke of Penance,* another vernacular text, the author discusses confession in terms of showing and opening:

> þe toþer point is shrift of mouþ
> to make to prest our synnis couþ
> opinli ham to knaw.
> wiþ-out glosing truli to shaw.
> & atte þis point be trew & lele
> hit fallis þer-til þingis fele.

·   ·   ·   ·   ·   ·   ·   ·   ·

Shrift is opin shewing of brest
laghfulli made be-fore preste
of synnis þat man myn of mai.
& is als mikil for to say.
als of man hert an opining wide
þat man can shew wiþ-outen hide.[24]

The repetition of the terms *shewing* and *open* suggests, perhaps, that this writer is concerned that his readers might not be willing to reveal their sins to the priest.[25]

Although these texts anticipate problems with penitents' speech, the problems are understood within the framework of "discerning" rather than "speaking." In this way, resistances to confession are always imagined as resistances to the category of sin, not to the category of speech. For example, the writer of the *Fasciculus Morum* tells a story about a virgin who has been thought to be devout but is seen after her death accompanied by devils. When asked why she is damned, she says, "Solebam, inquit, contra matrem meam insurgere et murmurare, et non credidi illud esse grave peccatum, cum tamen sit directe contra Dei preceptum. De isto nolui confiteri, unde dampnata sum et sic crucior sine fine." (I used to get angry and murmur against my mother, but I did not think it was a grave sin, though it goes directly against God's commandment. I would not confess that, so I am now condemned and tormented without end.)[26] This story imagines the difficulty of confessional speech as a result of willful disobedience to one of the Ten Commandments. Similarly, the same author details difficulties with "truthful confessions" as speech related—those who excuse their sins, or blame them on someone else, or blame them on God.[27] These penitents have accepted the category of sin; they have merely assigned it to someone else. While the vernacular handbooks give the problems of confessional speech less attention, they have a similar outlook. The *Boke* warns against "quaint wordis," which seem to be the euphemisms with which penitents disguise their sin: "lette for na shame / ne wiþ na quaint wordis of sliȝt / agh þou noȝt to shew þi pliȝt."[28] And the writer of *Jacob's Well* includes one exemplum after his discussion of confession about a woman who refuses to confess. What causes this resistance is shame; her understanding of her sin is apparent because she prays, does penance, and makes restitution.[29]

Up to this point, I have focused on penitential manuals, and one might argue that these have a somewhat self-selecting readership: those readers, whether clerical or lay, who have already accepted the importance of the penitential scheme. It is necessary, therefore, to turn to vernacular sermons, although, as I have mentioned, the distinction between sermons and penitential manuals in the vernacular is somewhat arbitrary. These sermons demonstrate that pastoral instruction more generally does not give attention to the problems of speaking the interior before the debates associated with Wycliffism. In these sermons, the church's teaching on confession is based primarily on the exposition of Jesus' actions in healing the afflicted (as discussed in the first chapter). These expositions refer only to showing, not to speech, as in the vernacular penitential manuals discussed above. For example, in the exposition of the Canaanite woman (who begs Christ to heal her daughter, Matt 15:22), an author writes, "She ranne to Crist, þe best leche of all, and forsoke hure countrey and shewed hure sekenes and askyd medecyne."[30] Similarly, the story of the publican and the Pharisee (Luke 18:10–14), a story often used to explain confession, describes the publican's actions: "And in þat þat he knokked so on is breste was vndurstonde an oppon confession."[31] We also find directions to "verely and oponly knalage þou trespasse."[32] This concern with opening also occurs in the fifteenth-century *Speculum Sacerdotale:* "Alle this is to be schewid and to be sorowed that he may after siche verrey knoweliche of his synne fynde God merciful to hym. For in knowlegynge of his synne, he shall fynde ekynge of grace."[33]

Even the directions to confess that play with figural language elide the function of speech. In this category, we could place the use of vomiting as a metaphor for confession: "Neuerþeles it is tau3th in fisike þat a vomyte is a profitabull medecyn to suche dronkon men. And þis vomyte to oure porpose is the sacrament of confession, to þe wiche I counceyll euery man þat is seke in anny maner þat I haue spoke of þat he draw to itt."[34] Clearly vomiting takes up the governing metaphors of confession: the priest is the doctor; the penitent is the patient; and the sickness and remedies are read as physical manifestations of emotional states.

Resisting Confession

In their polemic against confession, Wycliffites draw attention to the problem of speaking about the interior and, in this way, distinguish themselves from the problem of discerning sin, the subject of handbooks for priests, or the problem of understanding and making use of those categories, the subject of the penitentials for laypeople. In addition, they raise a number of new questions about the speaking subject: In what power relationship will individuals speak of their faith? What language is best suited to describe the interior? How will speakers represent their interior thoughts if they reject the language of discernment disseminated in the penitential manuals? The shift is most strikingly apparent is the redefining and retheorizing of the term *confession*. Whereas in Latin *confiteor* can (and does) refer to speaking about the self (to a priest, to God, to another layperson), Wycliffite writers introduce a number of distinctions between these kinds of speaking and, at times, translate them differently.[35] The Wycliffite sermons use the word *confession* to mean confession either as public proclamation or as private speech with God. Confession to a priest is redefined as a kind of whispered conversation, "rownyng."[36] For the first, confession as a public speech, a writer of the *English Wycliffite Sermons* states, "Here we schal vndurstonde, þat confession þat Crist nameþ here, is not rownyng in prestis heere, to tellon hym synne þat wee han doon, but it is grawntyng of trewþe þe whiche is *apertly* [openly] seyd."[37] While this confession is certainly a kind of speaking about the interior, it does not provide much insight into how that interior is imagined except, quite generally, as "trewþe." Nevertheless, we might note that the writer separates "synne" from "trewþe," whereas, in penitential manuals (and even in the *Nota*, discussed below), the truthful confession does indeed concern itself with "synne þat wee han doon," in contrast to the sin that we try to blame on others (see the discussion of the *Fasciculus Morum* above). In this way, the writer suggests that sin may no longer be the appropriate language to describe the interior, at least for the faithful, whose interior is imagined as a place of truth. As a result, we have two possible relationships between the interior and speech: "rownyng" in the priest's ear goes with an interior imagined as sin, but an interior imagined as truth goes with speaking "apertly."

In Wycliffite writers, the openness of confession has to do with its publicity rather than with its capability to manifest (that "opining" or "schewyng" in vernacular handbooks) what is contained inside. In this way, the Wycliffites redirect concerns about openness to the context of speaking (where and when the penitent speaks) and away from the content of the speech (whether what the penitent says "shows" his or her heart, in the language of the *Boke*). To be sure, the Wycliffites probably imagine that the two kinds of "open" confessions belong together and may, therefore, be guarantees of one another. Nevertheless, the discussion of openness occurs almost exclusively within expositions of the martyrs; this writer does not need to consider the possibility of a public, deceitful confession.

It might be useful to pause to examine why the Wycliffites are so concerned with the context of the speech act rather than the quality or content of the speech itself. In Wycliffite polemic, the corruption that pervades auricular confession has created a crisis of speaking about the interior to anyone except for God. For example, in an early statement of Lollard beliefs, "Twelve Conclusions of the Lollards" (1395), the author writes:[38]

> Þe ix conclusiun þat holdith þe puple lowe is þat þe articlis of confessiun þat is sayd necessari to saluaciun of man, with a feynid power of absoliciun enhaunsith prestis pride, and ȝeuith hem opertunite of priui calling othir þan we wele now say. For lordis and ladys ben arestid for fere of here confessouris þat þei dur nout seyn a treuth, and in time of confessiun is þe beste time of wowing and of priue continuaunce of dedli synne. þei seyn þat þei ben commissariis of God to deme of euery synne, to foulin and to clensin qwom so þei lyke. þei seyn þat þei han þe keys of heuene and of helle, þei mown cursyn and blissin, byndin and unbyndin at here owne wil, in so miche þat for a busschel of qwete or xii.d be ȝere þei welen selle þe blisse of heuene be chartre of clause of warantise, enselid with þe comown sel.[39]

While this conclusion is most clearly an attack on the commercialism inherent in the practice of confession (and therefore an attack related to antifraternalism), it also suggests the consequences of this corruption for the penitents' speech.[40] The confession described here is an opportunity not for the penitent's speech but rather for the priest's "priue calling," his private conversation. Moreover, this kind of confession is described as impeding rather than making available a language with which the penitent might describe that interior "trewthe" discussed above. The conversation does not define the penitent's sin and his or her interior state of contrition but produces sin by enhancing the priest's pride and motivating lustful thoughts. It seems to me that the bleakness of this portrait of confession stems not merely from the greedy and lustful confessor but also from the fact that speech, the very instrument that is supposed to alleviate sin by defining it and ultimately remedying it, produces more sin, a situation that seems to condemn the penitent to a silence marked by spiritual danger. It is worth recalling Chaucer's dig at the Friar in the *General Prologue* to the *Canterbury Tales:* "Therfore in stede of wepynge and preyeres / Men moote yeve silver to the povre freres."[41] Here "in stede" reveals that money has replaced both contrition and speech, a perspective made explicit in Wycliffite texts.

This disruption of the traditional (and discernible) relationship between speech and the interior is intensified in the second use of the term *confession* in Wycliffite writings, the private confession to God along the lines of David: "And ʒif þe feend [the established church] alegghe þe salm þat Dauyd roos at mydnyʒt to confesse to his God, why schulde not we now do so?"[42] Here this author is aware that David's confessions to God in the Psalms are often read as traditional confessional practice (as apparent in the citation from the *Fasciculus Morum* above), and he asserts the importance of taking this psalm literally. This form of confession is also translated as "knowlechyng" in another Wycliffite tract, the *Nota de Confessione,* which defines confession as "knowlechynge [acknowledgment or recognition] of synne," "truly by herte or mouthe."[43] The term *knowlechyng* asserts the importance of the penitent's role in speaking: it is the speaker's responsibility to make his or her interior known by putting it into language.[44]

This self-consciousness about speaking is even more apparent in the biblical exposition concerning David, in which the author of the *Nota* responds to the traditional readings of this confessional subject. I cite at length to make this author's response clear:

It were to witt to assoyle skils þat antecrist makiþ aʒens þis waye. ffurst he seiþ þat heretikes wolen distruyʒe þe seuen sacramentis; for þat stondiþ in confessioun of mouþ, & sorow of hert, & a-seet makyng, and herfor seiþ david in his boke: "þou god þat art my god, I shal synge to þe in an harpe." an harpe haþe þre partis of hym; þe ouermost in which ben stringis wrastid, þe secounde is þe holow part of þe harpe, þe þridde knytteþ þise two to-gidre. Riʒt so in þis sacrament mut be contricioun for þe furst part, & aftur a man mut synge to god in voice for þe secound part, and þe þridde tyme he must make a-seeþ & knytt þise two partes to-gidre. what

herityke or fool is he þat wold distruȝe þis gostly harpe? here men
seyen þat trewe entent shuld be to declare riȝt beleue, hou men
shulden harpe here to god, as david did & oþer seyntis; for many
kunne not wrast þis harpe, & oþur kunne not harpe whenne it is
diȝt. Suche wittis gyuen to goddis worde ben goode whenne þei
ben wele taken; and þis witt þat here is seid telliþ þat a man shulde
shriue hym to god, & makiþ no mynde of rownynge shrift, þat is
late brouȝt inne bi þe pope. and iche man þat holdiþ beleeue grant-
eþ þat a man shuld shriue him to god, ȝe, & to man, bi voice of
mouþe, and haue sorow for his synne, & þerfor make to god a-seeþ
for synne; but þis is don apertly to prestis, when þei ben good &
louen more þe heele of mennes soules þenne her goodis by coueytise. but here men shulden vndurstonde þat þe curtesie of god askiþ
not of iche man to shriue him þus bi voice of mouþe; for as many
synne greuously wiþ-inne in herte, as did þe fend, so many men
maken aseeþ bi sorow of herte, þat may not speke or wanteþ opor-
tunytee to shryue hym to man bi voice.[45]

In this passage, the author accepts the figural interpretation of David's harp-
ing as the three-part penitential scheme (contrition, confession, and satisfaction) only to raise the problem of where speaking fits into the interpretation.
This is a discussion much expanded from that offered by the author of the
sermon quoted above, who merely reinforces David's literal speech to God
as a model for the literal speech of his listeners. For this author, the confession itself, when David harps to God, is not merely the opening up of the
interior—the showing of sorrow and sin. In fact, sorrow and the expression
of it are not at all the same thing, and the author underlines this fact with
the phrase "voice of mouth," as if to emphasize that he does mean the penitent's literal voice and not the voice of his or her heart. Once he has noted
this important distinction between literal and figurative voices, he can acknowledge that there may be problems with speaking the interior and that
God allows for these problems. Indeed, his departure from the traditional
interpretation occurs quite gradually: he first states the obvious meaning of
the passage, that each man should confess to God by voice of mouth (a traditional interpretation) and then introduces his new qualification with a
"but," thus changing the directive entirely. One does not, in fact, need to
speak at all.[46]

Although the views in this passage could be read as entirely in line with orthodoxy, in that every penitential manual recognizes the possibility that one might not have the opportunity to confess to a priest, the emphasis here is quite different. In this passage, the author states that one does not need "voice of mouth" and, at the same time, observes that many sin within their hearts. In other words, the author establishes a distinction between speaking and thinking. It is as if the author's meditation on confession has led him to the recognition that some sins may not have a language associated with them, may not, in fact, be discernible when placed within the systems of definition associated with the established church. The limitations of this language's representational power are made most apparent in his observation that "whenne a man wiþ contrite herte shriueþ him opynly to god or man, þenne his voice, þat is token of his hooly sorowe of herte, may be called a sacrament."[47] For this writer, language can be only a token of the sorrow, not the "opening" or "showing" of the sorrow itself, as suggested by the *Boke of Penance* and *Jacob's Well*.

In this way, the Wycliffites introduce a division in the kinds of confession, a division where there was previously continuity. Traditionally, confession to a priest, public confessions (such as those of the martyrs), and private confessions (such as those that occur in the Bible, between David and God, or sinners and Jesus) are read as exactly the same kind of speech. Each act of speaking has the same potentialities for describing the interior, and each shares the same problems (the refusal to conform to the standards set by the priest). In challenging the traditional confessional models, the Wycliffites focus new attention to the confessional self.

William Thorpe's Resistance

The orthodox penitential manuals and sermons provide examples, most obviously in the exempla, of penitents' own experience of confession, however ideologically overdetermined these examples might be.[48] What matters here is not whether these exempla are mimetic in Erich Auerbach's sense (representations of reality) but whether they were perceived as instigating imitation on the part of the listeners.[49] As such, they offer illustrations of the declarations that penitents would make in confession. While the orthodox texts contain, then, illustrations of their ideology of confession in action, the

Wycliffite texts seem to offer no such illustrations, aside from the brief mention of David or the martyrs in the sermons. How, then, are we to investigate this crisis of the speaking subject that I have identified? One place to look would be to Wycliffite "confessions," as they define the term—that is, the testimony of Wycliffites who found themselves "martyrs" to the established church; these are the *Trial of Richard Wyche* and *The Testimony of William Thorpe*.[50] Here I shall concentrate on the latter because I am particularly interested in the subject who speaks in the vernacular.[51] While Thorpe's testimony has received increasing attention from scholars, a short summary might be useful here: the text records an encounter between William Thorpe and Archbishop Arundel in 1407. Thorpe acts as both commentator and participant during the examination: he frames his account of the trial with a short prologue in which he describes the four reasons for his writing (all concerning his desire to provide a good example for friends and fellow Lollards) and then organizes the text around the five questions Arundel asks at the trial, concerning the Eucharist, images, pilgrimages, tithes, and swearing.[52] Thorpe answers each question in great detail, thus providing both an outline of Lollard belief and, ultimately, a model for a rhetorical triumph over the established church (as represented by Arundel). Indeed, the text should be read as a kind of Lollard hagiography.[53] Thorpe certainly sounds like a fifteenth-century English St. Cecilia lecturing her inquisitor on the nature of belief, and one must assume that later readers, such as John Foxe, saw this aspect in this text; hence its inclusion in *Acts and Monuments*.[54] Of course, Thorpe's rhetorical triumph seems all the more powerful because his version of the examination is the only one we have; outside the text he has written, Thorpe's identity and his fate remain a mystery.[55]

While Thorpe's text certainly disseminates identifiably Lollard views and in this way is linked generically to other Lollard treatises on the Eucharist or pilgrimages, its structure—the examination—thematizes the act of speaking. Although this text has not been read as a response to the practice of auricular confession in particular, I shall argue here that it should be.[56] Thorpe is not alone in using the confession defined as public proclamation (often the subject of hagiography) to respond to concerns about confession defined as speaking about the self. Chaucer's *Canterbury Tales* also offers this pairing in the exemplary speech of St. Cecilia and the bleakly pessimistic confession of the Canon's Yeoman.[57]

When read as both a Wycliffite confession and a rejection of the traditional confessional self, Thorpe's text illustrates the debate over subjectivity and language at this particular historical moment. Perhaps it is best to begin by pointing out the ways in which the text takes up and expands the Wycliffite concerns with confession discussed above: the first is its resistance to "rownynge" and its interest in public confession; the second is its attention to the context and significance of the act of speaking. The first is made most apparent in the dialectic between what happens in the text (the examination itself) and the text's address to its readers. That is, Thorpe's text offers two opposing views of confession: Arundel's and his own. The text itself becomes the open confession, directed to its readers against Arundel's efforts within the text to reduce Thorpe's examination to a private conversation, the "rownynge." In this way, Thorpe's publication reverses the movement of the trial, which begins with Arundel's exclusion of the "myche peple" and "seculer men" in his "greet chaumbre," when he withdraws into a "priuy closet" with Thorpe, a physician, and two masters of law (29). Indeed, the scene that takes place within the "closet" resembles traditional auricular confession. When Thorpe opens the "priuy closet" to the public eye, we see Arundel invoking his authority over Thorpe: "if þou wolt now mekeli and of good herte wiþouten ony feynynge knele doun and leie þin hond vpon a book and kisse it, bihotinge feiþfulli, as I schal here charge þee, þat þou wolt submytte þee to my correccioun and stonde to myn ordinaunce, and fulfille it dewli bi alle þi kunnynge and þi power, þou schalt fynde me gracious and frendli to þee" (29–30).[58] Arundel's attempt to assert his authority as Thorpe's confessor is, of course, challenged both within the text, when Thorpe insists upon speaking his mind, and outside the text, when Thorpe addresses his readers. He writes so "þat alle men and wymmen occupieden feiþfulli alle her wittis in knowynge and kepynge of Goddis heestis, ablynge hem so to grace þat þei miȝten vndirstonde truli þe truþe" (27). In claiming his text as a vehicle for "Goddis heestis," Thorpe promotes his text's similarity to the process of confession itself, which is intended to enable penitents to "know and keep" God's commandments. His repeated claim in his Prologue to write "boþe myn aposynge and myn answeringe" (24, 25, 27) suggests, similarly, the questions and responses of a penitential handbook. Moreover, Thorpe even imagines a kind of absolution that his text can offer (as the confessor offers one to the penitent): "For to siche feiþful louers specially, and pacient suers of Crist [i.e., his readers], þis Lord sendiþ his wisdom fro aboue" (27–28).

In publishing his text for his followers, Thorpe not only replaces "row-nynge" with the Wycliffite version of confession but also changes the relationship that structures the traditional confessional—the confessor as the discerner and the penitent as the wounded. As a result, he provides a new meaning for the "open confession." As discussed above, directives to be open meant that the penitent should show his or her interior (often described as a heart) to the priest. An open confession, in this sense, was an honest and complete confession that facilitated the priest's discernment of the penitent. In contrast, Thorpe follows another, Wycliffite view of an open confession, the "apertly" of the sermon mentioned above. Here the speaker speaks publicly so that an audience can hear. In this way, Thorpe points to the changing role of discernment in the confessional self. For the Wycliffite confession, the priest does not impose a language on the penitent's wounds (or heart); that imposition is here described as the "correccioun" and "ordinaunce" that Arundel offers and Thorpe rejects. Rather, the discernment is imagined taking place outside the confessional relationship, in the readers who test Thorpe and ultimately themselves against the scriptural models to determine their relationship to the truth Thorpe repeatedly invokes.

The text demonstrates a second Wycliffite concern with traditional confessional speech (and therefore with the traditional confessional self) in Thorpe's attention to the context of speaking in the discussion of auricular confession that happens within the examination itself. It is important to note that this discussion is set apart from the other doctrinal discussions that occur as the five questions of the trial, set apart because Thorpe has already been asked the fifth and final question about swearing and because of the personal nature of the question. Indeed, this event precipitates a kind of confessional crisis for Thorpe, whereas the other questions seem merely to serve as vehicles to discuss Lollard views. The episode begins when a clerk asks Thorpe, "Whi on Fryday [þat] last was counseiledist [þou] a man of my lordis þat he schulde not schryue him to a man but oonli to God?" (80). It is suddenly clear to Thorpe that he is no longer in control of the discussion, that Arundel knows more than he does; he has sent a spy to get Thorpe to reveal in private what he might not admit in public. Thorpe reacts powerfully:

And wiþ þis axynge I was astonyed, and anoon þanne I knew þat I
was sotilly bitraied of a man þat came to me into prisoun on þe
Fryday bifore, comownynge wiþ me in þis mater of confessioun.
And certis bi his wordis I gessid þat þis man cam þan to me of ful
feruent and charitable desyre, but [now] I knowe þat he came to
tempte me and to acuse me—God forȝeue him if it be his wille þis
treesoun, and I do wiþ al myn herte! And so þan, whanne I had
þouȝt þus, I seide to þis clerk, "Sere, I preie ȝou þat ȝe wolde fecche
þat man hider, and alle þe wordis as niȝ as I can reporte hem which
I spak to him on Fridaie in prisoun I wole reherse here now bifore
ȝou alle and bifore him." (80)

This incident makes the audience (and, perhaps Thorpe himself in the narrative of the examination) aware of the problems associated with confessional speech. It is significant that Thorpe associates the practice of confession with deceitful speech (after all, no one has tried to trap him privately in
his beliefs on the Eucharist, as the knight does in Richard Wyche's trial).[59]
Here Thorpe is particularly interested in emphasizing the nature of the
speech between the two men rather than the matter of his authority or lack
thereof as a preacher: Is this conversation "comownynge" or a true "confessioun"? Indeed, it seems that Thorpe narrates this incident to demonstrate
the way in which he has been trapped against his will in a kind of traditional
confessional self, in allowing another (the spy and ultimately Arundel) to
"discern" his interior (his beliefs about confessional practice). His solution
is to regain control over his speech outside the context of this personal exchange by speaking about it publicly. In this way he would place discernment outside the confessional relationship (onto the audience), but his fear
lingers in his request to speak again, which repeats anxiously the act of
speech itself: "wordis," "reporte," "spak," "reherse."

    In focusing on the problems accompanying the second stage of the
penitential scheme, the act of confession itself, and not so much the first
and third (contrition and satisfaction), Thorpe (and his fellow Wycliffites)
certainly seem to accept the importance of contrition, and therefore one of
the traditional schemes for understanding the interior. And, indeed, this is
the case; when Thorpe responds to the spy who has asked him about confession, he sounds very much like an orthodox priest:

Ser, I counseile ȝou for to absente ȝou fro al yuel companye, and to drawe ȝou to hem þat louen and bisien hem to knowe and to kepe þe heestis of God. And þanne þe good spirit of God wole moue ȝou for to occupie bisili alle ȝoure wittis in gederynge togedere of alle ȝoure synnes, as ferforþ as ȝe cunne biþinke ȝou, schamynge greet-ly of hem, and sorowynge ofte hertli for hem—ȝhe, sere, þe Holi Goost wole þanne putte into ȝoure herte a good wille and a feruent desir for to take and holde a good purpos, to hate euere and to fle aftir ȝoure cunnynge and ȝoure power euery occasioun of synne. And so þanne wisedam schal come to ȝou from aboue, illumynynge wiþ dyuerse bemes of heuenly grace all ȝoure wittis, enfourmynge ȝou how ȝe schulen triste stidefastli in þe mercy of þe Lord, knowl-echinge to him al holy al ȝoure viciouse lyuynge. (81–82)

As this passage makes clear, Thorpe seems to accept the traditional models for describing the interior: the sorrow and shame that define contrition and the sins themselves. Nevertheless, there is an important difference here: this description of the interior changes the relationship between the process of discerning (the priest's duty to inquire about and then name and define sin and contrition) and the act of speaking (the penitent's duty to make a com-plete and detailed confession), which occur in tandem in the traditional con-fessional process. One could argue that in this case the penitent is supposed to take over both roles—acting as both the speaker and the discerner simul-taneously. Nevertheless, if one looks closely at this passage, one will see not only that Thorpe is uninterested in the role of speech in this process ("knowle-chinge" could be a spoken or unspoken recognition) but that he has sepa-rated the process of discernment from the penitential scheme itself. Clearly Thorpe is still interested in how the penitent will know that he has sinned, but here that process of learning comes when the penitent "draws" himself to those that keep God's commandments (and, presumably, learns them by example). This act of discernment (choosing the good from the evil com-pany) allows contrition and the process of self-examination (with the help of God's spirit).[60] While Thorpe might still find some of the traditional pasto-ral requirements useful (the command to think of one's sins, for example), he has removed many of the basic elements of confessional practice as they are described in vernacular handbooks: the necessity of a complete confes-sion, the definition of circumstances, and the evaluation of contrition. All of these also belong to the act of discerning but are here omitted.[61] The discernment that he does endorse (learning from others' actions about God's commands, thinking of sin "as ferforþ" as you can) is curiously unmediated by speech of any kind. Perhaps one must think of sin only as much as one can in the absence of conversation about it. Indeed, he seems to posit a knowledge of oneself that is unmediated by language, whose limitations will be overcome by the spirit of God and the Holy Ghost.

While this discussion of auricular confession certainly describes the interior, it does not address the relationship of language to this interior. Indeed, the one possible mention of speech in this description, "knowlechinge," is rather confusing, since the list of similar clauses seems to suggest that it modifies "wisedam" instead of "ʒou." Thorpe's view of this relationship can be found elsewhere in the text: when he is more directly concerned with confession defined as public proclamation than with confession as recognition of sins. Like his "confessional crisis" discussed above, these instances consistently underline the difficulties of speaking. Although Thorpe certainly provides insight into his interior both by describing his thoughts in the text and by invoking other models, Susannah or Paul's inner man, this access always seems to point at the same time to the failure of speech to represent his experience. In this way, the access Thorpe does provide falls short of the total knowledge offered by the categorizing mechanisms of traditional discernment. Instead, Thorpe's investigation of his interior suggests that the distinction between inner and outer is perhaps unbridgeable—that showing and opening the heart (or the internal wounds of sin) in language may well be impossible.

In these instances the interior with which Thorpe concerns himself is one that grows out of resistance to the questioner and not in response to him (as would be imagined in traditional penitential practice). But we must see this resistance not only in terms of Thorpe and Arundel but in terms of the larger question posed by the confessional experience itself—what if the speaker's experiences do not match the language of sins and wounds that he is given to describe them? This is, of course, a problem that the penitential manuals, with their exhaustive lists of possible circumstances and variations of sin, just do not imagine.

Thorpe investigates his interior on two occasions in the text, and both times these investigations are signaled to the reader by mention of his silence in the face of a threat (and his silences are remarkable because during the rest of the testimony he speaks at great length). Both occur early in the text, when Thorpe and Arundel are establishing what kind of confession this will be—an admission of error or the public proclamation of a martyr. The first time Thorpe decides not to speak comes in response to Arundel's requirement that he "forsake alle þe opynynouns whiche þe sect of Lollers holdiþ and is sclaundrid wiþ, so þat aftir þis tyme neiþir priuyli ne apeertli þou holde noon opynyoun whiche I schal, aftir þat þou hast sworun, reherse here to þee" (34). What is striking about this demand is the way in which it drains speech of any particularity. The Lollards' opinions are merely that; they will be "rehearsed" rather than stated or outlined, as if each of the opinions were only a repetition of the previous. In addition, Arundel's statement suggests that these opinions are only language, that they do not have the capacity to represent Thorpe's own experiences and beliefs (Thorpe's own particularity), because Thorpe is not going to be asked to describe them himself. While Arundel's statement certainly emphasizes his view of Lollard opinions as heretical (and as such perhaps undeserving of the kind of detail with which one would describe true belief), the reader is also confronted with the way in which this statement frames the discussion of belief throughout the text. For Thorpe, these opinions are beliefs, beliefs that are, in fact, quite close to orthodoxy, as his opening statement makes quite clear. From this perspective, Arundel's statement suggests that Arundel (and, therefore, the established church that he here represents) is completely uninterested in the relationship of the individual believer (his particular experience of belief) and the statement of belief, a situation that directly contradicts the purposes of annual auricular confession. This practice is, at least in part, supposed to monitor the successful internalization of the requirements of the faith (those six things in the *Lay Folks' Catechism*), and it is perhaps part of the polemical intent of this text to demonstrate the way in which the words of orthodox belief are perceived to be in some way deficient: a mechanistic, outdated system that is interested only in submission to its discourses and not in the capacity of that discourse to describe or interpret the experiences of church members.

Thorpe's silence in response to this demand must be read not only as fear in the face of Arundel's power but as the inadequacy of anything he might say (all of which will be read into Arundel's structure of Lollard opinion). He turns to himself: "And I heerynge þese wordis þouȝte in myn herte þat þis was an vnleeful askynge, and I demed mysilf cursid of God if I consentid herto; and I þou3te how Susanne seide 'Angwysschis ben to me on euery side,' and forþi þat I stood stille musynge and spak not" (35).[62] It should come as no surprise that Thorpe, a Wycliffite, uses a scriptural model in imagining his interior. But here the story not only provides an interpretive scheme for Thorpe's threatened virtue and the evil scheming of an authority figure but also draws attention to the failure of speech. For Susannah is a figure trapped in a situation in which her speech has been falsely contextualized for her, and therefore she has no power to determine that it will be understood properly. Susannah's words may represent her interior (the secret of her innocence), but the context (the scheming of the elders) ensures that the audience will not be able to discern the truth behind her speech. In this way, Thorpe uses the story of Susannah to demonstrate the uselessness of any speech that is constrained.[63] In addition, Susannah's story nicely demonstrates the opposition between two kinds of confessional speech. First, the private speech of Susannah and the elders in her garden functions as a kind of "rownynge" because it is motivated by the elders' lust (analogous to the "wowyng" described in the Ninth Conclusion of the Lollards). Second, Susannah's appeal to God at her trial functions as an example of a confession to God, a true representation of her interior: "Lord God, without bigynnyng and ende, that art knowere of hid thingis, that knowist alle thingis bifore that tho knowen alle thingus byfore thei be maad; thou wost, for thei han born fals witnessinge a3eines me. And loo! Y dye, whann Y dide nou3t of these thingus, whiche these maliciously maken to gydre a3einus me."[64] For Thorpe, like Susannah, the interrogation provides a context in which true speech cannot be discerned as true. In the story of Susannah, the presence of the divine spirit (in Daniel) ensures that truthful speech is finally discerned and upheld, and the reader of Thorpe's text can assume that Thorpe the commentator (as opposed to Thorpe the participant in the encounter) functions as a kind of Daniel. Nevertheless, the Susannah story provides a far more pessimistic view of the limitations of confessional speech than another exemplary figure might have done, perhaps a martyr whose speech would at least have had the power to convert others, such as St. Cecilia in Chaucer's *Second Nun's Tale.*

In focusing our attention on the limitations of speech and audience discernment, the silencing described above seems to describe a dead end, rather an odd place to begin the account of an examination in which readers are to be made aware of Thorpe's virtue. Yet Thorpe's second refusal to speak, after he has been threatened with burning, invokes a new model for speaking and guaranteeing truth—that of the martyr:

> And at þis seiynge I stood stille and spak not. But in myn herte I þouȝte þat God dide to me a greet grace if he wolde of his greet mercy brynge me into suche an eende, and [in] myn herte I was no þing maad agast wiþ þis manassynge of þe Archebischop. But more herþoruȝ myn herte was confortid and stablischid in þe drede and loue of God. And I lokinge biheeld inwardli þe Archebischop, and I considride þese to þingis in him: oon þat he was not ȝit sorowful forþi þat he hadde maade Wiliam Sautri [at Smeþefelde] to be wrongfulli brent, and also I considride þat þe Archebischop þirstide ȝit aftir þe schedynge out of more innocent blood. And anoon herfore I was moued in alle my wittis for to holde þe Archebischop neiþir prelat ne preest of God; and, forþi þat myn inner man was altogidre þus departid from þe Archebischop, me þowȝte I schulde not haue ony drede of him . . . and, whateuer þing þat I schulde speke, þat I miȝte haue þerto trewe autorite of scripture or open resoun. (36–37)

The threat of martyrdom opens up a language to describe Thorpe's experience in a more detailed manner than any other the reader encounters in the text. On the one hand, this passage uses traditional language to map the interior: Thorpe repeats the term "in myn herte," a phrase that also becomes "in alle my wittis or sense," terms that appear regularly in traditional descriptions of confessional selves, such as those in the *Boke of Penance* or *Jacob's Well*. On the other hand, the passage does not retreat into this interior space; it retains its focus on the world outside. Thorpe can see inside the archbishop (or he has internalized the archbishop's thoughts; either sense would work grammatically with *inwardli*), and within this interior space he meditates on a current event—the significance of Sawtry's execution. Even the term *inner man* gestures outside as well as inside; for the term refers not only to an inner Thorpe but to an inner, scriptural, authority to rival Arundel.[65] And this interior space has a direct effect on the way in which he chooses to mediate his experiences both to Arundel and, later, to his audience: the inner man allows him to deny that the archbishop is a prelate or priest of God during the examination and connects him to the readers who are also separate from this exchange but observing it as they read. Finally, and perhaps most significantly, this episode demonstrates the workings of a particular historical moment upon the interior. This interior is imagined, not as a space set apart from the workings of time (an imagined space that seems to connect both the stinking pit of *Jacob's Well* and the heart in the *Boke of Penance* to the inner self separate from history that contemporary selves are so fixated upon), but as fully contingent upon the topical for its mapping.

What I would like to suggest is that Thorpe and his fellow Wycliffites who wrote on confession transform the debate about confession into a debate about speaking.[66] This statement may sound rather odd, considering that the Foucauldian understanding of confession describes it very much in terms of speaking the interior, the interior defined as the secrets forced out of us. As Foucault writes in the *History of Sexuality*, "[O]ne confesses one's crimes, one's sins, one's thoughts and desires, one's illnesses and troubles; one goes about telling, with the greatest precision, whatever is most difficult to tell. . . . When it is not spontaneous or dictated by some internal imperative, the confession is wrung from a person by violence or threat; it is driven from its hiding place in the soul, or extracted from the body."[67] Traditional descriptions of auricular confession do concern the interior, as the consistent references to the heart, the internal pit, and even vomiting make clear. But this is an interior that can easily become exterior—revealed, scooped out, or purged—actions that underline the ease with which these interior conditions are translated into a language whose representational power is never questioned. Even Foucault's list of possible confessions resembles nothing so much as scooping out the secrets or vomiting forth details. In this way, Foucault sets at one the secret and the body itself in a manner that reminds one of the countless stories of saints, such as St. Ignatius, whose hearts are found to contain after their death golden letters stating their belief: "þat nyght ne daye ne cesed neuer spekynge of loue ne of þe swetenes of Ihesu Criste; and noȝthe spake he but as was in ys herte. In tokenynge where-of, when þat he was dede and ys herte was departed, þan was founde written in ys herte with letters of goold, 'Ihesus est amor meus—Ihesus ys my loue.'"[68] For both Foucault and traditional medieval accounts of confession, the heart, once opened, speaks clearly and completely.

This connection between Foucault and orthodox sermons underlines the strength of his argument about the continuity of confessional selves, but it is an argument that does not take into account the disruptions of the late medieval period, represented here by the Wycliffites. As I have tried to show above, the Wycliffites reposition the debate over confession around language itself, arguing that confession does not work as a practice not only because people do not accept the categories and understand the sins but because it relies on a context—the relationship between priest and confessor—in which language is never merely instrumental, the means to discovering sin. That the Wycliffites were not alone in their finding—that the more one attempts to describe the proper kind of language to define belief and lapses in belief, the more it seems to recede into the distance (except, of course, in those exceptional cases of martyrs)—is surely attested in a text written directly in response to Lollardy: Nicholas Love's *Mirror of the Blessed Life of Jesus Christ.*[69] It seems quite fitting to end a discussion of Thorpe's text with Love's text because both writers are connected through Archbishop Arundel; the villain of Thorpe's text has approved Love's for circulation.[70] One can even posit a chain of influence from Thorpe to Arundel to Love if one agrees that Arundel's encounter with Thorpe led him to draft the *Constitutions* (1409), under which Love's text would be the only form of the Bible allowed to the laity.[71]

Love includes in his life of Christ an account of the conversion of Mary Magdalene, a biblical text commonly interpreted to figure auricular confession (Luke 7:36–50).[72] In his exposition, Love departs from authors of earlier sermons and handbooks, whose interpretations reveal an unquestioned assumption of the passage's relevance to the practice. Discussions in these texts are generally quite brief; Magdalene appears, often along with others, as a sinner who confesses and is forgiven in the quick and easy reference in the *Fasciculus Morum,* cited above, or the opening to the *Boke of Penance.* Even sermons, which provide a bit more detail than the penitential handbooks, do not dwell upon the speech itself; they are often far more interested in her sin or her contrition.[73] Love, in contrast, writes with an awareness of the Lollard view of confession: he incorporates his response to the "fals opinyon of lollardes" in his exposition and indicates this perspective in the marginal note in Latin: "Contra lollardos nota de confessione" (92). The pressure to refute the Lollards and to return to an earlier, uncontested reading of this passage makes Love's text deeply conflicted. As much as he tries to assert the orthodox exposition, he expands his discussion of the biblical text far more than orthodox writers had done in the vernacular, thus granting the Wycliffites an interpretive power over the passage that he explicitly denies.[74] Nowhere is the influence of Lollardy more apparent than in the emphasis Love places on speech in this exposition.

Like the writer of the *Nota*, Love's deviation from traditional interpretation occurs only gradually. He begins in accordance with the traditional reading, that Mary Magdalene is contrite: she approaches Jesus *"with sorow of herte* withinforþe for hir synnes" (90; the italicized portion is a translation of the biblical text). From this point, Love's additions begin to distinguish this reading. Although he is still drawing on the traditional language of confession (the heart) when he writes that she "spake in hir herte to him," he continues the sentence in a new direction: "þenkyng *as it were* in þis manere" (90, my emphasis). This phrase self-consciously signals an insertion into the story, a speech in which Mary Magdalene says (among other things), "I knowlech soþely þat my synnes bene without noumbre as þe grauele of þe see" (90). In effect, Love has provided Magdalene with a confession, although he also signals that this confession does not occur in the text of Scripture. After finishing the story, he states its edifying nature as an "ensaumple of trewe repentance & penance" (92). The pressure to explain how exactly this story works an example of "trewe" (as in orthodox) repentance and penance, which requires "shrift of mouþe," causes him to create an interpretive tangle around the story:

> Bot here perantere sume men þenken aftur þe fals opinyon of lollardes þat shrift of mouþe is not nedeful, bot þat it sufficeþ onely in herte to be shriuen to god, as þe forseide woman was, for þe gospel telleþ not þat she spake any worde by mouþe, & ȝit was hir sinne fully forȝiuen as it is seide, & as it semeþ þis is a gret euidence for þat opinion. Bot hereto is an answere resonable þat oure lorde Jesus to whome she made hir confession in herte was þer in bodily presence verrey god & man, to whom by vertue of þe godhede was also opune þe þouht of hert as is to man þe spech of mouþe. . . . Wherfore þe þouht of herte onely was *þan* to him als miche as is *now* þerwiþ spech of mouþe to man bodily. . . . And siþen we haue not here his bodily presence as Maudleyn hade þerfore in his stede vs behoueþ to shewe to þe preste by worde þat we haue offendet him as man. (92–93; my emphasis)

In this passage Love again concedes that the Bible provides an example only of being "shriuen in herte to God," but he comes up with a way to interpret that internal confession as external. Whereas other orthodox views of confession merely take up the showing and opening of hearts and transfer this advice to the reader (as evident in the passage cited from the *Boke of Penance* above), Love must interpret this opening specifically as speech in order to refute the Lollard charge. He does this by introducing historical change— between the time the text was written, "þan," and the time of his readers, "now." What separates the reader from Mary Magdalene, what separates these showings/openings, is language itself. In acknowledging that something has changed between Jesus' time and the present, Love concedes a point to the Lollards. After all, the Lollards call the reader's attention, quite relentlessly, to the gap between the early church and the church of the late fourteenth century, which is defined as "new"—new sects (friars) and new laws (such as auricular confession).[75]

In his attempt to answer Lollard and traditional views of this passage, Love's text ends up satisfying neither. On the one hand, Love's interpretation insists on its literalness—Magdalene did confess "by mouþe" because thoughts are the same as words when Jesus is there. This insistence answers the Lollard charge that Magdalene confessed to God in her heart and that therefore penitents should do the same today. On the other hand, Love invokes traditional readings of the passage, in which penitents must show their sins as did Magdalene, and the nature or specificity of that showing in the scriptural text is not discussed. Love complicates both readings, both of which might be described as literal, with a quasi-figurative component: his attention to Jesus, who transforms literal thoughts into literal words. This transformation sounds much like the figurations discussed in chapter 1, and Love's distinction between Jesus' bodily and divine presence only underlines the sense that Love is attempting to solve the problem created by two conflicting literal readings of this passage with a figurative one—except, of course, that Love everywhere insists that his interpretation is literal. It is as if Love wanted to have it both ways: the literal (and here Lollard) reading that would require Magdalene to speak (hence the insertion of a confession) and a figurative reading that would allow him to maintain the pre-Lollard view of confession.

Finally, the insistence upon speech in this passage suggests its alignment with Lollard more than earlier traditional concerns. It is worth emphasizing that the Magdalene's example was traditionally invoked to support confession as such, not the nature of speaking. Yet Love takes her story and makes it about her speech: he inserts her confession as a monologue (as opposed to describing her interior state of sorrow) and repeats the phrases "worde by mouþe," "spech of mouþe," and "by worde." In this way, Love's text asserts that confession is about speaking as such, not necessarily the contrition of the penitent or her sins (although these are certainly important). Even though it asserts the efficacy of traditional confession, Love's text reveals that the debate has shifted to Thorpe's (and the other Wycliffites') concerns about the nature of speaking and its capacity to represent the interior. After all, despite Love's equation of "thought of heart" and "speech of mouth," the phrases reveal their own oppositional nature; in Love's universe there seems to be no speech pertaining to the heart.

Love's text attempts to repair the damage done by Wycliffite writings, which consistently expose the absence of speech in biblical texts justifying confession, by inserting speech into the foundational text. But what it cannot do is heal the breach that the Wycliffites have created between the practice of auricular confession and the process of self-definition. Indeed, it does not attempt to do so and, in this way, perhaps concedes the greatest point to the Wycliffites. For, in rewriting Jesus' life story, Love offers his readers a self defined in relation to the story of Christ's life (however orthodox that story turns out to be): "Ande more ouer þer is no synne or wikkednesse, bot that [he] schal want it & be kept fro [it] þe whiche byholdeþ inwardly & loueþ & foloweþ þe wordes & the dedis of that man in whome goddes sone 3aff himself to vs in to ensaumple of gode leuyng" (9–10). This is a form of self-definition with which the Wycliffites were in complete agreement.

Chapter Three

CHAUCER'S PARSON AND THE LANGUAGE
OF SELF-DEFINITION

The last two chapters have proposed that the Wycliffite heresy should be read as an extreme example of a late medieval crisis in the language of self-definition. To do so is to suggest a shift in how medievalists approach Wycliffite texts—from focusing on their heretical (or not so heretical) positions on doctrine to focusing on the consequences of those positions for their program of reform. Perhaps more importantly, it is to suggest a shift in our approach to late medieval responses to Wycliffism, particularly representations of Wycliffites in texts that are considered to be orthodox. Quite a number of late-fourteenth- and early-fifteenth-century texts invoke "lolleres"—William Langland's *Piers Plowman*, Gower's *Confessio Amantis*, Chaucer's *Canterbury Tales*, *The Book of Margery Kempe*, and John Lydgate's *Fall of Princes*, to name a few of the more well-known examples.[1] These texts are clearly not Wycliffite, but does their invocation of "lolleres" suggest an interest (however condemnatory) in Wycliffism? That interest cannot be understood merely doctrinally; after all, few of the texts investigate Wycliffite views sympathetically, particularly those that marked the Wycliffites as heretics, such as those on images, pilgrimages, or the Eucharist. Nevertheless,

the absence of an interest in the Wycliffites' heretical views does not preclude another kind of interest—in the ideological power of identification or
the capacity of language to represent the interior, the Wycliffite concerns
discussed in chapters 1 and 2.[2] In other words, the impact of Wycliffism on
late medieval writers may have less to do with the authors' embrace or rejection of Wycliffite positions than with an embrace or rejection of interpretive
concerns that the Wycliffites brought into focus for their contemporaries.
Indeed, the wide variety of contexts and sympathies in which these late-
fourteenth- and early-fifteenth-century "lolleres" appear should suggest that
what late medieval writers "do" with Lollards may indicate their response to
the interpretive challenges raised by the Lollards. This chapter shall take up
perhaps the most famous literary "lollere," Chaucer's Parson, to examine the
way in which he responds to Wycliffism, particularly the relationship between Wycliffism and self-definition with which this study is so concerned.

In arguing for the relevance of Wycliffism to Chaucer's Parson, I might
seem to be returning to an older debate about whether the Parson is meant
to be a Lollard.[3] But to engage in this argument seems to miss the point—
that Chaucer establishes this figure as a contradiction: he is meant to evoke
both sides of the contemporary religious debate, not to be definitively identified as one or the other. On the one hand, it should be clear that Chaucer
wanted his readers to think of his Parson in relation to Lollardy. After all,
Chaucer has both the Shipman and the Host accuse the Parson of heresy in
the Epilogue to the *Man of Law's Tale*. The Host calls the Parson a "Lollere"
twice: once in response to the rebuke about swearing and the second time in
anticipation of a "predicacioun."[4] The Shipman builds on this association
between the term *Lollere* and preaching:

> . . . "heer schal he nat preche;
> He schal no gospel glosen here ne teche.
> We leven alle in the grete God," quod he;
> "He wolde sowen som difficulte,
> Or springen cokkel in our clene corn."
> (II.1179–83)[5]

In this exchange between the Host and the Shipman, the term *Lollere* is so
clearly defined in relation to preaching that we can be sure that Chaucer
knew what he was about in using it. Moreover, the accusation of Lollardy

cited above seems to be confirmed by the portrait of the Parson in the *General Prologue*. This Parson "Cristes gospel trewely wolde preche" (I.481), and his single-minded adherence to interpreting and teaching the gospel (apparently the Shipman's definition of heresy) supports the term *Lollere*.[6] On the other hand, the *Parson's Tale* does not confirm the heretical tendencies suggested by the Parson's earlier appearances. Rather, as a penitential manual that reinforces the necessity of auricular confession, it concerns itself with one of the practices vehemently opposed by the Wycliffites.

Scholars have come up with a number of ways for resolving this apparent contradiction between the Parson's religious beliefs, mainly by privileging the *Tale* as more definitive, perhaps because it has come to be seen as closely allied with Chaucer's own voice.[7] The end result is to confirm the Parson's orthodoxy. As the note in *The Riverside Chaucer* asserts, "Chaucer had friends who were Lollards, and he may have been sympathetic to some aspects of the movement. . . . The Parson's Tale, however, is perfectly orthodox."[8] The argument for the Parson's orthodoxy depends upon eliding or resolving the questions raised by his earlier appearances and appeals to the *Tale* as the final proof of what Chaucer wanted his readers to think of the Parson. Although some scholars have drawn attention to the Parson's inconsistencies, viewing the *Tale* as an oblique criticism of the Parson, whose words do not fit the ideal portrait given in the Prologue, these are few and far between.[9] Others explain these inconsistencies by reading the *Tale* as a mistake, following Charles A. Owen Jr., who claims that the *Parson's Tale* "was perhaps not an ending ever intended by Chaucer" but an independent work appended at the time of Chaucer's death.[10] However, few scholars have discussed these inconsistencies in terms of what they might say about the Parson's religiosity.[11] Indeed, the variety of solutions offered by recent scholarship for the Parson's inconsistencies (and the textual problems associated with the tale) are remarkably unified in that they all ultimately maintain Chaucer's orthodoxy, and in this way Chaucer's orthodoxy seems to have become a kind of Chaucerian orthodoxy.

It is worth asking what it would mean to retain the contradiction that characterizes the Parson. One could argue that this contradiction is far more indicative of the religious climate in the 1380s and 1390s than the label *orthodoxy*. After all, as scholars of religious practices have demonstrated, the orthodoxy of late medieval England was a fluid and changing set of practices and not a static set of propositions.[12] To say, therefore, that the Parson is orthodox means relatively little, since orthodoxy was in the process of defining itself in relation to a heterodoxy that had only recently appeared.[13] Opening the question of Chaucer's contradictory Parson once again allows us to pay renewed attention to the ways in which Chaucer might be specifically interested in the contemporary religious conflict initiated by the Wycliffites and the effect of this conflict on the traditional languages of self-definition.[14] In this chapter, I shall argue that the split between the Parson of the *General Prologue* and that of the *Tale* allows Chaucer to explore a debate over the language of lay instruction, a debate brought into sharp focus by Wycliffite calls for reform. In this way, the Parson's two appearances reflect an uneasy and unresolved dialectic between, on one side, the demands for a reformed language with which to define the self and, on the other, the limits of clerical language to enact that reform. The incompatibility of these two appearances reflects the larger incompatibility of two objectives found in lay instruction at this particular historical moment: to reform its language and to provide a language for reform (of both the self and the larger community of the church).

Wycliffism and the *General Prologue*

To argue that the Parson of the *General Prologue* is a response to Wycliffism and to the crisis in the language of lay instruction that it revealed, I want first to establish that the Parson is not merely a traditional ideal, as he is commonly understood. To be sure, the elements of the Parson's ideal nature have their roots in older traditions of estates satire, as Jill Mann has made clear in her important study *Chaucer and Medieval Estates Satire*.[15] And Larry Scanlon has shown how the Parson grows out of an anticlericalism Chaucer shares with John Gower, whose hatred of Lollards remains unquestioned.[16] But to understand Chaucer's Parson only in terms of this older model of estates satire (to which both Gower and Wycliffite polemic are indebted) is to pass up the opportunity to see how Chaucer's anticlericalism might fit with the "new" anticlericalism that Wendy Scase has discussed in relationship to *Piers Plowman*.[17] Moreover, linking Gower and Chaucer to the same version of orthodoxy disguises the important differences between their representations of the clergy. A comparison with Gower's ideal priesthood will indicate how close to Wycliffism, and how far from Gower, Chaucer's Parson stands in the portrait of the *General Prologue*. Even Gower's view of the clergy suggests that it was next to impossible for any writer in the 1380s and 1390s to invoke a traditional anticlericalism without thinking of and responding to the Lollards. In the Prologue to the *Confessio Amantis*, Gower splits his discussion of the clergy into two parts: what clergy used to be like and what they are like now. He begins:

> To thenke upon the daies olde,
> The lif of clerkes to beholde,
> Men sein how that thei weren tho
> Ensample and reule of alle tho
> Whiche of wisdom the vertu soughten.[18]

Gower repeats the importance of the priest's example and links it to the preaching material:

> Wherof the poeple ensample tok;
> Her lust was al upon the bok,
> Or forto preche or forto preie,
> To wisse men the ryhte weie
>
> .   .   .   .
>
> And thus cam ferst to mannes Ere
> The feith of Crist and alle goode.
> (Prol. 229–37)

Although Gower does not explicitly name "the book," one must assume that he refers to the gospel, since he emphasizes with "and thus" that people come to hear of the "feith of Crist" through the preaching of priests. In this passage love of the book, preaching, and praying all contribute equally to guiding men in "the ryhte weie." After describing this original state, Gower signals a shift to the state of the church nowadays with "Bot now men sein is otherwise" (240) and discusses the failure of the church for about a hundred lines. It is in this section that Gower attacks Lollardy:

> And so to speke upon this branche,
> Which proud Envie hath mad to springe,
> Of Scisme, causeth forto bringe
> This new Secte of Lollardie,

> And also many an heresie
> Among the clerkes in hemselve.
> It were betre dike and delve
> And stonde upon the ryhte feith,
> Than knowe al that the bible seith
> And erre as somme clerkes do.
>   (Prol. 346–55)

This attack on Lollardy comes after Gower has articulated an ideal that shares quite a bit with the Lollard ideal—back in the old days, priests were not covetous, studied "the book," provided good examples, and taught people the "feith of Crist" (Prol. 237). For this reason, Gower's attack seems designed to preempt (and reject) any connection between his ideal and that of the Lollards. Gower adds an extra defense of his orthodoxy here because there is nothing inherent to this ideal (as he has stated it) that would mark him as unquestionably orthodox: he has not talked about the sacraments as he does in the *Vox Clamantis*, where an attack on Lollardy is not necessary to reinforce his orthodoxy. In this way, Gower himself shows his reader that his ideal is no longer timeless but reflects the specific debates over priests' duties in late-fourteenth-century England.

After denouncing the Lollards, Gower finds that he cannot return to the ideal he first suggested; after all, it has led him to worry about its connection to Lollardy. As a result he modifies his ideal priest for a present in which competing ideals have become more and more polemically charged. In the passage cited above, he separates "ryhte feith" from "al that the bible seith" so that these are no longer coterminous as they were in the first part of his discussion. In so doing, Gower describes a faith that exists independently of Scripture; clergy should no longer have their "lust al upon the book" because that would make them Lollards. Therefore, the Bible is reduced in importance: there are "betre" ways of following belief.[19]

Gower finds his way out of this dilemma, how to be anticlerical but not Lollard, by coming up with a new ideal priest that is not based on Christ's example, or even Christ's apostles, both of which can be found in traditional and Wycliffite writing about priests. Instead, despite his lengthy discussion of sheep and shepherds, terms that certainly allude to Jesus himself, Gower chooses Aaron (Prol. 437). Aaron is a traditional ideal for a priest, as the mention in a contemporary devotional handbook, *The Book of Vices and Vir-*

tues, makes clear.[20] But Gower's reference to Hebrews 5.4 in his Latin note implies what the description of Aaron in *The Book of Vices and Virtues* states explicitly—that priesthood is here particularly concerned with the sacraments of the altar and not with a priest's duties in preaching and teaching: "Aaron and his children . . . betoknen þe ministres of holi chirche, þat scholde be cloþed in cloþes of lynen cloþ of chastite" but "þe wikkednesse of þe mynestre ne apeiret not þe sacrament."[21] Aaron's actions provide a defense of the priest's sacramental nature in defense of the anticlerical attack on priestly corruption. Gower's choice of Aaron reinforces, therefore, the sacramental aspect of the priesthood as Jesus may not. Gower *knows* that any ideal for the clergy based solely on Jesus' deeds has already been infected with the reforming zeal of the Lollards, that it is not possible to draw priestly examples from the gospels without invoking or echoing Lollard calls for reform. Hence his interest in distancing himself from "this new Secte" (Prol. 349). Gower's text shows that once Lollards have laid claim to the traditional anticlerical ideal, the established church must come up with a different ideal for lay members to follow. Gower creates, therefore, a more sacramental ideal by invoking Aaron; and the trajectory he begins leads eventually to Nicholas Love, twenty-odd years later, who revises Christ's life for lay instruction so that it is not about preaching and teaching but about suffering and the Eucharist.[22]

In sum, Gower's view of the clergy reveals a struggle between his desire for reform and his desire to distance himself from the Lollards, a struggle that he resolves, relatively uneasily, by attacking them. In addition, he sets aside the biblical aspect of this reform to invoke nonbiblical traditions, the "matiere / Essampled of these olde wyse" (Prol. 6—7) that he holds quite dear. Gower is well aware that any insistence on the Bible coupled with calls for reform looks suspiciously like Lollardy.

In contrast to Gower, Chaucer does not seem to be at all concerned about whether his ideal is viewed as Wycliffite; instead, he simply gives us a portrait of a reformed priest in his *General Prologue* to the *Canterbury Tales.* Most important in this portrait of reform is its scriptural basis:

> This noble ensample to his sheep he yaf,
> That first he wroghte, and afterward he taughte.
> Out of the gospel he tho wordes caughte.
>
> (I.496–98)

Chaucer not only connects the Parson's teaching specifically to the gospel three times in the course of the description but describes the Parson's use of the Bible as a direct consequence of his education: "He was also a lerned man, a clerk, / That Cristes gospel trewely wolde preche" (I.480–81).[23] There is here none of the anti-intellectualism that informs Gower's portrait and that of other estates satires, in which learning is not always necessary for a good priest.[24] In addition, Scripture provides the past ideal and therefore the authority over priestly duties; the Parson is specifically imitating both Christ and the apostles and not Gower's "lif of clerkes" in some undefined "daies olde."[25] In thus emphasizing the biblical authority and origin for the Parson's preaching, Chaucer draws attention to the absence of the church. In addition, as both David Lawton and Larry Scanlon have noted, there are no references to the institution of the church and to the pastoral language associated with it, such as the sins, which figure so largely in his *Tale*.[26] Chaucer also underlines the Wycliffite undertones of this portrait by making it quite clear that the Parson's duties are focused on lay instruction, a focus that the Host and Shipman respond to quite vigorously in the Epilogue to the *Man of Law's Tale*. As David Aers has noted, there is no mention of any of the sacraments in this description, especially not the Eucharist, but not even the sacrament of penance, surprisingly enough, though it is the matter for his tale.[27] Finally, unlike Gower, Chaucer does not include anything in his description to distance the Parson's portrait from Lollardy, nor does he include any indication that this ideal is in danger from the Lollards.

If one accepts the Parson's Wycliffite nature, one can see what is particularly Chaucerian about this portrait: Chaucer was a very good reader of Wycliffite discourse in much the same way that he was a good reader of antifeminist satire or fabliaux. In this brief description, Chaucer not only demonstrates the Wycliffites' reformed priesthood but also draws our attention to the consequences of this reform for the language of lay instruction. For it is not this version of the Parson who tells the *Parson's Tale*, although his commitment to lay instruction through preaching has been made quite apparent not only here in the *General Prologue* but also in his second appearance in the Epilogue to the *Man of Law's Tale*. In other words, this version of the Parson remains voiceless, not, as I shall argue, because Chaucer changed his mind by the time he got to the *Tale* but because this Parson's reformed language is troubled by an interpretive incapacity—the absence of interpretive links between the text and the self-definition of his listeners, such as those found in the orthodox sermons discussed in chapter 1. The absence is apparent in the Parson's description; the use of biblical language—gold, shepherd, sheep—indicates that the Parson is the biblical text; he does not necessarily interpret it. This identity between the Parson and his text also indicates that in the Parson's ideal world words and deeds have an unproblematic relationship. This relationship is evident both in the description of his "noble ensample" (I.496) and in the last line of the portrait, in which doing and saying become the same thing: "Cristes loore and his apostles twelve / He taughte; but first he folwed it hymselve" (I.527–28). For the Parson, words have no separate status from actions because both point back to the foundational text of the gospels.[28] In this way, the relationship between language and what it denotes is absolute; language has been pared down to an unproblematic representation of the truth contained in the gospels.[29] There are no questions here about the potentialities and problems of biblical exposition, of making sense out of God's word for the laity, of using biblical interpretation to aid the self-definition of the listeners.

If we agree that the Parson's appearance is troubled by what I am calling an interpretive incapacity, then it is worth understanding why it is there. I shall demonstrate below that this incapacity is a function of the Parson's association with Wycliffism and the Wycliffite approach to Scripture.[30] Perhaps the most obvious similarity between the Parson and the Wycliffites is quite simply the access to the Bible that he promises in both his preaching and his very existence; these are a pastiche of scriptural allusions.[31] Certainly, the writers of the *English Wycliffite Sermons* were similarly concerned with disseminating the gospel widely: "*alle* cristene men han nede to knowe byleue of þe gospel, and so to knowe þe lif of Crist, and þe wisdam of hise wordis."[32] To use Wycliffite phraseology (which also draws upon the traditional language of feeding the flock), the Parson represents an access to the Bible imagined as a common pasture: "he tawȝte apostlus to feede his schep in pasturis of holy wryt, and not in rotone pasturis, as ben fables and lesyngus and lawis of men."[33] Like the Wycliffites, he is concerned with what is (or should be) common knowledge rather than the enclosed field belonging to the clergy.[34] This openness of access means that the text itself is open, that interpretation for both his parishioners and himself will be uncomplicated.[35] But, as I shall demonstrate below, Chaucer's attempt (in following the Wycliffites) to imagine preaching and reading Scripture without interpretational guidelines leads to a circularity of words and their meanings.

This problem becomes apparent when one begins to consider the similarity between the kind of interpretive guidelines the Parson offers his listeners—his insistence on the absolute relationship of words and their meanings—and those of the Wycliffites. Like the Parson, the Wycliffites consistently claim a unity of words and deeds: "For alle werkys of Crist ben good lore to cristen men to techen hem how þey schal lyue for to gete þe blisse of heuene."[36] Here the author equates "werkys" with "lore" so that the deeds and the words are the same. In itself, this claim is unsurprising and echoes both Gower's and Chaucer's understanding of exemplarity: that Christ or the Parson, respectively, illustrates his words with his deeds. But when the Wycliffite author approaches the biblical texts of the sermons, he must interpret the "werkys" and "lore." He is then faced with an interpretive problem: a circularity of reference that is particularly noticeable in the sermons on the Sunday Gospels, in which Jesus is invoked as the model for the preacher. Despite its status as model, Jesus' preaching lacks literal content: it is always interpreted figuratively to refer to preaching. For example, the sermon for the Fifth Sunday after Trinity contains the story of Simon (Peter) fishing.[37] In this story, the nets are read figurally as the matter of preaching: "þese nettys þat fyscherus fysche wiþ bytoknen Godys lawe in whyche vertuwes and trewþus ben knytted," and the action of the fishers is read as the action of preachers: "Þese fyscherys of God schulden waschen þer nettys in þis ryuer, for Cristys prechowres schulden clenely tellen Godys lawe and not medle wiþ mannys lawe þat is trobly watur."[38] But the river's figuration is ambiguous: it is opposed to "mannys lawe" in that it is clean, and it is also said to represent "a wondurly ful burthe."[39] This figuration does not make any sense because it opens up the possibility that both the water and the nets have the same function—to convert believers; in this way, the story that "fishermen catch fish in the water with nets" could mean either that preachers catch believers with God's law or that preachers should wash God's law in God's law. In short, the interpretation has collapsed under the weight that the writer wishes to give God's law, and this collapse makes it impossible for the listener to see the relationship of the elements clearly.[40] Even if we can make sense of the figuration, we still have not been told what God's law actually contains, nor have we been told what this interpretation means for the laity or for the priests (besides further preaching of God's law). Despite the repeated calls for the necessity of preaching God's law, the sermon leads the listener away from its content. Such interpretations of Jesus' action, and there are many in the Wycliffite sermon cycle, prevent the listener from actually getting at the interpretations of what he said.[41]

The circularity of interpretation in this sermon indicates both a resistance to traditional modes of interpretation and, at the same time, a reliance upon them. While Wycliffites certainly rejected the figurations that function both ideologically and psychologically to link listeners to the church (as I discussed in chap. 1), they are still dependent on figuration. Figuration was seen as part of the literal sense, but the Wycliffites were well aware of the uses to which it was put in contemporary orthodox sermons.[42] As one author remarks, "And heere anticristis truauntis spekyn aȝen þe newe lawe, and seyen þat literal witt of it shulde neuere be takun but goostly witt; and þei feynen þis goostli witt aftir shrewed wille þat þei haue."[43] There is clearly a desire here to limit the space for interpretation to the category that the Wycliffites call "literal witt."[44] And one could imagine that the sermon writers had to think hard about exactly what kind of figuration they were willing to accept and promote, which figures counted as the rejected "goostly witt" and which as "literal witt." As the Wycliffite sermon above indicates, this is a figuration that is trying hard not to be figural, in that it reproduces what happens at the narrative level—Jesus' own analogy between his actions and those of the fishermen.

The implications of this interpretive confusion are quite clear for potential lay listeners of the sermons, who are provided this form of interpretation and encouraged to shape their behavior around it: the scriptural exposition they are offered informs them to enact the text itself, like the Parson, and not an interpretation of it. One must remember that traditional scriptural exposition uses figural interpretations to direct the laity to perform certain practices—the healings read as confession, the loaves and fishes as almsgiving—that are not literally in the text.[45] John Wyclif's exposition of this same passage is quite interested in this kind of figuration, particularly of the nets: "Supposito hoc sensu allegorico accedendo ad sensum tropologicum, notandum quod triplex est rete, primum est rete Christi. . . . Secundum est rete diaboli . . . sed tercium est rete seculi." (Adding to this allegorical sense, approaching the tropological sense, it should be noted that the net is threefold: the first is the net of Christ. . . . The second is the net of the devil . . . but the third is the net of the world.).[46] Finally, he states that Christ's net works by way of the seven works of spiritual mercy: "irretitus in septem operibus spiritualis misericordie" (netted in the seven works of spiritual mercy), which he then goes on to list and discuss.[47] In accordance with the traditional mode, Wyclif extends his discussion of what preachers/ fishermen are supposed to do (catch the faithful) to include how they are supposed to do it (with the seven works of mercy). In contrast to Wyclif's sermon, the Wycliffite sermon conflates these two aspects, the biblical text about what to do and the interpretation about how to do it, thus demonstrating the same kind of interpretive incapacity as Chaucer's Parson.

I have tried to show here that the Wycliffite emphasis on the gospels produces an interpretive cul-de-sac, the circularity evident in preaching about preaching.[48] Despite the constancy of God's law across these sermons, it tends to remain an empty vessel—its meaning evacuated. If the words that Jesus speaks stand only for "Holy Writ" always and in every circumstance, they lose the specificity with which they were first spoken. This loss of specificity can be attributed to the polemical nature of Wycliffite writing, the necessity of reading the contemporary circumstances into all biblical passages. In this way, Jesus seems always to be preaching about the Wycliffites rather than the other way around. While this version of Jesus is certainly empowering, it is also hermetic and, in a certain way, voiceless, since it eternally repeats and reproduces a model whose only language is received from the Bible. It is this hermeticism that Chaucer dramatizes in the Parson of the *General Prologue.* The Parson invokes a particular ideal, but it is one that seems unable to extend reform beyond itself. Even his isolation from the other pilgrims reveals a certain hopelessness about the possibility of his reforming influence.[49]

The *Tale* and the Limits of Orthodox Language

In the *Tale,* Chaucer's concern with the language of lay instruction shifts to the other side of the debate: language authorized by the church. Here Chaucer uses the Parson to explore an orthodox response to Wycliffism, a language that is reformed and enables reform but does not threaten the authority of the church. For Chaucer, this is the language of the penitential tradition. The Parson's new (or renewed) commitment to orthodoxy is apparent both in his statements in the Prologue and in the genre of his *Tale:* the penitential handbook.[50] In his Prologue, the Parson separates himself from his earlier appearances by reasserting the authority he derives from the institutional church. First, he takes pains to defend the orthodoxy of his language. He insists that he will sow wheat—"Why sholde I sowen draf out of my fest / Whan I may sowen whete, if that me lest?" (X.35–36)—a statement that appears to be a direct response to the Shipman's earlier accusation: "He wolde sowen som difficulte / Or springen cokkel in our clene corn" (II.1182–83). In invoking wheat (in contrast to "cokkel"), the Parson opposes himself (and what he is sowing) to the heretics who sow tares, known as *lollia* in Latin, a word that resonates with (and informs) *lollere*.[51] Second, the Parson asserts that he will accept others' authority over his language: "this meditacioun / I putte is ay under correccioun / Of clerkes, for I am nat textueel" (X.55–57). This last claim is quite at odds with the portrait of the gospel preacher we get in the *General Prologue*. If he follows Scripture, then he is "textueel" and to that degree is not susceptible to correction. Moreover, by accepting another clerk's authority over his language, he might be invoking the institutional authority of the church, which is altogether absent in the *General Prologue*. At the very least, he is asserting his place within a larger estate (the clergy) from which his earlier portrait seemed to separate him.

His commitment to orthodoxy in the Prologue is, however, undermined somewhat by what seems to be a return of Wycliffism: his rejection of fables. Indeed, this rejection is perhaps the most ambiguous and troubling aspect of the shift from a "Wycliffite" to an orthodox Parson.[52] From the perspective of the *General Prologue,* his disavowal of fables could be consistent with the Wycliffite undertones of his characterization:

> Thou getest fable noon ytoold for me,
> For Paul, that writeth unto Thymothee,
> Repreveth hem that weyven soothfastnesse
> And tellen fables and swich wrecchednesse.
>
> (X.31–34)

At first glance, this passage echoes Wycliffite polemic, which sharply divides fables (exempla) from scriptural texts: "Cryst ȝuueþ auctorite furst to hise disciples . . . *'He þat heruþ ȝow, in þat he heruþ me'*" and "by þis cause schulde men worshipe prechowrus, and dispuyson hem þat prechen fables or lesyngus."[53] Both uses, the Parson's and the Wycliffites', set doctrine (here Paul's letter to Timothy) and fables asunder. If the Parson were indeed a

Lollard, then his rejection of fables, which we can assume to be the exempla used in preaching, would have two consequences for his tale: the embrace of Holy Writ and the rejection of identifications that exempla enable, as discussed in chapter 1. But the Parson does not replace fables with "Cristes loore" (527), the material he preaches according to the *General Prologue*. Rather, he sets aside narrative of all kinds, even the biblical narratives that seem to appear consistently in narratives of the penitential tradition—the publican and the Pharisee or Mary Magdalene.

The orthodoxy of the *Parson's Tale* depends, of course, on the nature of its genre—as a penitential handbook. In insisting on the necessity of auricular confession and the means to do it, the Parson embraces a practice that the Wycliffites rejected. But this invocation of orthodox language should be appreciated for its oddness (or its anxiety) in that the Parson sets aside two of the *pastoralia*, the Ten Commandments and the Pater Noster, both of which regularly appear in vernacular sermons and penitential manuals as part of a penitent's self-definition, and he does so for the same reason—that they are above his ability. For the first, he claims that "so heigh a doctrine I lete to divines" (X.956) and for the second, "The exposicioun of this hooly preyere, that is so excellent and digne, I bitake to this maistres of theologie" (X.1043).

Despite the boundaries he draws around penitential language, this choice addresses the concern raised by his "Wycliffite" appearance in the *General Prologue*—about the ability of a reformed language to shape its listeners/readers. The Parson's language in his *Tale* is surely reformed, although not necessarily from a Wycliffite perspective, in that it offers a moral and doctrinal language for salvation through a figure whose own moral authority cannot be questioned. Although his appearance in the *General Prologue* certainly offers a reformed language, it is never imagined in relation to its listeners. In contrast, the *Tale* is very much concerned with shaping listeners' sense of themselves as sinners and as participants in the practices of the church. In his explanation of penitence, the Parson states,

> Manye been the weyes espirituels that leden folk to oure Lord Jhesu Crist and to the regne of glorie. / Of whiche weyes ther is a ful noble wey and a ful convenable, which may nat fayle to man ne to womman that thurgh synne hath mysgoon fro the righte wey of Jerusalem celestial; /and this wey is cleped Penitence, of which man

sholde gladly herknen and enquere with al his herte. . . .
And now, sith I have declared yow what thyng is Penitence, now
shul ye understonde that ther been three acciouns of Penitence.

(X.79–81, 95)

Here the Parson offers listeners an interpretive path (a way) with which to
approach not a text but their lives, and this way requires the "yow" to perform certain actions.

The Parson's choice of penitential language, along with his outright rejection of narrative, suggests that he has separated narrative from the process
of self-definition. This move must be understood as neither Wycliffite nor
orthodox, but something new that responds to the pressures of both. From
the Wycliffite perspective, a limited number of narratives, such as those concerning Christ's deeds and particular martyrs (consider William Thorpe),
were central to the process of self-definition. Indeed, the "Wycliffite" characterization of the Parson in the *General Prologue* as a living example of
Christ's deeds should demonstrate an embrace of precisely these (and only
these) narratives. From the orthodox perspective, narrative was absolutely
essential to lay instruction, as the sermons and handbooks discussed throughout this study have made clear. Perhaps the Nun's Priest's "moral" provides a
succinct justification of the way in which doctrine and narrative are inti-
mately connected, especially because his invocation of Paul's authority mirrors the Parson's:

But ye that holden this tale a folye,
As of a fox, or of a cok and hen,
Taketh the moralite, goode men.
For Seint Paul seith that al that written is,
To oure doctrine it is ywrite, ywis.

(VII.3438–42)

Clearly, the Parson distances himself from the Nun's Priest's perspective, as
well as the Wycliffite perspective on narrative, but, equally clearly, he responds to both perspectives throughout. In ensuring that the *Tale* is read as
a response, Chaucer seems to propose that a reformed clergy (the Parson's
ideal), even if it does not embrace Wycliffism, will have to make some sacri-
fices—and that sacrifice is imagined as narrative. Indeed, it is worth noting

the Parson's contrast with another of Chaucer's pilgrims, through whom lay instruction is examined more extensively than in the case of the Nun's Priest, and that is the Pardoner. The contrast between the Pardoner and the Parson can certainly be read in terms of their characters: the Pardoner is both unreformed and unrepentant, mired in the corrupt practices of the established church, whereas the Parson is an ideal. But the contrast between these figures is also generic, despite their similar interest in confession. The Pardoner embraces both the confessional and the narrative mode as completely intertwined: his narrative extends the "confession" from his *Prologue,* and it encourages the identifications and confessions of his audience: "For lewed peple loven tales olde; / Swiche thynges kan they wel reporte and holde" (VI.437–38). The Parson, in contrast, shows that penitential self-definition can succeed only in the rejection of narrative.

The attempt to make the language of penitential self-definition safe (both from the threat of Wycliffism and from the excesses of the established church, represented by "fables") does not eliminate these threats entirely. In what follows I shall argue that despite its orthodoxy the *Parson's Tale* is haunted by the Parson's earlier incarnation and his association with Wycliffism.[54] Although Chaucer's Parson does use the language of the penitential tradition to speak to the pilgrims, it is a voice that is interestingly fragmented, not only between the two main sources, Raymond of Pennaforte's *Summa de Poenitentia* and William Peraldus's *Summa Vitiorum,* but also within the translation of those sources.[55] Although an earlier scholar considered the *Tale* a "clumsy combination of two religious treatises," this view seems to have fallen out of favor, replaced by Lee Patterson's claim for "theoretical cohesion" of the parts.[56] Yet neither of these approaches has explored the possibility that Chaucer's work of lay instruction might be (might have to be) disunified because of the particular pressure on the language through which that instruction would be articulated. It is almost certain that Chaucer did make revisions to his sources and, in doing so, made his work more cohesive, but he did not quite succeed (or finish) in unifying the Parson's voice.

The *Tale*'s disunity can be read as responding to Wycliffism in two ways, each of which matches one of the main sources. In the first section, the Parson explores the language of contrition through translating Pennaforte's *Summa.* As I have already mentioned in chapter 2, the Wycliffites were very much concerned with the role of contrition in confession, arguing that contrition alone absolves sin and that confession to a priest is, therefore, unnecessary. In translating this tract, Chaucer does not continue to promote the Parson's association with Wycliffism. Instead, he has shifted to considering what it means to talk about contrition—to discover a language for it in English.[57] This section seems to be a positive move, an endorsement of the church's thinking about the capacity of language to describe individual and interior experience. Indeed, in this section the Parson is particularly concerned with providing a language of interiority, as is apparent in his six steps to contrition. All of these require thought and remembrance: "shame and sorwe for his gilt" (X.134); realization of "thraldom" (142); "drede of the day of doom and of the horrible peynes of helle" (158); "sorweful remembraunce of the good that he hath left to doon here in erthe, and eek the good that he hath lorn" (231); "remembrance of the passioun that oure Lord Jhesu Crist suffred for oure synnes" (255); a "hope of three thynges; that is to seyn, foryifnesse of synne, and the yifte of grace wel for to do, and the glorie of hevene" (283). Patterson has discussed the changes from Raymond of Pennaforte's *Summa*, the source for the section on contrition, which Chaucer has greatly expanded and varied.[58] It would seem that Chaucer is here answering the Wycliffite charges in which they separate "sorowe of hert" from the speech act of confession; here sorrow does find a voice and a language that can be translated and disseminated.

Moreover, in doing so, Chaucer far surpasses the language of contrition circulating in the vernacular. For example, in the *Boke of Penance*, included in the *Cursor Mundi*, the author devotes only 126 lines to contrition, whereas he devotes the majority of the treatise to his discussion of the other two stages of penitence (confession and satisfaction).[59] First he discusses the three degrees of contrition (shame, thought, and dread):

Þarfor agh sinful man and wijf
On þis maner þair hert to rijf,
And stand it if it nede to be
Wit thorn, glaiue, nail, wit al thre,
Wit quilk þat crist for us was stongen.[60]

One can see from this small section that this author's discussion is far less nuanced than Chaucer's. This different approach to contrition might be best described as informational and pragmatic: here is what you need to know about contrition (rather than Chaucer's approach, which also responds to the question "What does it mean to feel contrite?"). Moreover, the author reinforces the separation between his reader (assumed to be a layperson) and the priest when he ends the discussion of contrition with a warning to the "lewd" readers not to question the necessity of "shrift of mouth":

> Bot þou sal not þe queþer vnder-tak
> That reuth allan forgiues þe sak,
> Bot crist him-self thoru reuth allan,
> That inwardli in hert es tan.[61]

The author emphasizes that penitents should not be the ones to judge the level of their contrition and reminds readers that they should not assume that contrition (here "reuth") can achieve forgiveness. In other words, readers are not supposed to think deeply about the role of contrition in their own penitential process, the trajectory through different inward states, but to understand simply that it is necessary.

Unlike the author of the *Boke*, the Parson constructs a detailed portrait of self-examination out of the authoritative language he has received from Pennaforte. The Parson rejects the familiarity of the *Boke* (the "thou" and "us") in order to retain the sophistication of the original. For example, the Parson describes what should be done using the third person: "The causes that oghte moeve a man to Contricioun been sixe. First a man shal remembre hym of his synnes" (X.133). In rejecting the "realistic and hortatory" language of the penitential tradition, Chaucer distances himself from some of the vernacular forms of lay instruction with which he would have been familiar: Wycliffite polemic and orthodox penitentials.[62] This apparent distance does not mean, however, that there is no space for a personal voice, and, in fact, the Parson's own voice intrudes upon his subject. There are the Parson's comments on his own work, such as "And now, sith I have declared yow what thyng is Penitence, now shul ye understonde [etc.]" (X.95).[63] This first kind of "I" is generalized, with no interest in revealing the Parson's interior. But there is a second kind of "I" that is penitential and formed of all the various "I's" in his authorities to construct a voice that we assume to be the Parson's own. For example, in the first cause of contrition he quotes Ezekiel: "I wol remembre me alle the yeres of my lyf in bitternesse of myn herte" (X.135).[64] Although this interiority is patched together out of a variety of authorities, Ezekiel, St. Bernard, Seneca, and Job, the Parson seems to be building up a sense of what happens inside the sinner: "I shal have remembrance" (X.256); "I wol remembre" in "myn herte" (X.135); and "I may a while biwaille and wepe" (X.176).

This second kind of "I" underlines the possibilities for the penitential voice: when the Parson reaches the end of this section on contrition, an "I" appears that is radically different from the other "I's" in the tale.[65] Here the Parson cites a passage from Augustine, one quite similar to those from Ezekiel, "I wot certeynly that God is enemy to everich synnere," (X.303) and then explicates it:

> And how thanne? He that observeth o synne, shal he have foryifnesse of the remenaunt of his othere synnes? Nay. / And further over, contricioun sholde be wonder sorweful and angwissous; and therfore yeveth hym God pleynly his mercy; and therfore, whan my soule was angwissous withinne me, *I* hadde remembrance of God that my preyere myghte come to hym. (X.303–4, my emphasis)

This "I" is not Augustine speaking. Moreover, this "I" does not appear in the source for this section, the *Summa* of Pennaforte.[66] Despite its similarity to Jonah's complaint (Jonah 2.8), the Parson does not indicate that he is quoting an authority, as he does with his other authorities' first-person voices.[67] We can only assume, therefore, that this is the Parson's own voice and that he refers to his own sins. This slippage demonstrates that in the space between the dutifully translating and commenting "I" and the "I" of biblical authority the Parson (and perhaps his readers/penitents) can build his own interiority.

Chaucer's emphasis on contrition underlines the interiority of the penitential process and, more importantly, its independence from the relationship between priest and penitent. Indeed, this section is completely uninterested in that relationship. The Parson does not reject the priest, nor does he indicate that self-examination should lead toward the priest (in contrast to the *Boke*, which imagines that the self-examination generated by this poem is channeled into the proper institutional forms). Perhaps, more importantly, this self-examination is one that precedes and is not explicitly linked to the detailed exposition of the sins. Although the tract imagines an interiority created around sin, as the penitent feels shame and sorrow for sins, sin retains its broadest possible meaning; it is not categorized and defined. It would seem, then, that the discussion of contrition not only is unaffected by this crisis in lay instruction but asserts the promising possibilities of translating clerical language into the vernacular.

When the Parson reaches his discussion of confession (and leaves the *Summa* behind), his tone shifts. In this section, he relies on two different (even contrary) approaches to sin, which correspond to the parts of his discussion: "it is necessarie to understonde whennes that synnes spryngen, and how they encreessen, and whiche they been" (X.321).[68] The first approach informs all three parts and provides the same kind of theoretical (and sophisticated language) that he used in the section on contrition. The second approach, which informs the catalog of sins from the *Summa Vitiorum* and their remedies from the *Postquam*, focuses even more thoroughly on "whiche they been" and introduces an extensive taxonomizing of sin.[69] While the first approach to sin explains its relevance to the individual sinner, the second approach, the catalog of sins, raises questions about the limits of personal reform through penitential language. In the first part, the Parson maps out the progress of sin just as he has mapped out the progress of contrition: "The firste thyng is thilke norissynge of synne of which I spak biforn, thilke flesshly concupiscence. / And after that comth the subjeccioun of the devel. . . . / And after that, a man bithynketh hym wheither he wol doon or no thilke thing to which he is tempted" (X.350–52). Here the Parson continues his focus on the inner life of the penitent as indicated in the words *norissynge, subjeccioun, bithynketh.* But when he comes to cataloguing the sins, he abruptly changes his tone. Indeed, he seems so caught up in taxonomizing that there is no space for relating sin as a theoretical concept to the person sinning. For example—and almost any example will do—in the section on Pride, he writes, "For certes, swiche lordes sellen thanne hir lordshipe to the devel of helle, whanne they sustenen the wikkednesse of hir meynee. / Or elles, when this folk of lowe degree, as thilke that holden hostelries, sustenen the theft of hire hostilers" (X.439–40). In this passage, "man" has changed to "swiche lordes" and "this folk," and the interest has shifted from making listeners aware of how they might understand their sin to the overwhelming presence of their sin.

We are back to the question about the lack of unity in the treatise, but perhaps now we can see it from a different perspective. The catalog of sins reinforces the reader's sense of the difficulty of finding a language for con-

fession, the second step of the penitential process, not incidentally the part
that the Wycliffites rejected almost absolutely. In other words, Chaucer fails
to connect the language of sin and contrition with the language of confession. This failure is important because it is not typical for penitential manuals.[70] Here we might look at *The Boke of Penance,* which Patterson cites as
having a similar structure. Like the *Parson's Tale,* this tract is made up of a
discussion of the three parts of shrift: "reuþ," "shrift," and "buxum beting of
misdide."[71] Like Chaucer's Parson, the author inserts a discussion of the
seven sins into the discussion of shrift. Yet there is an important difference:
after itemizing the sins, the author includes a guide on how to confess them:
"Bot nu sal I tell þe her nest / Hu þu sal sceu þi scrift to preist."[72] For example, the formula for confessing pride is as follows:

Qua þat o sin o pride wil rise,
He sal him scriue on þiskin-wise,
Til our lauerd crist and þe,
"Mi gastli fader, yeild i me
Plighti for my syn o pride
In pointes þat i sal vn-hyde."[73]

The author then closes this discussion by giving the reader a prayer to recite
"Apon þi scrift."[74] Clearly, this author is very much concerned with how to
put sin into language and, therefore, how to establish the language of confessional practice.[75]

The Parson's discussion of sin also reasserts the necessity of putting the
experience of the penitent into the received language of sin; after all, the
section on the sins follows the discussion of confession. But there is something lost in his version, since the discussion of sin is never explicitly linked
to speaking—either that of the priest or that of the penitent. Instead, the
catalog of sins resembles a diatribe with no other stated object than "Now is
it bihovely thyng to telle whiche been the sevene deedly synnes, this is to
seyn, chieftaynes of synnes" (X.387). One might well ask why is this list "bihovely"? To what use is the list going to be put? Moreover, its distance from
the speaking "I" is made clear in the absence of the "I" that characterizes the
section on contrition. Here we only have the commenting "I"—yet wol I
shewe a partie of hem" (X.390)—not the interior "I" of Ezekiel and of the
other authorities. The failure of language is also made clear at the end of the

treatise on sin: "Now after that I have declared yow, as I kan, the sevene deedly synnes, and somme of hire braunches and hire remedies, soothly, if I koude, I wolde telle yow the ten comandementz / But so heigh a doctrine I lete to divines. Nathelees, I hope to God, they been touched in this tretice, everich of hem alle" (X.956–57). It was quite common for penitents to con- fess according to the Ten Commandments, as a glance at *Handlyng Synne,* Thomas of Chobham, and Jean Gerson reveals. One must ask, then, why Chaucer has his Parson abandon one form of confessional speech when he maintains the language of the sins. Perhaps the attempt to describe every conceivable sin has exhausted the Parson or thrown him into a kind of apo- ria in the face of the *pastoralia* he is required to transmit.

In Chaucer's section on the seven sins, sin does not enable a discussion of the self, the "I," as has the section on contrition. This aspect of the tale becomes clear only when the reader sees how easy it is to set aside the rest of the *Parson's Tale* and to use the catalog of sins to order the pilgrims in the *Canterbury Tales,* to reduce them to "lust" or "sloth" without regard for the nuances with which they were created. The exegetical critics who happily matched up the sins of the *Parson's Tale* with the pilgrims of the *Canterbury Tales* indicate the ways in which a language intended to reveal the workings of the self may actually end up concealing from us who we are. This concern over the limits of late medieval pastoral language appears in both orthodox and Wycliffite writers alike—in Julian of Norwich, who does not see the sins as they are most commonly categorized, and in the writers of the *En- glish Wycliffite Sermons,* who struggle to articulate a new, reformed language for describing the self.[76]

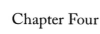

Chapter Four

THE RETREAT FROM CONFESSION

While Chaucer's Parson might be seen as a somewhat sympathetic response to Wycliffism, writers more virulently hostile to Wycliffism also use "lolleres" to explore the crisis of self-definition that the Wycliffite heresy reflected and generated. In this chapter I shall turn to two poems that vilify Lollards in the context of confessions, John Gower's *Confessio Amantis* and Thomas Hoccleve's *Regiment of Princes,* in order to examine the impact of Wycliffism on the way in which these authors represent confessional practice. In discussing these two poems together, I am underlining not only their structural similarity, particularly the use of the confessional dialogue, but also their kinship, in that Hoccleve's poem responds to Gower's, as his mention of Gower as "maistir" reveals.[1] Despite the poems' shared use of confession as a genre, in the first in the dialogue between Genius and Amans and the second between the narrator and the Old Man, scholars have largely ignored the poems' specifically confessional nature.[2] Instead, scholars have focused on another important similarity, the poems' collections of exempla, particularly in the "mirrors for princes" tradition.[3] Perhaps this neglect of confession springs from the assumption that confession is a known entity, a traditional language, and therefore that the authors' use of it is unproblematic. At least

for Gower's poem, investigation into confession seems merely to have confirmed his orthodoxy, his indebtedness to conventions.[4] Yet, as I shall demonstrate, attention to confession as a mode of self-definition in each poem
reveals it as a threatened practice. In this chapter, I argue that these poems
demonstrate the shifting fortunes of the confessional genre in the late medieval period, fortunes tied particularly to Wycliffism.

The relationship between Wycliffism and confession in each poem reflects at least in part the particular historical moment at which the poem was
written, and, as a result, the poems can be mapped onto a pre-Wycliffite to
post-Wycliffite spectrum. That is, at the time when Gower was writing the
Confessio in the 1380s, Lollards were clearly perceived as a danger (the division that so troubled Gower) but had not yet officially been hereticated.[5]
Gower's poem and its portrait of confession belong to a period in which debate over the modes of lay instruction could still take place largely without
consequences. To be sure, Lollard doctrines had been condemned in 1382 at
the Blackfriars' Council, but there was no sustained attempt by the church
to control lay instruction—to ensure that those doctrines were no longer discussed or disseminated.[6] For Hoccleve, writing in 1410–11, the debate over lay
instruction was no longer possible in the same terms it was for Gower.[7] After
all, the more than twenty years that separate Hoccleve from Gower saw an
increasing amount of attention to Lollards and the threat they posed to the
established church: the burning of the first Lollard, William Sawtry, in 1401;
the statute to burn heretics in 1401 *(De heretico comburendo)*; Arundel's *Constitutions* (1409), which severely restricted writing in the vernacular; the examination of William Thorpe (1407); and the trials and recantations of
famous Lollards, such as John Purvey.[8] This brief but by no means exhaustive list should suggest not only that Lollardy had become far more dangerous to uphold or even imagine but also that the boundaries between heterodox
and orthodox beliefs on lay instruction had become more clearly defined for
Hoccleve than for Gower (or even for Chaucer).

My chapter shall, therefore, consist of two parts, focusing first on
Gower's poem, then Hoccleve's. First, I shall argue that Gower's text stages
a pre-Wycliffite confession, despite his awareness of and anxiety caused by
the Wycliffite threat. For Gower, Lollardy might threaten the context of
confession (the world in which it takes place), but it does not threaten its
structure or its capacity to describe human experience and console the penitent. Second, I shall argue that Hoccleve's poem, in contrast, stages a retreat

from the practice of confession, identifying it as, ironically, too fraught with
Lollard concerns. Hoccleve, therefore, empties confession of its authority
over the penitent and democratizes its effects.[9] In this way, Hoccleve's text
mirrors "Lollard confession" (in form if not content) as I defined it in chapter 2, in its attempt to respond to Lollardy and promote orthodoxy.[10]

   To read these poems as engaged with contemporary debates over confession and self-definition generated around Wycliffism is, of course, to limit
my discussion of the poems rather severely. These are massive poems, and
any approach to both in the space of a chapter would necessarily have to be
selective. I should emphasize here that I am less interested in offering a com-
prehensive reading of these poems than in identifying the manner in which
they take up and participate in these debates. I locate that participation in
the structure of the confession, not in the details of the exempla; for those
details, I refer the reader to the extensive scholarship on both Gower and
Hoccleve.[11] The premise of this chapter is that each writer chooses the confessional genre in the face of contemporary concerns about self-definition
that he details in the poem.[12] This choice should not be understood as re-
flecting the writer's own Lollard beliefs: neither writer is particularly sympathetic to Lollard belief as Chaucer might be said to be. In fact, the orthodoxy
of these writers is not in question: neither the orthodoxy of the doctrinal positions they offer (Gower's use of the seven sins, for example, or Hoccleve's
view of images and the Eucharist) nor that of the stories they tell (exempla
that would have been familiar from a variety of sources). That said, the appearance of Lollards in each text should not be dismissed as peripheral; it
suggests central concerns about the modes of self-definition available to each
writer in his particular historical moment.

Gower's Confession

Gower's *Confessio Amantis* uses the confessional genre as a mode of self-
definition in the face of the divisions threatened by the contemporary world,
including the Lollards. There can be no doubt that Gower wants the reader
to understand Amans's confession, which occupies books 1 through 8 of a
very long poem, in terms of the practice as he knew it (inflected as it might
be with Ovidian concerns).[13] If one were in doubt, one might merely turn
to Gower's earlier work, the *Mirour de l'Omme,* which includes a passage

describing confession almost exactly as one would find it in penitential hand-books such as those discussed in chapter 2.[14] The historical resonance of this particular confession, or the relationship between confession inside and out-side the *Confessio*, has, perhaps, been underemphasized in the scholarship, quite simply because Amans's confession is not sacramental or even particu-larly religious and instead, as John Fisher once noted, has to do with courtly love.[15] Thus it is no wonder that scholars have been far more interested in tracing his indebtedness to the traditional language of love poetry or ethical analysis than to the language of confession. Nevertheless, it is worth empha-sizing the way Gower's poem invokes the language of confessional practice and demonstrates its workings. This indebtedness is apparent quite simply in the way Gower describes Amans's "maladie."[16] For example, Genius uses the language of the seven sins and the five wits (although only two are dis-cussed), and Amans speaks of his "contricioun" and the desire to be "schriven" (1.214 and 219 and throughout), echoing penitential manuals such as Man-nyng's *Handlyng Synne*.[17] Similarly, Amans asks for "an absolucion" (8.2892) at the end of the poem and receives both Genius's "pardoun" (8.2896) and his own penance, "[a] Peire of Bedes blak as Sable" (8.2904).

In addition, Gower uses the priest/penitent relationship of confessional practice in which the priest is the authority over the penitent's self-definition, as Amans makes clear throughout the text:

> Mi fader, I woll noght foryete
> Of this that ye have told me hiere,
> And if that eny such manere
> Of humble port mai love appaie,
> Hierafterward I thenke assaie:
> Bot now forth over I beseche
> That ye more of my schrifte seche.
>
> (1.3426–32)

In this way, Gower invokes the rhetoric of penitential submission to demon-strate Amans's subjection to Genius, and to love more generally. One could argue that Genius is not meant to be a Christian priest from Gower's own world, but Gower presents his priestly authority in precisely the same terms as if he were, as made evident in Venus's statement to Amans:

Mi will is ferst that thou be schrive;
And natheles how that it is
I wot miself, bot for al this
Unto my prest, which comth anon.

(1.190–93)

And she refers to Genius as "myn oghne Clerk" (1.196).[18] Moreover, Genius's use of the seven sins, although it is not his "comun us" (1.267), underlines that this language is unquestionably a part of any process of self-definition.[19] Indeed, the sins seem to be the method by which difficult ideas are made "plein," so that "thou schalt knowe and understonde / The pointz of schrifte and how that thei stonde" (1.282, 287–88).

The confessional self-definition in this text is not limited to the language of sin and contrition but includes narrative. This dual emphasis shows a significant debt to the traditional languages of confessional practice.[20] Indeed, Gower seems to be a good student of the mode of encouraged identification, familiar in vernacular sermons and penitential manuals, in which the priest directs listeners or readers to inhabit what Benveniste calls "empty forms" and see themselves in relation to both the language of sin and contrition and the virtuous or sinful figures of exemplary narratives (see chap. 1). This mode recurs throughout the poem, and I have selected only one example:

And thus as touchende of lachesce [procrastination],
As I have told, I me confesse
To you, mi fader, and beseche
That furthermor ye wol me teche;
And if ther be to this matiere
Som goodly tale forto liere
How I mai do lachesce aweie,
That ye it wolden telle I preie.

(4.65–72)

Here Amans defines himself not only in terms of "lachesce" (the language of the sins) but also in relation to the exemplary narratives that Genius provides to illustrate it. Indeed, this link between the two is central for his understanding, as Amans confesses himself guilty of this sin but still desires the specificity of the story to understand his own particular relationship to "lachesce." In making use of this aspect of lay instruction, Gower draws attention to the ways in which the narratives function as models to imitate, and both Genius and Amans invoke the names of the characters to define Amans's own sins:

> [Genius:] "Mi Sone, be thou war withal
> To seche suche mecheries [thievishness],
> Bot if thou have the betre aspies
> In aunter if the so betyde.
> As Faunus dede thilke tyde,
> Wherof thou miht be schamed so."
> [Amans:] "Mi holi fader, certes no."
> (5.6936–42)

Finally, Gower's use of traditional confessional self-definition underlines its capacity to provide absolution/consolation and return the penitent to "[t]his large world" (8.2972).[21] This consolation is apparent not only in the pardon Amans/Gower receives from Genius and the mercy he receives from Venus but in his description of his state:

> I stod amasid for a while,
> And in my self y gan to smyle
> Thenkende uppon the bedis blake,
> And how they weren me betake,
> For that y schulde bidde and preie.
> And whanne y sigh non othre weie
> Bot only that y was refusid,
> Unto the lif which y hadde usid
> I thoughte nevere torne ayein:
> And in this wise, soth to seyn,
> Homward a softe pas y wente.
> (8.2957–67)

In the end, Amans/Gower accepts his state—in both his smile and his return home. This return is also an exit from the fiction of both Amans and his confession because at this point the poem returns to the same world that Gower has defined in the Prologue—the problems of the three estates—as he describes each one in turn, in a kind of coda to the Prologue. The poem's circularity underlines both what is the same at the end of the confession (the world is still beset by division) and what has changed (Gower himself).[22] But this time the penitent Amans/Gower does not set aside the world in the face of its problems; he will spend his days praying: "I thenke bidde whil y live" (8.2970). In this way, Gower suggests that confessional self-definition not only has the power to reform the penitent but also can infuse him with hope for the social world: "I hope that men schuldyn se / This lond amende" (3004–5). Gower's own amendment thus generates insight into the means by which the amendment of the world around him might take place:

> If these astatz amendid were,
> So that the vertus stodyn there
> And that the vices were aweie:
> Me thenkth y dorste thanne seie,
> This londis grace schulde arise.
>
> (8.3049–53)

Gower recalls the language of penitential tradition, virtues and vices and grace, but assigns it to Gower's "lond," England, not just to Gower himself. Indeed, it forms a neat parallel with the confession of the seven sins in *Piers Plowman*, discussed in chapter 1, in which confession is the mode to reform both the individual and the entire social world.

Up to this point, I have focused on Gower's indebtedness to the traditional language of confession, in a sense confirming his orthodoxy, but Gower is also intensely aware of the ways in which topical concerns interrupt and affect traditional languages, such as the exempla. Indeed, Gower's topicality has already been extensively examined in the exempla, which raise questions about the king and the clergy in Gower's own time.[23] I would like to suggest that these topical pressures are not limited in their influence to the exempla but also inform the larger structuring devices of the poem, most notably in the generic division between its two parts: the estates satire of the Prologue and the confession of books 1 through 8. As Gower repeatedly emphasizes with "now" (Prol. 118, 126, 163, 168, passim), the Prologue details the problems of the contemporary world. But this "now" belongs only to the estates satire, and Gower indicates that he will set it aside in the confession:

> I may noght strecche up to the hevene
> Min hand, ne setten al in evene
> This world, which evere is in balance:
> It stant noght in my sufficance,
> So grete thinges to compasse,
> Bot I mot lete it overpasse
> And treten upon othre thinges.
> Fro this day forth I thenke change
> And speke of thing is noght so strange,
> Which every kinde hath upon honde,
> And wherupon the world mot stonde,
> And hath don sithen it began,
> And schal whil ther is any man;
> And that is love, of which I mene
> To trete, as after schal be sene.
>
> (1.1–16)

Here love is unifying force, or at least a universal one (belonging to "every kinde"), in contrast to the division Gower has described in the Prologue: "That love is falle into discord" (Prol. 121). In addition, love is here timeless (in contrast to the "now" of the Prologue) because it has shaped the world "sithen it began." The contrast between the Prologue and the confession (books 1–8) is all the more apparent in that Gower does not directly address the causal relation between the two matters (division and Amans's confession of love) but sets the division aside—"I mote lete it overpasse." In this way, the gap between the two genres suggests that confession is at this moment a kind of retreat from the present threat of Lollardy and schism into a self solipsistically concerned with love.[24] Although the lover's confession may be a retreat from the world of the Prologue, it is still a response, one that asserts the efficacy of the language of confession for discussing the individual (if not the larger community of the estates satire) in the face of the division and schism that threaten that practice in the here and now.

As a response (however oblique), the lover's confession cannot eliminate the threat of the contemporary world completely, and there are moments at which the world of the Prologue interrupts the confession. These moments are so important precisely because they signal the way in which the poem can no longer conceal or integrate the divisive forces of the present that it has attempted to set aside.[25] Genius's discussion of homicide within the sin of wrath, for example, takes him far from courtly love back to the world of "holi cherche":

> And forto loke on every side,
> Er that thou falle in homicide,
> Whiche Senne is now so general,
> That it welnyh stant overal,
> In holi cherche and elles where.
>   (3.2525–29)

The word *now* in relation to "holi cherche" instantly returns the reader to the division of "holy cherche" articulated in the Prologue:

> Bot it is seid and ever schal,
> Between tuo Stoles lyth the fal,
> Whan that men wenen best to sitte:
> In holy cherche of such a slitte
> Is for to rewe un to ous alle.
>   (Prol. 335–39)

Similarly, Lollardy first appears as a concern in Gower's contemporary world, identified in the Prologue as "[t]his new Secte of Lollardie" (Prol. 349), and its recurrence in Amans's and Genius's conversation demonstrates its threat to confessional self-definition. In book 5 Genius includes Lollardy in his discussion of the Christian faith; I cite from the text at length to examine its workings closely:

> Bot this believe is so certain,
> So full of grace and of vertu,
> That what man clepeth to Jhesu
> In clene lif forthwith good dede,
> He mai noght faile of hevene mede,
> Which taken hath the rihte feith;

For elles, as the gospel seith,
Salvacion ther mai be non.
And forto preche therupon
Crist bad to hise Apostles alle,
The whos pouer as nou is falle
On ous that ben of holi cherche,
If we the goode dedes werche;
For feith only sufficeth noght,
Bot if good dede also be wroght.
Now were it good that thou forthi,
Which thurgh baptesme proprely
Art unto Cristes feith professed,
Be war that thou be noght oppressed
With Anticristes lollardie.
For as the Jwes prophecie
Was set of god for avantage,
Riht so this newe tapinage [skulking]
Of lollardie goth aboute
To sette Cristes feith in doute.
The seintz that weren ous tofore,
Be whom the feith was ferst upbore,
That holi cherche stod relieved,
Thei oghten betre be believed
Than these, whiche that men knowe
Noght holy, thogh thei feigne and blowe
Here lollardie in mennes Ere.
Bot if thou wolt live out of fere,
Such newe lore, I rede, eschuie,
And hold forth riht the weie and suie,
As thine Ancestres dede er this:
So schalt thou noght believe amis.
Crist wroghte ferst and after tawhte,
So that the dede his word arawhte [explained];
He yaf ensample in his persone,
And we the wordes have al one,
Lich to the Tree with leves grene,
Upon the which no fruit is sene.

(5.1788–1830)[26]

This passage understands Lollardy and self-definition as integrally connected. First, and most obviously, this is a confession, and Genius is asking Amans to define himself in terms of Lollardy, specifically by rejecting it ("be noght oppressed"). In this way, Lollardy becomes a kind of sin, like "lachese," in relation to which Amans should define himself (although no exemplary story is given). Second, Gower's interest in Lollardy is only in terms of its effect on self-definition. That is, Gower does not take this opportunity to excoriate the Lollards for their incorrect beliefs on the Eucharist, images, or swearing, beliefs typically associated with Lollards, nor does he even mention these doctrinal matters in relation to the Lollards, like Chaucer before him and Hoccleve after him. Gower locates the danger of Lollardy in the process of listening to it, not in the holding of false beliefs as such. What is important in understanding Lollardy for Gower is the relationship between people and belief, not the beliefs themselves. This may seem to be a hairsplitting distinction, but it marks an important boundary between polemic, with which Gower is quite familiar, given his *Vox Clamantis,* and the exploration of the effect of those views on readers/listeners, which Gower imagines here. For Gower, then, the danger of Lollardy cannot be combated only by rejecting its "lore" but by ensuring that one defines oneself according to examples that are undoubtedly orthodox—in this case following the saints and ancestors. Indeed, Gower not only opposes Lollards to saints but compares them—in stating that the saints are "betre," he underlines that what is at stake here is whom to imitate.

Gower's juxtaposition of saints and Lollards would certainly seem to suggest a clarity about whom to imitate, but that clarity falls apart as the passage proceeds in its description of how to imitate. On the one hand, Gower follows the language of the instructional mode, offering "empty forms" to the reader (here Amans) for appropriation: the "ous" and "thou" in the discussion of saints and ancestors. On the other hand, Gower's references to Christ interrupt this process. Jesus is, of course, the foundational example for imitation, but his example is here never mobilized for encouraged identification, offering neither the better belief of the saints (1806) nor the right way (1822) of the ancestors. It is as if Gower wants to emphasize that Jesus provides the theory for imitation but that for practice we should turn to saints and ancestors. In fact, the choppiness of the transitions reveals a choppiness in Gower's thinking: the relationship between Jesus' example and that of the other orthodox examples has been disrupted by the very subject under discussion—Lollardy. After all, Jesus has a special status for Lollards as an example; he is often invoked in opposition to the examples of most saints and ancestors, which are consistently described as fables and lies (see chap. 1).

Finally, the passage contains an odd echo of the Lollard resistance to confession, although it never directly mentions the practice of confession. When Gower describes Lollard deceit as blowing in men's ears, one cannot help but think of it as a reversal of the Lollard account of auricular confession: "rownyng" (whispering) into men's ears. Here the Lollards are the ones whispering, but in both instances the whispering itself is a sign of the communication of wrong belief. Moreover, the response to whispering is the same in both instances—the following of examples, as I discussed in chapter 2. Indeed, one could read this moment as a kind of return of the repressed—although Lollardy is successfully disarmed within the confessional mode, the passage suggests that it has already infected Gower's thinking about confession.

Despite the anxiety that pervades this discussion of Lollards, they seem very much out of place in the conversation between Amans and Genius, and this out-of-place quality should suggest how carefully Gower has crafted this confession to respond to the division described in the Prologue, where they do not seem at all out of place. On the most obvious structural level, the divisive power of the Lollards is nullified: although they appear in the Prologue as a threat to the social world, they do not reappear at the end in Amans's/Gower's return to that world from the confession. In this way, Gower suggests that the dangerous influence of Lollards and the division they represent can be answered and disarmed by confession.

Hoccleve's Lollard Confession

For Thomas Hoccleve, writing in the early fifteenth century, Lollards were a very different kind of problem, and his zeal in attacking Lollard beliefs suggests a certain opportunism not shared by Gower.[27] Nevertheless, Hoccleve's understanding of the relationship between confession and self-definition has been profoundly affected by Lollardy (and concerns shared with Lollardy).[28] Indeed, one cannot, as one can with Gower, discuss Hoccleve's representation of confession without addressing Lollardy because Hoccleve frames his own confession to the "Old Man" with an account of the heretic John Badby.[29] This frame links two versions of resistance to confession: despair and heresy, as I shall argue below. Although Hoccleve does not show the sympathy for the latter resistance that he does for the former, the juxtaposition hints at a deeper similarity: that Lollardy may be just another form of despair at the church's program for salvation.[30]

For Hoccleve, heresy and confession seem to be inextricably linked. Indeed, the Old Man introduces his story of Badby with advice to confess:

> The verray cause of thyn hid maladie
> Thow moot deskevere and telle out al thyn herte.
> If thow it hyde, thow schalt nat asterte
> That thow ne falle shalt in sum meschance;
> Forthy amende thow thy governance.
>
> Be waar of thoght, for it is perillous;
> He the streight way to desconfort men ledith;
> His violence is ful outrageous;
> Unwys is he that bisy thoght ne dredith.
> In whom that he his mortel venym schedith,
> But if a vomyt aftir folwe blyve,
> At the port of despeir he may arryve.
>
> Sone, swich thoghte lurkynge thee withynne,
> That huntith aftir thy confusioun,
> Hy tyme it is to voide and lat him twynne.
>
> (262–76)

On first glance, one notes the traditional language of confession—"deskever," telling the heart, vomiting, and voiding—in essence drawing out and showing what is "withynne."[31] In this way, the language calls to mind the instructions given to the penitent in vernacular penitentials, as discussed in chapter 2. Even while asserting confession's efficacy in traditional terms, the Old Man introduces a confessional problem, despair, that threatens the practice of confession from the inside, as it were, and might affect Hoccleve's own confession. The problem with despair is that it will prevent the penitent from confessing. As Lee Patterson writes, presumption and despair "are the prime elements of the medieval understanding of the impenitence that constituted the unforgiveable sin against the Holy Spirit—unforgive-able not because of its heinousness but because of the inner dynamic by which the presumptuous and/or despairing sinner refuses to ask for for-giveness."[32] In pointing out this potential for an impenitence caused by de-spair, the Old Man draws attention to the way in which Hoccleve might re-sist confession even before he has begun. This resistance is made even clearer in Hoccleve's desire to have nothing to do with the Old Man: "talke to me no more" (139).[33]

It is, of course, important to note that this resistance is typically under-stood in purely personal terms (as it is here): someone refuses to confess out of despair and thereby damns him- or herself. The person does not call the general efficacy of confession into question, only the efficacy for him- or her-self. An exemplum for this kind of refusal appears in John Mirk's *Festial* and the *Middle English Sermons:* a woman will not confess out of shame, and Jesus appears to her and sticks her hand in his wound.[34] As these sermons suggest, hers is a resistance that the church anticipates and attempts to ad-dress in devotional literature. Indeed, this anticipation demonstrates that despair is endemic to the confessional system, as Patterson points out, in that "despair actually arises from the self-confrontation that initiates penance and is disturbingly close to the genuine spiritual impulses that lead to salva-tion."[35] From this perspective, Hoccleve's account of despair seems to fit within the traditional devotional mode: the Old Man states that Hoccleve can avoid the "port" of despair by talking to him. Nevertheless, despair here takes on a heightened importance, even a tautological emphasis, because the Old Man himself can be understood not as alleviating despair but as figur-ing it in his intertextuality with another story about penitential despair and another Old Man.[36] That is, the language of the Old Man initially echoes Chaucer's description of the rioters in the *Pardoner's Tale,* suggesting that this Old Man, like Chaucer's, may only be a penitential dead end.[37] To be sure, Hoccleve abandons the allusive quality of his Old Man as the conver-sation continues; nevertheless, the echo of the Pardoner's Old Man certainly runs the risk of generating confusion about this Old Man's ability to console this particular rioter (perhaps he will only lead him to death!), even about the possibility of the Old Man's own despair.[38]

Whether or not one wants to read this despair as threatening Hoccleve's own confession, one cannot overlook the fact that this potential resistance is juxtaposed with another form: heresy (in the story of Badby). Like despair, heresy is described within a confessional structure, in terms of Hoccleve's own self-definition (whether his despair has led him to Lollardy or not). As in Gower's *Confessio*, Lollardy (here the Lollard) is understood as a threat to orthodox self-definition, both its content (belief) and the practices by which believers know themselves as orthodox. The Old Man begins with a warning about Badby, similar to Genius's command to "Be war" of false beliefs:

> Sum man for lak of occupacioun,
> Musith ferthere than his wit may strecche,
> And, at the feendes instigacioun
> Dampnable errour holdith, and can nat flecche
> For no conseil ne reed, as dide a wrecche
> Nat fern ago, which that of heresie
> Convict and brent was unto asshen drie.
>
> The precious body of our Lord Jhesu
> In forme of brede he leeved not at al;
> He was in nothyng abassht ne eschu
> To seye it was but brede material.
> He seide a preestes power was as smal
> As a rakers [street cleaner][39] or swiche anothir wight,
> And to make it hadde no gretter might.
>
> (281–94)

Lollardy concerns a specific person ("sum man" and a "wrecche") and a specific doctrine (the Eucharist) that may have a bearing on Hoccleve personally, since the Old Man goes on to ask him, "thow art noon of tho / That wrappid been in this dampnacioun?" (372–73). Raised in the confessor's questions, Lollardy becomes another sin, perhaps even the sin of despair, that one must reveal in confession. Moreover, by connecting Lollardy with thought, Hoccleve (or the Old Man) characterizes it as afflicting the individual from the inside rather than threatening church unity from the outside, the "tapinage" of Gower's Lollards who "blow" false information into wayward ears.

Unlike despair, heresy signals a resistance to confession that threatens to undermine the system: Badby does not submit to the authority of the prince, does not confess his error to him:

By any outward tokne resonable,
If he inward hadde any repentance,
That woot He that of nothyng hath doutaunce.

(320–22)

The language clearly echoes the confessional—making the "inward" state of repentance known via tokens—a process that Badby rejects. What is most important is not only that the Old Man gives an account of that resistance but that he describes the reasons for it, his words becoming an odd parody of Lollard belief: that only God can know the state of Badby's contrition, as in the Wycliffite passage cited at the opening of chapter 2: "þi confessour can nouȝt wyte wheþer þou be bound or soyled."[40]

Using the story of Badby's resistance within a confessional structure would, at first glance, seem to neutralize Badby's resistance in the same way that Gower's invocation of "Lollardie" within Amans's confession has the potential to neutralize that threat. One should note, however, that Hoccleve's poem understands "Lollardie" not as a generalized, abstract threat (as Gower does) but as a particular Lollard, Badby. His integration of this threat is far more personal, and the poem is that much more interested in detailing a confession concerned with Hoccleve's belief, whereas Amans quite simply never mentions his. That Hoccleve understands Lollardy's threat as deeply personal is underlined in the Old Man's closing remarks on the subject of Badby:

And first I was ful sore agast of thee,
Lest that thow thurgh thoghtful adversitee
Nat haddest standen in thy feith aright.

(389–91)

While it makes perfect sense to describe heresy as thought because false beliefs are, after all, thoughts, the threat of heresy is more often described as external. For example, Gower consistently describes Lollardy as an abstraction that lurks on the outside, threatening to come in (through the ears). In contrast, Hoccleve's poem demonstrates that Lollardy has already arrived on the inside, and the problem is how to get it out. In this way, the poem shows that confessional practice can amend (or correct) the internal state of the penitent (including his heretical thought). And we see this correction implied in Hoccleve's conversation with the Old Man: "And meekly yow by-seeche I of pardoun, / Me submittyng unto correccioun" (755–56), a submission juxtaposed with Badby's refusal to "discover," "void," or "vomit"—to make his inner contrition apparent by a token. This emphasis on correction within confessional practice makes sense: if Lollardy in this poem concerns a purely individualized belief, and not schism more generally, then confession is pre-cisely the means for resolving it. After all, as the Decrees of the Fourth Lat-eran Council reveal, one of the functions of annual auricular confession was to "suppress heresy."[41] From this perspective, Hoccleve's poem appropriates the resistance to confession, Badby's obduracy, into another confession, his own, thus demonstrating a victory for the confessional genre.

Despite this attempt to integrate Lollardy into the practice that it threat-ened, the poem does not, indeed cannot, ultimately demonstrate the success of that integration. Rather, the poem consistently reveals the assimilation or reproduction of Lollard concerns. I shall argue here that Hoccleve's text ul-timately ends up being "Lollard" in its approach to self-definition, that the poem enacts a retreat from confession as it has been traditionally defined. It is worth emphasizing the nature of this retreat: it is not, as it is in Gower's poem, a retreat *into* confession, one that extends for the duration of the lover's confession but returns Amans/Gower ultimately to the world of the *Prologue,* but a retreat *from* confession as unsuited to the demands of the poem Hoccleve is writing. First, I shall demonstrate the way Hoccleve rede-fines confession as a site of solely personal, private concerns, disconnected from the authority of the institutional church. Second, I shall argue that his poem ultimately abandons the confessional genre entirely in favor of exem-plary narrative as the site of self-definition. As my discussion of confession in chapter 2 makes clear, this is the structure of the Lollard redefinition of confession, although surely not its content.

Hoccleve's redefinition of confession begins with his conversation with the Old Man. On first glance, this conversation reproduces the discourses of confession unproblematically: the questions, the language of sins, the ex-empla. Indeed, Hoccleve seems to demonstrate the same kind of efficacy of confessional self-definition that Gower has described—the use of examples to link the moral world he is describing to the personal experience of the lis-tener. Warnings to "Be a treewe housbounde" (1683) and to "Waar advoutrie" (1690) are illustrated with stories about Abraham and David. Similarly, the discussion of poverty takes up both its theoretical importance and exempla about the king of Sicily and Scipio Africanus, who rejected wealth. Yet the similarity to confession seems more asserted than set into motion. Although Hoccleve uses all the terms of confession, as reflected in the Old Man's commands to "deskevere and telle out al thyn herte" (263), he is far less interested in representing encouraged identification, as Gower has done. As the penitent, the speaker in the poem does not see himself in relation to the stories, as has Amans; indeed, it seems as if the Old Man makes a point of invoking the stories' relevance to Hoccleve only to set that relevance aside. In the Old Man's discussion of marriage, he includes exempla about David and Abraham and then states:

> Of swiche stories cowde I telle an heep,
> But I suppose thise schul souffyse,
> And forthy sone, wole I make a leep
> From hem and go wole I to the empryse
> That I first took. If thow thee wel avyse,
> Whanne I the mette and sy thyn hevynesse,
> Of confort, sone, made I thee promesse.
>
> (1765–71)[42]

The Old Man suggests that all the exempla he could tell in this process of self-definition do not necessarily aid in defining Hoccleve's problem or offer him "confort."

The lack of encouraged identification suggests that Hoccleve does not accede to the Old Man's authority, and, in fact, the poem does not reproduce the penitent's subjection to institutional authority.[43] Indeed, this confession occurs outside an institutional context, and the Old Man's advice directs Hoccleve to the prince, not to the church:

> "Wryte him nothyng that sowneth into vice
> Kythe thy love in mateere of sadnesse.
> Looke if thow fynde canst any tretice
> Growndid on his estates holsumnesse.
> Swich thyng translate and unto his hynesse,
> As humblely as that thow canst, presente.
> Do thus, my sone." "Fadir, I assente."
>
> (1947–53)

Hoccleve's submission to the Old Man, whom he calls "father," leads seamlessly to submission to the prince. It is worth comparing this directive to the prince with Gower's address to Richard II in his *Confessio*, although Gower removes the mention from Richard II from the second version of his poem. In Gower's poem, the king is located only in the "contemporary world" of the Prologue and the end of book 8, not in the confession itself. For this reason, the authority of Richard II never impinges in any way on Genius's, and Genius remains the confessor-authority throughout.

In addition, the Old Man's efficacy (and authority) as a confessor is entirely personal, based on the similarity of his and Hoccleve's personal history, not his clerical or even learned status. The trajectory of that history is riotous living (without repentance) to repentance and poverty:

> Whan I was yong, I was ful rechelees,
> Prowd, nyce, and riotous for the maistrie,
> And among othir, consciencelees.
> By that sette I nat the worth of a flie;
> And of hem hauntid I the conpaignie
> That wente on pilgrimage to taverne,
> Which before unthrift berith the lanterne.
>
> There offred I wel more than my tythe,
> And withdrow Holy Chirche his duetee.
> My freendes me conseillid often sythe
> That I with lownesse and humilitee
> To my curat go sholde and make his gree,
> But straw, unto hir reed wolde I nat bowe
> For aght they cowden preyen all or wowe!
> (610–23)
>
> But nevere thoghte I in al my yong lyf
> What I unjustly gat for to restore,
> Wherfore I now repente wondir sore.
> (661–63)
>
> Now is povert the glas and the mirour
> In which I see my God, my sauveour.
> (690–91)

Although refusal to submit to a curate is a sign of the Old Man's youthful recklessness, his repentance in old age occurs without reference to the institutional church. Indeed, the signs of his repentance, his poverty and his gown of russet (675), also suggest his distance from the institutional clergy as they are commonly described. Given the Wycliffite associations of poverty and russet, they are markers of an outright rejection of the established church.[44] After all, poverty is a common marker of anticlerical satire, as Wendy Scase has demonstrated in *Piers Plowman and the New Anticlericalism*.[45] One might then ask whether the Old Man is a kind of idealized poor priest who has renounced his goods and is wandering around in a robe of russet, a reminder of the failure of the clergy in the established church. Although the Old Man himself includes a brief bit of anticlericalism that describes priests' greed (1409–44), he does not retain a consistently anticlerical perspective: he does not link his own poverty to anything other than his personal history, and he quite clearly states his submission to "Holy Chirche."[46] In this way, these anticlerical markers float somewhat freely; they function both to invoke the clergy and to distance the Old Man from them.

The Old Man's ambiguous relationship with the clergy and with anticlericalism is underlined by the echoes of Chaucer's *Pardoner's Prologue* and *Tale*. Indeed, one can read the Old Man as a kind of converted Pardoner who is riotous and lecherous and holds a "lucrative" office (659) at the beginning of his life and who repents at the end. It is fitting that Hoccleve imagines a converted Pardoner figure through the Old Man of the *Pardoner's Tale* because, as Lee Patterson has argued, "The penitential meaning of the Pardoner's history, with its tortuous inner complexities, is most powerfully expressed in the uncanny figure of the Old Man."[47] If Hoccleve has rewritten the Old Man/Pardoner as repentant, then, one would think, he has resolved some of the penitential problems surrounding this figure, specifically his despair at the limitations of the institutional church.[48] And it is true that Hoccleve's Old Man does not share the bleak vision of Chaucer's Pardoner. Like "covetise," the despair of Hoccleve's Old Man seems to have been resolved by poverty, which spurs his repentance. Moreover, the Old Man seems to become the effective confessor that the Pardoner was not—providing "confort" to Hoccleve, as the Pardoner was so clearly unable to do for any of the pilgrims in the *Canterbury Tales*. Nevertheless, Hoccleve's "solution" to the Pardoner's (and Old Man's) exclusion from penitence takes place outside the institutional church or at least in a deeply ambiguous relationship to it. There are hints that we are supposed to read the Old Man as a cleric in his reference to "the Carmes mess" (2007), perhaps even a Carmelite, as Derek Pearsall has suggested.[49] But these hints are just that. In leaving the Old Man's status ambiguous, Hoccleve sidesteps a central issue raised by the *Pardoner's Prologue* and *Tale*—the relationship between the penitent and institutional authority that is created in the practice of confession and the power of that institutional authority to console.

Moreover, in invoking the Old Man of the *Pardoner's Tale*, Hoccleve suggests that his Old Man has no value outside his figurative importance to Hoccleve's sinful past, the *vetus homo* of Pauline tradition.[50] Indeed, he makes the link between his own past and Hoccleve's perfectly clear:

> "I cowde of youthe han talkid more and told
> Than I have doon . . ."
> "Telle on anoon, my goode sone."
>
> (743–47)

In drawing attention to their psychological, or personal, parallel, Hoccleve emphasizes the immateriality of the Old Man's authority. This immateriality forms, of course, a striking contrast to the overwhelming materiality of the Pardoner's authority: "And thanne my bulles shewe I, alle and some. / Oure lige lordes seel on my patente" (6.336–37). These material documents stand in for the institution of the church, as they are clearly linked to popes, cardinals, patriarchs, and bishops (6.342–43).

In distancing the Old Man from the clergy and making him a personal authority, Hoccleve makes his Old Man the most obvious example of the laicization of confession in the poem. This laicization distinguishes Hoccleve's confession from Gower's and links it more closely to Lollardy. Although Genius is also not a priest in Gower's *Confessio*, the difference between these confessors should be clear in the names: the Old Man is clearly a man with no institutional status (as I have indicated above), whereas Genius is an abstraction from the world of courtly love, certainly more of an authoritative tradition than a man.[51] It is Genius's separation from the contemporary world that ultimately makes the exact nature of his priestly status outside the world of love irrelevant—he is a priest in the world of love, and that world is quite distinct from the world of the clergy as described in the Prologue. In contrast, Hoccleve sets his Old Man within his contemporary world, thus drawing attention to the relationship between that world and the practice of confession.

The removal of confession from institutional authority is further emphasized by the larger movement of the text—from Hoccleve's confession to the Old Man to his confession to the prince (the intended reader)—a movement made evident in the Old Man's command to "Conpleyne unto his excellent noblesse, / As I have herd the unto me conpleyne" (1849–50). Although the poem directly suggests that the prince is the ultimate authority over confession, it enacts a kind of democratization of confession, as the Old Man, Prince Hal, and Hoccleve himself all serve as confessors: the Old Man to Hoccleve, Prince Hal to Badby (and ultimately to Hoccleve), and Hoccleve to the prince.[52] This last relationship is not represented in the text explicitly, and it clearly causes Hoccleve some discomfort to be offering himself as an authority, as the insistence on his humility and "meeknesse" (2023) reveals. Nevertheless, Hoccleve's directions to the prince necessarily identify him as an authority not only over the moral language (such as avarice) and the stories that illustrate that moral language but also over the prince himself.[53] This authority is clear in his opening discussion of the dignity of a king (and one could choose many such examples):

> First and forward, the dignitee of kyng
> Impressith in the botme of your mynde,
> Consideryng how chargeable a thyng
> That office is, for so yee shul it fynde.
>
> (2164–67)

And he follows this discussion of this morality with a story: "Ones ther was a kyng, as I have rad" (2171). This authority might be understood as that of the advisor, not that of the confessor, as the "mirrors for princes" tradition indicates, but these roles seem to overlap. This overlap is apparent in the confessional dialogue with the Old Man, who offers himself both as a "gyde" (210) and as a confessor, in the commands to "telle on thy grevance" (232). It is also apparent in one of Hoccleve's sources or influences: Gower's *Confessio*.[54] Indeed, Gower's text makes the convergence between the princely advisor and the confessor even more notable by placing the "mirror for princes" in the mouth of Genius, the confessor (in book 7), not in Amans (the figure for Gower himself), thus emphasizing the continuity between these authoritative roles.[55]

Reading Hoccleve as a potential confessor to the prince underlines the way in which all successful confessions in this poem are imagined in terms of a voluntary submission to authority. This is true for Hoccleve, who submits to the Old Man only because he recognizes his personal authority/wisdom: "And meekly yow byseeche I of pardoun, / Me submittyng unto correccioun" (755–56) because "Your wys reed hope I hele shal my wownde" (775). And it is also true for the prince, as Hoccleve imagines the prince submitting to the authority of the poem because he recognizes its value:

And if I nat the way of reson holde,
Folwe me nat; and if that I do, thenne
Do as I shal reporte with my penne.
                    (2189–91)

The prince may choose to submit to Hoccleve's authority (understood here as the "way of reson") or not.

The redefinition of confession identified here—its democratization (or laicization) and its voluntary nature—echoes the Lollard redefinition in two ways. First, it removes the authority of the priest, and, second, it replaces that authority with the authority of virtuous examples (both living and textual). William Thorpe's response to the "spy's" questions about confession, discussed at length in chapter 2, can serve as an example of this Lollard redefinition:

Ser, I counseile ȝou for to absente ȝou fro al yuel companye, and to drawe ȝou to hem þat louen and bisien hem to knowe and to kepe þe heestis of God. And þanne þe good spirit of God wole moue ȝou for to occupie bisili alle ȝoure wittis in gederynge togedere of alle ȝoure synnes, as ferforþ as ȝe cunne biþinke ȝou, schamynge greetly of hem, and sorowynge ofte hertli for hem—ȝhe, sere, þe Holi Goost wole þanne putte into ȝoure herte a good wille and a feruent desir for to take and holde a good purpos, to hate euere and to fle aftir ȝoure cunnynge and ȝoure power euery occasioun of synne. And so þanne wisedam schal come to ȝou from aboue, illumynynge wiþ dyuerse bemes of heuenly grace alle ȝoure wittis, enfourmynge ȝou how ȝe schulen triste stidefastli in þe mercy of þe Lord, knowlechinge to him al holy al ȝoure viciouse lyuynge.[56]

For Thorpe, confession is purely voluntary; it does not require the presence of the priest, only the presence of virtuous people who keep God's commandments. Indeed, the imitation of virtuous people will generate the different stages of confession—contrition, acknowledgment, and absolution ("heuenly grace")—a process that reverses the traditional form in which confession generates the imitation of virtuous examples (see the discussion of *Handlyng Synne* in my introduction).

Hoccleve's Lollard echoes point to a limiting of confessional language and an expansion of the role of exemplary narrative and exemplary figures. And indeed, the generic shift in the poem, from the confessional dialogue to the "mirror for princes" with its extended use of exempla, underlines the separation between these two forms of self-definition. It is worth recalling here that for Gower exempla are never detached from their place within the confessional dialogue, even in the "mirror for princes," book 7 of his *Confessio*. Whereas Gower's poem thus emphasizes the links between the "empty forms" (or subject positions) of narrative and the language of sin and virtue through the capaciousness of the confessional genre, Hoccleve's poem underlines the split. Indeed, the poem offers the links between these different discursive strands not in the confession at all but in the "mirror for princes." In addition, it is the second part of the poem that takes up the encouraged identification familiar from homiletics, in contrast to the failure of that identification in Hoccleve's own confession. This use is made clear in the mode of address:

> O worthy Prince, for to God eterne
> It ful plesant is; dooth your mercy heere,
> For to late is, aftir yee go to beere.
>
> Take heede, excellent Prince, of your grauntsyre,
> How in his werkes he was merciable.
> He that for mercy dyde qwyte his hyre.
> He nevere was in al his lyf vengeable,
> But ay forgaf the gilty and coupable.

Our lige lord your fadir, dooth the same;
Now folwe hem two, my lord in Goddes name!

(3344–53)

Here Hoccleve invokes the language of sermons and penitential manuals, "Take heede," and encourages the prince to identify with the moral (mercy) and imitate the examples (his grandfather and father). In this way, he assumes a kind of authority over the prince's moral fashioning, although it is an authority that exists outside an institution. It is important to note that Hoccleve's "mirror for princes" departs from his sources in placing the encouraged identification in relation to his exemplary sources.[57] Even Gower's "mirror," book 7 of the *Confessio*, which includes very similar exposition and exempla, does not use encouraged identification, quite simply because it is addressed only indirectly to Richard II (or Henry Bolingbroke) through Amans. To be sure, the version of exemplary self-definition in Hoccleve's "mirror" can in no way be understood as Wycliffite. The exempla themselves would be rejected as a means of lay instruction. Nevertheless, the interpretive approach to these examples reproduces the Lollard position: the examples are offered here as virtuous models with no guarantee except for the prince's good will that they will be imitated.

In redefining the role of confession, Hoccleve's text disrupts the workings of consolation and absolution, transferring it from the confessor to outside the text, the uncertainty of the prince's favor. In this way, Hoccleve's redefinition is accompanied by a limiting of its consoling potential and therefore its power to return a reformed penitent to the community.[58] To be sure, a Lollard redefinition would not necessitate these limitations. As the quotation from Thorpe demonstrates, confession, however redefined as "knowlechyng," will still bring grace from God: "so þanne wisedam schal come to ȝou from aboue, illumynynge wiþ dyuerse bemes of heuenly grace." But Hoccleve is not a Lollard, and therefore invoking the Lollard interpretive position does not allow a Lollard form of grace (or absolution). Rather, his exploration of confession suggests a precarious position between championing the efficacy of confession and recognizing its limitations. This divided nature is most clearly evident in the generic split in the two parts of the poem: between the Prologue/Hoccleve's confession, which promises comfort only to defer it, and the "mirror for princes," which continues a petition for grace from the prince whose outcome is uncertain. Although the Old

Man offers himself as a doctor to "[a]bregge" Hoccleve's "maladie" (217, 216), thus invoking the language of penitential tradition (see chap. 2), it is the prince who can offer absolution, an absolution that the Old Man has suggested, if we understand absolution as a kind of grace:

> O, my good sone, wilt thow yit algate
> Despeired be? Nay, sone, let be that!
> Thow shalt as blyve entre into the gate
> Of thy confort. Now telle on pleyn and plat:
> My lord the Prince, knowith he thee nat?
> If that thow stonde in his benevolence,
> He may be salve unto thyn indigence.
>
> (1828–34)

While the prince offers a kind of salvation (the gate of comfort) to Hoccleve, it is not one that the poem can represent; the promise of a "confort" is, therefore, only that. Indeed, the word *despaired* indicates the pessimism that underwrites this plea.

In this way, the generic divide in this poem can be read as a retreat from another aspect of confessional practice—its potential to return the absolved penitent to the social world. Once again, it is worth noting the way in which Hoccleve alters the trajectory of Gower's poem, which returns the penitent to the world after absolution. In contrast to Gower's poem, Hoccleve's returns the penitent to the social world (the world of the "mirror for princes") *before* he has received consolation, if, in fact, it has ever removed him from it. The confessional dialogue ends with an acknowledgment of the Old Man's powerlessness to help Hoccleve: "I deeme so syn that my long sermoun / Profitith naght—it sore me repentith" (1821–22). In this way, Hoccleve's resolution at the end of his dialogue, to write to the prince, does not end his repentance; it merely continues in another form to another addressee. This is made clearest when Hoccleve interrupts his "mirror" to remind the prince of his repentance: "I me repente of my misreuled lyf" (4376), and this reminder leads once more to a plea to be remembered:

> And worthy Prince, at Crystes reverence,
> Herkneth what I shal seyn and beeth nat greeved,
> But lat me stande in your benevolence.
>
> (4390–92)

The uncertainty of consolation affects Hoccleve's relationship to his contemporary world, to which his discussion of "counsel" (in section 14) recalls him. Indeed, he comes to the end of his exercise (the "mirror for princes") with a tone of defeat:

> More othir thyng wolde I fayne speke and touche
> Heere in this book, but swich is my dulnesse,
> For that al voide and empty is my pouche,
> That al my lust is qweynt with hevynesse,
> And hevy spirit commandith stillnesse.
> And have I spoke of pees, I shal be stille.
> God sende us pees, if that it be His wille.
>
> (5013–19)

This passage suggests that neither the dialogue with the Old Man nor the penitential exercise he has assigned (the "mirrors for princes") brings consolation for Hoccleve's "hevynesse." In addition, the return to the social world, in the prayer for peace, seems defeated even before articulated, as apparent in the stillness that it evokes. One might compare this failed consolation (and failed return) with the end of Gower's poem, in which confession (and the absolution it brings) returns a prayerful and hopeful Gower to "amende" his social world.

In disempowering the confessional mode and miring his poem in despair, Hoccleve's poem raises an important question about resistance to traditional forms, a question underlined by his inclusion of the Badby episode: To what extent could Hoccleve's poem be understood in terms of a Lollard resistance? Resistance here is, of course, resistance not only to the practice of confession but to the ways in which narratives are offered for confessional self-definition, as I demonstrated in my discussion of the Lollards in chapters 1 and 2. If the function of narratives in the confessional frame is to authorize certain selves (for example, the woman who refuses to confess but finally understands the wisdom of doing so), then releasing those narratives from that frame might generate new ways of defining the self, perhaps the refusal to confess at all. While such a release might be liberating for Wycliffites, necessitating a redefinition of the kinds of stories upon which individuals might model themselves, it would be seen as intensely dangerous for those wishing to distance themselves from the Wycliffites, as Hoccleve does. In this danger one might note another reason for Hoccleve's "hevynesse"—

that Hoccleve is worried about these stories once he has released them from
their institutional structure, because their relevance or purpose in self-definition can only be guessed at. Indeed, Hoccleve begins the poem quite concerned about identification and where it might take him:

> Whan to the thoghtful whight is told a tale,
> He heerith it as thogh he thennes were;
> His hevy thoghtes him so plukke and hale
> Hidir and thidir, and him greeve and dere,
> That his eres availle him nat a pere;
> He undirstandith nothyng what men seye,
> So been his wittes fer goon hem to pleye.
>   (99–105)

In its focus on the reader's response to narrative (instead of the power of the
narrative to illustrate a certain concept), this passage suggests the possible
failure of the interpretive underpinnings that allow readers to define themselves in relation to narratives. The success of the confessional genre depends, after all, on readers' identification with the characters and events in
the tale and with the language offered as a moral frame—their appropriation
of those "empty forms." Hoccleve, in contrast, describes a problem with identification, apparent in the ambiguity of the word *thennes*. Either his identification is so strong that it traps him inside the tale, if we understand the
thennes as Hoccleve's hearing the tale as if he were in it.[59] Or identification
fails if we understand *thennes* as "elsewhere"; in this case he hears the tale not
at all because he is carried away somewhere else.[60] Either way, he is unable to
understand the tale's illustrative or imitative potential for his own particular
condition, and his inability to hear what men say seems to suggest that he
cannot join in the interpretations that the tale generates among others.

Hoccleve's poem revises the confessional genre, emptying it of its power
to define the self and its power to console, and the poem details this transformation structurally in the shift from the dialogue with the Old Man to
the "mirror for princes." The pressure for this revision comes, of course, from
the contemporary world, which Hoccleve cannot seem to escape as easily as
can Gower. Despite these differences, the generic fissures of both poems
suggest that the divisions of this world, particularly the Lollard heresy,
threaten the traditional form of self-definition associated with the practice
of confession.

AFTERWORD

I have ended this study with Hoccleve's poem *The Regiment of Princes* because it marks a shift in how confession might be appropriated and represented by writers in the late medieval period. Indeed, the *Regiment* can be
seen as both a formal and a historical hinge: the poem itself contains a transition between the confessional genre and what replaces it, and, historically,
it is situated between the flourishing of interest in the language of lay instruction (or, as Nicholas Watson has suggested, "vernacular theology") in
the late fourteenth century and the crackdown on that "vernacular theology"
in the fifteenth century.[1] In this way, the poem gestures simultaneously toward a literary past in which authors found confessional language and practice informing and inspiring and toward a future that will be concerned
with containing the threat of Wycliffism.

Because this study began with the instructional handbooks, such as
Handlyng Synne, that defined and generated the link between confession and
self-definition in the vernacular, it is perhaps fitting to close with the official
attempts to limit instruction in the vernacular. The most important of these
is Archbishop Arundel's *Constitutions* (1409), which returns lay instruction
to a pre-Wycliffite status quo.[2] The *Constitutions* demonstrates throughout a
concern with regaining control over the language that has been provided to
the laity. The fourth article states:

> Item, quia turpis est pars, quae non convenit suo toti, decernimus et
> ordinamus, ut nullus hujusmodi praedicator, aut alia quaevis per-
> sona de sacramento altaris, matrimonio, peccatorum confessione,
> aliove quocunque sacramento eccliesiae, seu fidei articulo aliter
> doceat, praedicet aut observet, quam quod per sanctam matrem
> ecclesiam reperitur discussum. . . .

[Item, Forasmuch as the part is vile, that agreeth not with the whole, we do decree and ordain, that no preacher aforesaid, or any other person whatsoever, shall otherwise teach or preach [or adopt] concerning the sacrament of the altar, matrimony, confession of sins, or any other sacrament of the church, or article of the faith, than what already is discussed by the holy mother church.][3]

This article reveals a fear not only about what is officially preached or taught but what is adopted *(observet)*. In other words, it acknowledges that the danger lies not only in what the laity might hear from teaching and preaching but in what they might internalize, the adoption of beliefs contrary to the church.[4]

In this way, the *Constitutions* shares with Hoccleve's poem a shift in understanding the relationship between traditional institutional discourses and the self that must define itself in relation to them. From this perspective, one might approach anew other fifteenth-century writers, such as John Lydgate, and ask in what way they also renegotiate the language of self-definition. This renegotiation would respond not only to the Wycliffite heresy but also to the response to that heresy—the legislation and censorship that characterize fifteenth-century England. Does this shift away from one form of self-definition, that associated with confession, demonstrate that fifteenth-century writers have also abandoned what is tied up with this form for their fourteenth-century forerunners—the self in relation to the institutional church and its penitential doctrines, the process of identification (with the pastoral language of sin and contrition and with narrative), and possibilities for both individual and community reform? While each of these characteristics might be transferable in some form to other genres, such as the exemplum collection or hagiography, the particular potential associated with the confessional mode would be lost.

If, as I have argued here, forms of self-definition shift from the late fourteenth to the early fifteenth century, then the consequences could be found not only in the fifteenth century but also in the early modern period. While the early modern period has, historically, been constructed around a disruption—that of medieval to Renaissance—the shift I am suggesting is rather more subtle—from forms of self-definition generated by confessional language to those generated by the exempla. Although the early modern period and its selves/subjects have been much investigated, their relation to the medieval period and its selves/subjects remains obscure and understudied, as David Aers and Lee Patterson have noted.[5] While the early modern period has long proposed itself as the site of origin for a self remarkably modern in its consciousness, this book has proposed that the late medieval period is also a rich site for the investigation of multiple and sometimes conflicting forms of self-definition, of selves defined in terms of moral and doctrinal language and narrative.

In ending with the loss of one form of self-definition, demonstrated by Hoccleve's poem and the larger cultural shift of which it is a part, my study seems to reinforce a bleak perspective on this period in history—that the flourishing of lay devotion in the late fourteenth century came rather abruptly to a halt. Yet to view this disruption purely as a sign of loss or degeneracy is to ignore much of the hope that informs the writers with which this study has been concerned. It is worth noting that this period is marked as much by despair over the limitations of traditional languages as by the hope (particularly of the Wycliffites) that to change the language of the laity would be to reform the world. Indeed, it is this position between the hope for change and despair over the intransigence of received traditions that may have a relevance to our own time, one that may even be inspiring. In highlighting the purposeful disruptions of the Wycliffites, this project has demonstrated that practices for making and understanding the self are capable of shifting in response to the concerted efforts of calls for reform; Wycliffite writings indicate that the possibilities for change exist in our language and are, perhaps, waiting to be discovered and set into motion.

NOTES

Introduction

1. I will use the terms *Lollard* and *Wycliffite* interchangeably to indicate that I am referring both to the "academic heresy" that developed around John Wyclif and the vernacular version of that heresy as it moved outward from the universities. On the term *Lollard*, see Andrew Cole, "William Langland and the Invention of Lollardy," in *Lollards and Their Influence in Late Medieval England*, ed. Fiona Somerset, Jill C. Havens, and Derrick G. Pitard (Woodbridge, Suffolk: Boydell Press, 2003), 37–58; Anne Hudson, *The Premature Reformation: Wycliffite Texts and Lollard History* (Oxford: Clarendon Press, 1988), 2–4; and Wendy Scase, *Piers Plowman and the New Anticlericalism* (Cambridge: Cambridge University Press, 1989), 150–51. On the relationship of academic to popular and vernacular Lollardy, see Hudson, *Premature Reformation*, chap. 2; and Fiona Somerset, *Clerical Discourse and Lay Audience in Late Medieval England* (Cambridge: Cambridge University Press, 1998), 3–21.

2. On the Lollards/Wycliffites, see Hudson, *Premature Reformation;* Margaret Aston, *Lollards and Reformers: Images and Literacy in Late Medieval Religion* (London: Hambledon Press, 1984); and Kantik Ghosh, *The Wycliffite Heresy: Authority and the Interpretation of Texts* (Cambridge: Cambridge University Press, 2002). For work linking Lollards to their contemporaries, see the essays in Somerset, Havens, and Pitard, *Lollards and Their Influence,* as well as David Aers and Lynn Staley, *Powers of the Holy: Religion, Politics, and Gender in Late Medieval English Culture* (University Park: Pennsylvania State University Pres, 1996); Rita Copeland, *Rhetoric, Hermeneutics, and Translation in the Middle Ages: Academic Traditions and Vernacular Texts* (Cambridge: Cambridge University Press, 1991) and *Pedagogy, Intellectuals, and Dissent in the Later Middle Ages: Lollardy and Ideas of Learning* (Cambridge: Cambridge University Press, 2001); Ruth Nisse, "Cobham's Daughter: *The Book of Margery Kempe* and the Power of Heterodox Thinking," *Modern Language Quarterly* 56 (1995): 277–304, and "Staged Interpretations: Civic Rhetoric and Lollard Politics in the York Plays," *Journal of Medieval and Early Modern Studies* 28 (1998): 427–73; Somerset, *Clerical Discourse* and "'As Just as Is a Squyre': The Politics of 'Lewed Translacion' in

Chaucer's *Summoner's Tale*," *Studies in the Age of Chaucer* 21 (1999): 187–207; Paul Strohm, "Chaucer's Lollard Joke: History and the Textual Unconscious," *Studies in the Age of Chaucer* 17 (1995): 23–42; and Nicholas Watson, "Censorship and Cultural Change in Late-Medieval England: Vernacular Theology, the Oxford Translation Debate, and Arundel's Constitutions of 1409," *Speculum* 70 (1995): 822–64. This is by no means an exhaustive list of this sort of work.

3. Both Eamon Duffy and Richard Rex downplay the importance of the Lollards in *The Stripping of the Altars: Traditional Religion in England, c.1400–c.1580* (New Haven: Yale University Press, 1992), 61–62, and *The Lollards* (London: Palgrave, 2002), respectively, whereas much of the work cited in n. 2 understands the Lollards as central.

4. The medieval self has witnessed a great deal of attention from literary critics in the last fifteen years, as they have challenged long-standing claims that the Renaissance (or early modern) invented the individual. See, for example, Sarah Kay, *Subjectivity in Troubadour Poetry* (Cambridge: Cambridge University Press, 1990); H. Marshall Leicester, *The Disenchanted Self: Representing the Subject in the Canterbury Tales* (Berkeley: University of California Press, 1990); and Lee Patterson, *Chaucer and the Subject of History* (Madison: University of Wisconsin Press, 1991). Both Patterson and David Aers have issued a "call to arms" to medievalists interested in breaking down the boundary between the medieval and early modern periods, particularly in terms of the self/subject. See David Aers, "A Whisper in the Ear of Early Modernists; or Reflections on Literary Critics Writing the 'History of the Subject,'" in *Culture and History, 1350–1600: Essays on English Communities, Identities, and Writing*, ed. David Aers (Detroit: Wayne State University Press, 1992), 177–202; and Lee Patterson, "On the Margin: Postmodernism, Ironic History, and Medieval Studies," *Speculum* 65 (1990): 87–108.

5. Hudson, *Premature Reformation*, 9–10.

6. Wycliffites' writings stand in stark contrast to Chaucer's poetry, where much of the work on subjectivity has been done. See, for example, Leicester, *Disenchanted Self*, and Patterson, *Chaucer*.

7. Paul de Vooght argues that Wyclif did not advocate Scripture as the sole authority, *scriptura sola*, for the church but rather was close to his contemporaries in advocating the authority of Scripture and the authority of traditional interpretations. *Les sources de la doctrine chrétienne d'après les théologiens du XIVe siècle et du début du XVe* (Bruges: Desclée, De Brouwer, 1954), 168–200. In contrast, Michael Hurley argues that Wyclif's position can, in fact, be described as advocating *scriptura sola*. "'Scriptura Sola': Wyclif and His Critics," *Traditio* 16 (1960): 275–352. For the background to Wyclif's thinking, see Heiko Oberman, *The Harvest of Medieval Theology: Gabriel Biel and Late Medieval Nominalism* (Cambridge: Harvard University Press, 1963), chap. 11. For a discussion of Wyclif's and Wycliffite hermeneutics, see Ghosh, *Wycliffite Heresy*, chaps. 1 and 4, respectively.

8. Sermon E51, lines 107–10, in *English Wycliffite Sermons*, ed. Pamela Gradon and Anne Hudson, 5 vols. (New York: Oxford University Press, 1983–96). Hereafter

referred to as *EWS*, following the system of citation established by Pamela Gradon and Anne Hudson in their edition, sermon number/line numbers. In this passage, the thorn has been changed to "th."

9. "Sixteen Points on Which the Bishops Accuse Lollards," in *Selections from English Wycliffite Writings*, ed. Anne Hudson (1978; reprint, Toronto: University of Toronto Press, 1997), 19.

10. The foundational nature of this council is widely accepted. See, for example, R. N. Swanson, who writes that Lateran IV was the "formulation of a programme to disseminate and inculcate the Christian faith and Christian way of life." *Religion and Devotion in Europe, c.1215–c.1515* (Cambridge: Cambridge University Press, 1995), 41. Accounts of confession typically include a discussion of this council; see, for example, Patterson, *Chaucer*, 374, and Karma Lochrie, *Covert Operations: The Medieval Uses of Secrecy* (Philadelphia: University of Pennsylvania Press, 1999), 24–27.

11. Michel Foucault, *The History of Sexuality*, trans. Robert Hurley (New York: Vintage Books, 1978), 1:61–62.

12. See Marjorie Curry Woods and Rita Copeland, "Classroom and Confession," in *The Cambridge History of Medieval English Literature*, ed. David Wallace (Cambridge: Cambridge University Press, 1999), 376–406.

13. The phrase "technology of the self" comes from Foucault's essay "Technologies of the Self," in *Ethics: Subjectivity and Truth*, ed. Paul Rabinow, trans. Robert Hurley and others, vol. 1 of *The Essential Works of Michel Foucault, 1954–1984* (New York: New Press, 1997), 223–51. This term is useful because it emphasizes practice over knowledge. The phrase also informs Karma Lochrie's discussion of confession in *Covert Operations*, 18.

14. Foucault, *History of Sexuality*, 1:33. See Lochrie's discussion, *Covert Operations*, 16 and throughout chap. 1. Foucault's version of history has, of course, also been criticized for its totalizing nature: see Fredric Jameson, *The Political Unconscious: Narrative as a Socially Symbolic Act* (Ithaca: Cornell University Press, 1981), 90–92. See also Pierre J. Payer, "Foucault on Penance and the Shaping of Sexuality," *Studies in Religion* 14 (1985): 313–20.

15. Lochrie identifies "three disturbing aspects of Foucault's *History of Sexuality*: his nostalgic representation of the Middle Ages as the modern's 'other,' his own complex and paradoxical relationship to confession, and finally, his reduction of confessional discourse to the subject of sex" (*Covert Operations*, 14); see, further, 15–24. Carolyn Dinshaw also criticizes Foucault for his nostalgia; see *Getting Medieval: Sexualities and Communities Pre and Postmodern* (Durham, NC: Duke University Press, 1999), 191–206.

16. Foucault's importance to studies of subjectivity is made clear by Kaja Silverman, who writes that Foucault "insists that man as we know him is the product of certain historically determined discourses." *The Subject of Semiotics* (New York: Oxford University Press, 1983), 129. In *The Sublime Object of Ideology* (London: Verso, 1989), Slavoj Žižek identifies the poststructuralist subject as Foucauldian—"The great master of such analysis was, of course, Foucault: one might say that the main

point of his late work was to articulate the different modes by which individuals assume their subject-positions" (174)—and he contrasts the Foucauldian subject with the Lacanian. As will become clear below, the Foucauldian subject is perhaps as problematic for the medieval period as it is for the contemporary, but Lacan cannot be invoked to solve that problem.

17. "The term 'subject' designates a quite different semantic and ideological space from that indicated by the more familiar term 'individual'" (Silverman, *Subject of Semiotics*, 126). See further, 126–31, for the contrast between the humanist self and the subject.

18. Emile Benveniste, *Problems in General Linguistics*, trans. Mary Elizabeth Meek (Coral Gables, FL: University of Miami Press, 1971), 227. See also Silverman, *Subject of Semiotics*, 43–53.

19. Silverman writes, "Indeed, the subject has an even more provisional status in Benveniste's writings than it does in Lacan's, since it has no existence outside of the specific discursive moments in which it emerges. . . . Curiously, this very transience results in a much less totalized view of subjectivity than that advanced by Lacan. . . . This descriptive model thus enables us to understand the subject in more culturally and historically specific ways than that provided by Lacan—i.e. in terms of a range of discursive positions available at a given time" (*Subject of Semiotics*, 199).

20. While one could certainly make the argument that sacraments have a particular role in shaping selves, this shaping would seem to be quite different from the approach I have outlined here, which takes language as its focus. For a sacramental approach to subjectivity, see Sarah Beckwith's *Christ's Body: Identity, Culture, and Society in Late Medieval Writings* (London: Routledge, 1993).

21. See Constitution 10 in *Decrees of the Ecumenical Councils*, ed. Norman P. Tanner, 2 vols. (Washington, DC: Georgetown University Press, 1990), which states that the clergy are to assist "non solum in praedicationis officio, verum etiam in audiendis confessionibus et poenitentiis iniugendis" (not only in the office of preaching but also in hearing confessions and enjoining penances) (1:240). Although Swanson writes that "for the practicalities of medieval spiritual life, perhaps the most important decree of the IV Lateran Council was *Omnis utriusque sexus*" (*Religion and Devotion*, 26), Leonard Boyle, Eamon Duffy, and H. Leith Spencer emphasize that the connection between preaching and confession was central to the church's program of instruction. See Boyle's "The Fourth Lateran Council and Manuals of Popular Theology," in *The Popular Literature of Medieval England*, ed. Thomas Heffernan (Knoxville: University of Tennessee Press, 1985), 30–43; Duffy, *Stripping of the Altars*; and H. Leith Spencer, *English Preaching in the Late Middle Ages* (Oxford: Clarendon Press, 1993), 102–3. The friars played an essential role in putting the decrees of the Fourth Lateran Council into practice, since they were authorized to preach and to act as confessors. For a discussion of their preaching, see G. R. Owst, *Preaching in Medieval England: An Introduction to Sermon Manuscripts of the Period c. 1350–1450* (Cambridge: Cambridge University Press, 1926), chap. 2; and Spencer, *English Preaching*, 58–60 and 166–71.

22. See Woods and Copeland, "Classroom and Confession," 396–98, and W. A. Pantin, *The English Church in the Fourteenth Century* (1955; reprint, Toronto: University of Toronto Press, 1980), 211–12.

23. *The Lay Folks' Catechism*, ed. T. F. Simmons and H. E. Nolloth, EETS, o.s., 118 (London: Kegan Paul, Trench, Trübner, 1901), lines 59–68, pp. 20, 22. Archbishop Pecham's Constitutions detail the same six requirements and indicate that they should be preached four times a year: "Ignorantia Sacerdotum populum praecipitat in foveam erroris. . . . In quorum remedium discriminum statuendo Praecipimus, ut quilibet sacerdos plebi praesidens quater in anno, hoc est, semel in qualibet quarta anni, una die solenni vel pluribus, per se vel per alium exponat populo vulgariter absque cujus libet subtilitatis textura fantastica" (line 7 and lines 15–19, in *Lay Folks' Catechism*, pp. 5 and 7). For a discussion of Thoresby's program, see Jonathan Hughes, *Pastors and Visionaries: Religion and Secular Life in Late Medieval Yorkshire* (Woodbridge, Suffolk: D. S. Brewer, 1988), 149–53.

24. Spencer discusses the English reaction to Lateran IV (*English Preaching*, 201–7) and notes that it is difficult to distinguish sermons from pastoral manuals and scriptural commentary, since sermon collections were copied for use by individuals and preachers (33). See also Pantin, *English Church*, 191–95, and Leonard Boyle, "The Summa for Confessors as a Genre and Its Religious Intent," in *The Pursuit of Holiness in Late Medieval and Renaissance Religion*, ed. Charles Trinkaus and Heiko Oberman (Leiden: Brill, 1974), 126–30 (on manuals more generally).

25. Cited in Pantin, *English Church*, 192 n. 1.

26. Boyle, "Fourth Lateran Council," 31. See also Swanson, *Religion and Devotion*, chap. 3, and Duffy, *Stripping of the Altars*, chap. 2, for discussions of pastoral instruction.

27. Boyle writes that "it was the Fourth Lateran Council which gave both these parochial priests and the *cura animarum* or parishioners an identity and a self-awareness, and an honorable, recognized place in the Church at large" ("Fourth Lateran Council," 31).

28. The most well-known advocate of medieval religion as a unified, traditional religion is Duffy, *Stripping of the Altars*.

29. Scholars have been attentive to the role of one particular pastoral language in shaping selves: the language of sin. See, for example, Foucault, *History of Sexuality;* Mary Flowers Braswell, *The Medieval Sinner: Characterization and Confession in the Literature of the English Middle Ages* (East Brunswick, NJ: Fairleigh Dickinson University Press, 1983); J. A. Burrow, *Ricardian Poetry: Chaucer, Gower, Langland, and the Gawain Poet* (New Haven: Yale University Press, 1971), 106–10; and Jerry Root, *"Space to Speke": The Confessional Subject in Medieval Literature* (New York: Peter Lang, 1997).

30. These contents are relatively typical. See Pantin, *English Church*, chap. 9. The absence of the Pater Noster was noted and corrected in the Wycliffite version of the *Lay Folks' Catechism* published parallel to the other versions in Simmons's and Nolloth's edition.

31. *Lay Folks' Catechism*, lines 30–31, p. 4.

32. *Fasciculus Morum: A Fourteenth-Century Preacher's Handbook*, ed. and trans. Siegfried Wenzel (University Park: Pennsylvania State University Press, 1989), lines 11–12, p. 160; trans., p. 161.

33. Žižek discusses this emptiness in Lacanian terms: "What, then is the status of this subject before subjectivation? The Lacanian answer would be, roughly speaking, that before subjectivation as identification, before ideological interpellation, before assuming a certain subject-position, the subject is subject of a question" (178). He observes that religious confession is an obvious example (*Sublime Object*, 179).

34. *Fasciculus Morum*, lines 83–84, p. 162; trans., pp. 163, 165.

35. This text contains a far more sophisticated approach to narrative than most vernacular penitential manuals, but the instructions to imitate are nevertheless representative. For a discussion of its relation to confession, see D. W. Robertson Jr., "The Cultural Tradition of *Handlyng Synne*," *Speculum* 22 (1947): 162–85.

36. Robert Mannyng, *Handlyng Synne*, ed. Idelle Sullens (Binghamton, NY: Medieval and Renaissance Texts and Studies, 1983), lines 11653–682; spelling modernized.

37. Foucault, *History of Sexuality*, 1:61.

38. For studies of exempla, see J. A. Mosher, *The Exemplum in the Early Religious and Didactic Literature of England* (New York: Columbia University Press, 1911); G. R. Owst, *Literature and Pulpit in Medieval England* (Cambridge: Cambridge University Press, 1933), chap. 4; Charles Runacres, "Art and Ethics in the 'Exempla' of 'Confessio Amantis,'" in *Gower's Confessio Amantis: Responses and Reassessments*, ed. A. J. Minnis (Cambridge: D. S. Brewer, 1983), 106–34; Larry Scanlon, *Narrative, Authority, and Power: The Medieval Exemplum and the Chaucerian Tradition* (Cambridge: Cambridge University Press, 1994); J. T. Welter, *L'exemplum dans la littérature religieuse et didactique du moyen âge* (Paris: Occitania, 1927). Although Scanlon mentions the possibility for subjectivity (35), he does not explore it at length.

39. These texts will be discussed further in chap. 2.

40. Here I quote from MSR 3.8 Trinity College, Cambridge, in *Cursor Mundi*, pt. 1, lines 1–2 and 85–88. *Cursor Mundi*, ed. Richard K. Morris, 3 vols., EETS, o.s., 57, 59, 62, 66, 68, 99, 101 (London: Kegan Paul, Trench, Trübner, 1874–93); spelling modernized. In *Piers Plowman*, Sloth also opposes romances with religious material:

I kan noȝt parfitly my Paternoster as þe preest it syngeþ,
But I kan rymes of Robyn hood and Randolf Erl of Chestre,

. . . .

I haue leuere here an harlotrye or a Somer game of Souters,
Or lesynge[s] to lauȝen [of] and bilye my neȝebores,
Than al þat euere Marc made, Mathew, Iohan and Lucas.

William Langland, *Piers Plowman: The B-Version*, ed. George Kane and E. Talbot Donaldson (London: Athlone Press, 1975), 5.394–408. The parallel should suggest that the gospels are understood in narrative terms.

41. Mosher describes the popularity of the exemplum in terms of "our credulous story-loving ancestors" (*Exemplum*, 139). The most recent scholar, Scanlon, argues that the exempla are a concession to the laity, thus separating narrative and doctrine: "As it developed within the Church, the exemplum's narrative component came more and more to be identified with the lay audience and its *sententia* comes more and more to be identified with the doctrinal discourse of the Church" (*Narrative, Authority*, 14–15). This separation is, of course, possible only if one ignores biblical narratives, in which both are combined. In fact biblical narratives were often used very similarly to exempla, and when Scanlon defines the exemplum, he could just as easily be defining biblical narratives and their interpretation: the moral "would be better described as a moral law: a value which the exemplarist assumes already binds the community together, or which he or she is strenuously arguing should bind it together. In short, the exemplum is not a purely textual exchange between two discursive genres, the narrative and the interpretive. . . . In its narrative the exemplum reenacts the actual, historical embodiment of communal value in a protagonist or event, and then, in its moral, effects the value's reemergence with the obligatory force of moral law" (*Narrative, Authority*, 33–34).

42. Alasdair MacIntyre, *After Virtue: A Study in Moral Theory* (Notre Dame, IN: University of Notre Dame Press, 1981), 216.

43. Jameson, *Political Unconscious*, 13.

44. Foucault, *History of Sexuality*, 1:59.

45. The phrase is Foucault's (*History of Sexuality*, 1:59).

46. James Simpson has argued persuasively for the multiple and decentered nature of authority in late medieval England (in contrast with the sixteenth century): "a complex parcelling out and impersonation of authority." *The Oxford English Literary History*, vol. 2, *1350–1547: Reform and Cultural Revolution* (Oxford: Oxford University Press, 2002), 62. For this reason, I avoid the term *self-fashioning;* as Stephen Greenblatt describes the term, "Self-fashioning for such figures involves submission to an absolute power or authority." *Renaissance Self-Fashioning: From More to Shakespeare* (Chicago: University of Chicago Press, 1980), 9.

47. The inability to deal with historical conflict or disruption is, perhaps, one of the limitations of theories of subjectivity that assume the stability of the preexisting language into which subjects emerge and by which they are produced. This limitation is not inherent in the theories themselves; it is apparent only in the absence of any discussion of contradictions in the Symbolic Order or the discourses Benveniste discusses. Leicester notes this limitation as well: "But the modern critique of the subject has tended to share the reductionism of traditional positivism insofar as it too has not provided a satisfactory account of the *agency* of the subject" (*Disenchanted Self*, 22).

48. Pantin calls it "the age of the devout layman" (*English Church*, 1). See also Vincent Gillespie, "Vernacular Books of Religion," in *Book Production and Publishing in Britain, 1375–1475*, ed. Jeremy Griffiths and Derek Pearsall (Cambridge: Cambridge University Press, 1989), 317–44; and Nicholas Watson, "Censorship and Cultural Change."

49. K. B. McFarlane, *Lancastrian Kings and Lollard Knights* (Oxford: Clarendon Press, 1972), 204, quoted in Gillespie, "Vernacular Books," 317. See also Pantin's pithy remark that "[t]he fourteenth century is above all things an age of continual controversy, of which the familiar Wycliffite controversy is but the culmination" (*English Church*, 1).

50. *EWS*, 11/52–61. Thorns and yoghs have been modernized.

51. See, for example, the studies by Braswell, *Medieval Sinner*, and Root, "*Space to Speke.*"

52. See, for example, Peter Brooks, *Troubling Confessions: Speaking Guilt in Law and Literature* (Chicago: University of Chicago Press, 2000).

53. Benveniste, *Problems in General Linguistics*, 225. Consider, for example, Patterson's interest in "this dialectical relationship between the subject and history—between the inner self of desire and its external mode of self-articulation as a singular individual who traces a specific worldly career" (*Chaucer*, 10).

54. Of course, it should come as no surprise that a reader's perspective colors what he or she reads. My point here is that studies of medieval subjectivity have not perhaps been as attuned to the forms of subjectivity they are studying as they might be. In the medievalists' important corrective to the early modernist position (e.g., Aers and Patterson in n. 4), there is the assumption that the modern notion of self (as a private, interior one) is, in fact, the only one worth studying (or recognizing).

Chapter One.   Narratives and Self-Definition

1. R. Higden, *Polychronicon Ranulphi Higden*, ed. Churchill Babington and Joseph Rawson Lumby, trans. John Trevisa, 9 vols. (London: Longman, 1865–86), 1:5–7. Here Higden is clearly interested in the stories we tell about the past, since the Latin is *historia*. Nevertheless, the relationship between narrative and subject formation is the same.

2. *English Wycliffite Sermons*, ed. Pamela Gradon and Anne Hudson, 5 vols. (New York: Oxford University Press, 1983–96), sermon 94, lines 1–8. Hereafter cited as *EWS*, with sermon number/line numbers (unless referring to the introductions, which appear as volume number: page numbers). This passage occurs at the opening of a sermon in the Proprium Sanctorum, and the author is at pains to remind his audience that "þese festus of þese seyntus han þis goode bysyde oþre, þat man may wel telle in hem þe vndurstondyng of þe gospel" (94/8–10).

3. To be sure, the Wycliffites were not alone in their desire to draw distinctions between stories that were appropriate for the laity and those that were not. But tradi-

tional distinctions had more often to do with condemning the stories the laity wanted to hear, such as Robin Hood, and encouraging them to read the gospels. The Wycliffites distinguished between kinds of preaching material and were far more insistent than any other reformers, including John Wyclif himself, that only Scripture be taught to the laity. The reform they envisioned would have changed preaching material quite radically, since the orthodox pastoral syllabus relied to a great extent on nonbiblical moral instruction, such as the exempla and the seven sins.

4. *Parson's Prologue*, in *The Riverside Chaucer*, 3rd ed., gen. ed. Larry D. Benson (Boston: Houghton Mifflin, 1987), X.34. I will discuss the Parson at greater length in chap. 3.

5. A cursory glance at any of the treatises collected in vol. 3 of *Select English Works of John Wyclif*, ed. Thomas Arnold (Oxford: Clarendon Press, 1869–71), *The English Works of Wyclif Hitherto Unprinted*, ed. F. D. Matthew, EETS, o.s., 74 (1880; reprint, Millwood, NY: Kraus Reprint, 1978), or the sermons in the *EWS* will give a fair idea of their views: extrascriptural stories, such as the exempla, are repeatedly referred to as "fables" and "lesynges" (lies). A typical view appears in a tract on the office of curates: "þei ben fals prophetis, techinge fals cronyclis & fablis to colour here worldly lif þerby, & leuen þe trewe gospel of ihu crist" (*English Works of Wyclif*, 153).

6. Of course, these two aspects are inseparable for the Wycliffites themselves: God's word should be the only mirror offered to the laity. Nevertheless, the Wycliffites must still contend with the place of interpretation in that mirroring function, and that is my interest here.

7. For example, in the same sermon that I have quoted above, the writer goes on to describe the eternal nature of God's word, its existence outside the contingencies of both readers and textual production: "We schulde not trowe in þis enke, ne in þese skynnys þat is clepud booc, but in þe sentence þat þei seyen, whyche sentence is þe booc of lyf; for al 3if þer ben manye trewþus and diuerse resonys in þe gospelus, neþeles eche of þes trewþus is þe substaunce of God hymself" (*EWS*, 94/19–24).

8. Both Christina von Nolcken and Anne Hudson have explored the Wycliffites' rhetorical emphasis on the group. See von Nolcken's "A 'Certain Sameness' and Our Response to It in English Wycliffite Texts," in *Literature and Religion in the Later Middle Ages: Philological Studies in Honor of Siegfried Wenzel*, ed. Richard G. Newhauser and John A. Alford (Binghamton, NY: Center for Medieval and Early Renaissance Studies, 1995), 191–208, and Hudson's "A Lollard Sect Vocabulary?" in *Lollards and Their Books* (London: Hambledon Press, 1985), 165–80.

9. This view is articulated by G. R. Owst, who writes, "[T]his movement was in its own way as completely dependent upon traditional authority and the influence of the past as orthodox Catholicism itself. The infallibility of the Scriptural text had merely taken the place of the infallibility of an inspired organization which further professed to hold the one key to its correct interpretation." *Preaching in Medieval England: An Introduction to Sermon Manuscripts of the Period c. 1350–1450* (Cambridge: Cambridge University Press, 1926), 136. Nevertheless, Owst also sees Lollardy as "an advance towards the spiritual independence of the future" (136–37).

10. H. Leith Spencer, *English Preaching in the Late Middle Ages* (Oxford: Clarendon Press, 1993), 192. Spencer also recognizes that "[i]n great measure the conflict between the Lollards and their adversaries was a battle over education, specifically the education of the laity. And the history of sermons in the late fourteenth century and the fifteenth is inextricably bound up with the greater struggle that was then taking place over lay education and censorship" (5).

11. The relationship between language and subjectivity is a basic tenet in poststructuralist thinking in the tradition of Lacan and Benveniste, as I have discussed in the introduction.

12. For the history of preaching in England, I rely upon Spencer, *English Preaching*, and, to a lesser extent, G. R. Owst, *Preaching in Medieval England* and *Literature and Pulpit in Medieval England* (Cambridge: Cambridge University Press, 1933).

13. For a discussion of the historical relationship between narrative and theology, see Hans W. Frei, *The Eclipse of Biblical Narrative: A Study of Eighteenth and Nineteenth Century Hermeneutics* (New Haven: Yale University Press, 1974). See also the essays collected in *Why Narrative? Readings in Narrative Theology*, ed. Stanley Hauerwas and L. Gregory Jones (Grand Rapids, MI: William B. Eerdmans, 1989).

14. The most recent study of exempla is Larry Scanlon, *Narrative, Authority, and Power: The Medieval Exemplum and the Chaucerian Tradition* (Cambridge: Cambridge University Press, 1994). See also J. A. Mosher, *The Exemplum in the Early Religious and Didactic Literature of England* (New York: Columbia University Press, 1911); J. T. Welter, *L'exemplum dans la littérature religieuse et didactique du moyen âge* (Paris: Occitania, 1927); and Owst, *Literature and Pulpit*, chap. 4. Although I have found Scanlon's study of exempla quite useful, particularly for the discussion of their ideological aspect (see below), I disagree that narratives used in preaching are a "discursive concession" to the laity (*Narrative, Authority*, 80). Sermons preached to the clergy were just as much indebted to narratives (both biblical and exempla) as those preached to the laity. See, for example, the sermons that Bishop Brinton preached to the clergy, which contain exempla: *The Sermons of Thomas Brinton, Bishop of Rochester (1373–1389)*, ed. Sister Mary Aquinas Devlin, 2 vols., Camden 3rd ser. 85–86 (London: Offices of the Royal Historical Society, 1954). Moreover, as Beryl Smalley has shown, exempla have a long history in biblical exegesis, appearing in glosses starting in the late twelfth century. *The Study of the Bible in the Middle Ages*, 2nd ed. (Oxford: Basil Blackwell, 1952), 256–57.

15. Quoted in Owst, *Preaching in Medieval England*, 322–23. The *artes praedicandi* are full of examples of what to preach to whom. Gregory's *Cura Pastoralis* (influential in the *artes* tradition) lists thirty-six pairs of opposite "characters," such as men and women, rich and poor, with examples of what to preach to an audience containing both. John J. Murphy, *Rhetoric in the Middle Ages: A History of Rhetorical Theory from St. Augustine to the Renaissance* (Berkeley: University of California Press, 1974), 294–96.

16. The influential essays are, of course, Sigmund Freud's *The Ego and the Id*, trans. Joan Riviere, ed. James Strachey, introd. Peter Gay (London: Hogarth Press,

1962; reprint, New York: Norton, 1989), and Jacques Lacan, "The Mirror Stage as Formative of the Function of the I as Revealed in Psychoanalytic Experience," in *Écrits: A Selection*, trans. Alan Sheridan (New York: Norton, 1977), 1–7. See also Diana Fuss, *Identification Papers* (New York: Routledge, 1995), 1–19.

17. My understanding of the importance of "recognition" in ideology is based on Louis Althusser's famous essay "Ideological State Apparatuses," in *Lenin and Philosophy and Other Essays*, trans. Ben Brewster (New York: Monthly Review Press, 1971), 127–86. I am also indebted to Terry Eagleton's *Criticism and Ideology: A Study in Marxist Literary Theory* (London: Verso, 1978), chap. 3, and *Ideology: An Introduction* (London: Verso, 1991); and Slavoj Žižek's *The Sublime Object of Ideology* (London: Verso, 1989).

18. In my discussion of allegory in medieval biblical exegesis, I rely on the following studies: Smalley, *Study of the Bible; Medieval Literary Theory and Criticism, c. 1100–c. 1375: The Commentary Tradition*, ed. A. J. Minnis and A. B. Scott (Oxford: Clarendon Press, 1988); A. J. Minnis, "'Authorial Intention' and 'Literal Sense' in the Exegetical Theories of Richard Fitzralph and John Wyclif: An Essay in the Medieval History of Biblical Hermeneutics," *Proceedings of the Royal Irish Academy* 75, no. 1 (1975): 1–30; Henri de Lubac, *Exégèse médiéval: Les quatre sens de l'ecriture*, 4 vols. (Paris: Aubier, 1959–64); and David Aers, *Piers Plowman and Christian Allegory* (London: Edward Arnold, 1975). One should note that the vernacular sermons discussed here do not offer their listeners the same kind of extended allegorical expositions found in texts for clerics, such as the *Glossa Ordinaria*. *Biblia Latina cum Glossa Ordinaria: Facsimile Reprint of the Editio Princeps, Adolph Rusch of Strassburg, 1480/81*, ed. Karlfried Froehlich and Margaret T. Gibson, 4 vols. (Turnhout: Brepols, 1992). Nevertheless, they are informed by the same approach. As Smalley writes, "[T]he twelfth century . . . saw a great revival of popular preaching; allegory could be used for instructing the laity, for presenting to them the Church and her sacraments in a concrete and intelligible form" (*Study of the Bible*, 244). Fredric Jameson suggests the ideological uses of figurative readings in *The Political Unconscious: Narrative as a Socially Symbolic Act* (Ithaca: Cornell University Press, 1981), 30–31.

19. In the following discussion, I make use of two cycles contemporary with Wycliffite writings: John Mirk, *Mirk's Festial*, ed. Theodor Erbe, EETS, e.s., 96 (London: K. Paul, Trench, Trübner, 1905), and *Middle English Sermons*, ed. Woodburn O. Ross, EETS, o.s., 209 (London: Oxford University Press, 1960), both hereafter cited parenthetically in the text, the latter as *MES*. Mirk's *Festial* was a text taken up by the self-consciously orthodox in the fifteenth century, those who wanted to "display their distance from Lollard preaching by their willingness to tolerate *exempla*, similitudes, verses, and other non-biblical *curiosa*" (Spencer, *English Preaching*, 312). Although I do not want to argue that Mirk's *Festial* is what the Wycliffites had in mind as their antimodel, it certainly could be defined in Wycliffite terms as dependent upon "talus" from "seyntys lyuys" or from "wiþowton holy writ." Passages labeled "Narracio" fill the sermons, whereas scriptural quotation and exposition make up a very small percentage of the material. Indeed, Mirk has concentrated his energies

on the sermons for particular saints' days, occasions for the discussion of many miracles. Moreover, the *Festial* is at least an equally influential sermon cycle written during roughly the same time period, probably 1382–90. For the dating, see Alan J. Fletcher, "John Mirk and the Lollards," *Medium Aevum* 56 (1987): 216–24. Although not as influential or as polemical as Mirk, the *MES* combine both scriptural narratives and exempla and are, therefore, important for comparison. They are particularly relevant to a discussion of the *EWS* because some of the sermons were derived from the *EWS* and revised to reflect more orthodox teachings and sentiments (Spencer, *English Preaching*, 286). Sermons 18–21 and 44–46 derive from the *EWS* (308–11); therefore, I have not used these in my discussion. For the traditional approach, see also sermon 2 in *Three Middle English Sermons from the Worcester Chapter Manuscript F.10*, ed. D. M. Grisdale (Leeds: Titus Wilson of Kendal, 1939).

20. See Emile Benveniste, "Subjectivity in Language," in *Problems in General Linguistics*, trans. Mary Elizabeth Meek (Coral Gables, FL: University of Miami Press, 1971), 223–30, and Kaja Silverman's account in *The Subject of Semiotics* (New York: Oxford University Press, 1983), 43–53.

21. For example, Mirk writes, "þys tyme of Lenton ys ordeynt only to scowre and clanse your concyens of all maner roust and fulþe of synne þat scho ys defowled wyth, so þat ȝe may wyth a clene consyens receyue, on Astyr-day, þe clene body of our Lord Ihesu Crist" (92–93). Another vernacular sermon also picks up this theme: "Good men, þe tyme of Lenten entred, þe wiche tyme we must clense vs of all oure mysdedis þat we haue done before" (*MES*, 140). In this way, listeners are reminded of their responsibilities during Lent, responsibilities over which they have control: "your concyens" and "we must clense vs." It is the individual who has sinned and must then perform the required actions to cleanse him- or herself.

22. This is the view of sin found in confessors' manuals: as Thomas N. Tentler writes, "[I]mplicit in the thinking of Gerson, and everyone else, is that something outside of the rational self—something not controlled voluntarily—originates temptation. It could be the devil. It could be the corrupted flesh. But whatever it is, there is no avoiding it while we are in our earthly form." *Sin and Confession on the Eve of the Reformation* (Princeton: Princeton University Press, 1977), 150. See also Morton Bloomfield, *The Seven Deadly Sins: An Introduction to the History of a Religious Concept with Special Reference to Medieval English Literature* (East Lansing: Michigan State College Press, 1952), and Jacques LeGoff, "Trades and Professions as Represented in Confessors' Manuals," in *Time, Work, and Culture in the Middle Ages*, trans. Arthur Goldhammer (Chicago: University of Chicago Press, 1980), 113.

23. Jameson writes, "[A]s the ideologies of 'identification' and 'point of view' make plain, 'character' is that point in the narrative text at which the problem of the insertion of the subject into the Symbolic most acutely arises." "Imaginary and Symbolic in Lacan: Marxism, Psychoanalytic Criticism, and the Problem of the Subject," *Yale French Studies* 55/56 (1977): 381. I have also been influenced by Žižek, *Sublime Object*, 105–14.

24. Perhaps this relation of material and spiritual food grows out of the commentary in the *Glossa Ordinaria* in which the boy who offers the loaves and fishes is Moses. That they are not enough to feed the people signifies the insufficiency of the letter and the bodily senses: "Quasi legis littera, vel corporei sensus quid prosunt ad multitudinem in te creditorum: qui spiritualia alimenta sunt petituri quae omnem litteram omnemque corporeum sensum superant." Gloss on John 6.9, "Sed haec quid sunt inter," in *Biblia Latina*, 4:238. (So to speak, the letter of the law, or the bodily senses, what do they profit the multitude of those who believe in you, who are asking for spiritual food, which surpasses every letter and every bodily sense?) Here as elsewhere my translation. I am grateful to Father Joseph Lienhard of *Traditio* for his assistance with all translations from the *Glossa*.

25. The emphasis on the materiality of this almsgiving is enforced in both authors by the same exemplum: a rich man throws a loaf of bread at a beggar, and, when the rich man is on the verge of death, this unwitting act of charity persuades the assembled angels and devils to give him another chance. Both the exposition of the biblical narrative and the exemplum identify the recipients of these alms as the poor (those who come to hear Jesus or the beggar in the tale), and this identification disguises one of the possible recipients—the priest or friar who preaches this sermon and hears the audience's confessions.

26. Scanlon, *Narrative, Authority*, 34–35.

27. In the *Festial* the narrative appears in sermons for both the first and the second Sunday in Lent (sermons 20 and 21). In the *MES*, the narrative appears in the sermon for the fourth Sunday in Lent (sermon 38).

28. The parallels with Margery Kempe's opening episode (her failure to confess her secret sin) are startling. See Margery Kempe, *The Book of Margery Kempe*, ed. Sanford Brown Meech and Hope Emily Allen, EETS, o.s., 212 (1940; reprint, Woodbridge, Suffolk: Boydell and Brewer, 1997), 6–7.

29. This obviousness is, of course, "an ideological effect" (Althusser, "Ideological State Apparatuses," 171–72).

30. For Langland's relationship to traditional discourses, particularly preaching, Owst's *Literature and Pulpit* remains the primary study; see chaps. 2 and 9. See also Siegfried Wenzel, "Medieval Sermons," in *A Companion to Piers Plowman*, ed. John A. Alford (Berkeley: University of California Press, 1988), 155–72, and A. C. Spearing's *Criticism and Medieval Poetry* (New York: Barnes and Noble, 1972), 107–34. Recent scholars understand Langland's orthodoxy as more complicated than either the heterodoxy found by sixteenth-century readers or the orthodoxy found by readers until the late twentieth century. See, for example, David Aers, whose views inform mine: "[W]hile the informing ideology is indeed the received orthodoxy just described, his imaginative engagement with contemporary ecclesiastic realities acts in ways which go beyond conventional criticism of the *status quo* to undermine the very credibility of the ideology and organization he wished to preserve." *Chaucer, Langland and the Creative Imagination* (London: Routledge, 1980), 42.

31. See, for example, John Burrow, "The Action of Langland's Second Vision," *Essays in Criticism* 15 (1965): 247–68, and, more recently, James Simpson, *Piers Plowman: An Introduction to the B-Text* (London: Longman, 1992).

32. The literature on *Piers Plowman* is exhaustive; I have limited my citations, therefore, to texts that deal specifically with the confession of the Sins.

33. I focus on the B-text here, although there are important variants in the C-text, namely the autobiographical passage that prefaces Reason's sermon and the additional material in the confessions (transferred from the B-text's passus 13). The addition of the autobiographical passage changes the context for the confessions quite drastically and strengthens their association with the dreamer personally (as opposed to the society at large). For a discussion of the changes from B to C, see George H. Russell, "Poet as Reviser: The Metamorphosis of the Confession of the Seven Deadly Sins in *Piers Plowman*," in *Acts of Interpretation: The Text in Its Contexts, 700–1600: Essays on Medieval and Renaissance Literature in Honor of E. Talbot Donaldson*, ed. Mary Carruthers and Elizabeth Kirk (Norman, OK: Pilgrim Books, 1982), 53–65. For the changes from A to B, see Elizabeth Kirk, *The Dream-Thought of Piers Plowman* (New Haven: Yale University Press, 1972), 64–70.

34. Kirk, *Dream Thought*, 63, and Lee Patterson, "Chaucerian Confession: Penitential Literature and the Pardoner," *Medievalia et Humanistica*, n.s., 7 (1976): 157. Both see this paradox in psychological rather than ideological terms.

35. Langland's view of penance has not been much discussed in scholarship, as noted by Robert Adams, "Langland's Theology," in Alford, *Companion to Piers Plowman*, 101, particularly in light of possible connections with Wycliffism. Greta Hort notes his insistence on contrition in *Piers Plowman and Contemporary Religious Thought* (New York: Macmillan, 1938), 148–55. Pamela Gradon discusses his views of penance and contrition briefly, writing that "he is making a debating point to which his protagonists provide a perfectly orthodox answer." "Langland and the Ideology of Dissent," *Proceedings of the British Academy* 66 (1980): 193.

36. Burrow, "Action," 249.

37. *Piers Plowman: The B Version*, ed. George Kane and E. Talbot Donaldson (London: Athlone Press, 1975), 5.415–19, hereafter cited parenthetically in the text.

38. Some scholars have seen the confession of the sins as that of the dreamer (Kirk, *Dream Thought*, 49, and A. V. C. Schmidt, *The Vision of Piers the Plowman* (London: Dent, 1978), 316 n. 61, 184–85. This is a view that seems to be suggested by the odd lines following Wrath's repentance: "'*Esto sobrius!*' he seide and assoiled me after / And bad me wilne to wepe my wikkednesse to amende" (Langland, *Piers Plowman: The B-Version*, 5.186–87). Nevertheless, the Sins confess from a range of occupations, and it seems to me that the confession of the community is what is at stake here.

39. I have borrowed this term from Burrow, who writes, "Langland substitutes the personifications of the Seven Deadly Sins (representing the sins of the folk) for the penitents" ("Action," 251), because his term draws attention to the way in which Langland alters the traditional discourses. As Bloomfield notes, sins in personifi-

cation allegory do not usually confess, although he finds one other example in the *Speculum Christiani* (*Seven Deadly Sins*, 186; see also 425 n. 306).

40. Burrow, "Action," 249.

41. See, for example, sermon 9 in the *MES*, which also relates sloth to the clergy: "The iiii synne, þat letteþ þis iiii prayoure of þe Pater Noster, is slowȝth in Goddes serues. . . . þat may we se in all degrees but principally in prelates, prestes, and clerkes" (53). And the writer continues in the first person (which he uses for this sin only): "We ben to meche ȝeven to þe world and to worldely occupacions, and we ben to slowe aboute Goddes serves" (*MES*, 53).

42. As Aers writes, "[I]t is one of the greatnesses of Langland's poetry that instead of merely adding another voice to the conventional moral attack it displays the internal and external forces which made such criticism stillborn" (*Chaucer, Langland*, 48).

43. William Langland, *Will's Vision of Piers Plowman*, trans. E. Talbot Donaldson, ed. Elizabeth Kirk and Judith Anderson (New York: Norton, 1990), lines 122–28.

44. As Patterson writes, "Enviousness suborns and appropriates the contrition that is its only cure" ("Chaucerian Confession," 158).

45. The importance of these sermons to vernacular preaching in England cannot be doubted, as has been argued by Spencer in *English Preaching*, esp. 278–311, and Hudson in her introduction, *EWS*, 1:98–123. Written most likely in the late 1380s and 1390s, it is the most complete sermon cycle that has survived (*EWS*, 4:10–20). Only two other sermon cycles in the vernacular even come close to providing this many sermons: Mirk's *Festial* (with 90 sermons) and the *Northern Homily Cycle* (with 117 items). In addition, the Wycliffite cycle survives in thirty-one manuscripts (*EWS*, 1:9), a survival rate comparable with John Mirk's *Festial* (Spencer, *English Preaching*, 311 n. 123). What distinguishes the *EWS* from these other sermon cycles is that it emphasizes coverage of the entire year instead of privileging some occasions over others (*EWS*, 1:45). Given the number of sermons, the cycle is remarkably unified, and Hudson has suggested a single process of production, although most likely more than one author (*EWS*, 4:20–37). Finally, the influence of the *EWS* is impressive. They were copied and modified, particularly to make them more orthodox, and these derivatives certainly suggest that the influence of Wycliffism went far beyond the small number of people who may have considered themselves (or may have been considered) Wycliffites.

46. It is important to note that these sermons are not merely translations of Wyclif's sermons, that the Wycliffites develop their own approach to interpretation. First, the Wycliffites include far more polemic against the established church than Wyclif himself, and, second, they alter and reduce biblical exegesis. While Wyclif's biblical exegesis has received quite a bit of scholarly attention, that of the Wycliffites has not. For an exception, see Kantik Ghosh, *The Wycliffite Heresy: Authority and the Interpretation of Texts* (Cambridge: Cambridge University Press, 2001), chap. 4. Ghosh

focuses on the hermeneutics of the sermons and argues that they are beset by the same contradiction as Wyclif's writing in *De Veritate Sacrae Scripturae:* "an attempt to fix and define meaning theoretically while in practice retaining the creative prerogative of traditional exegesis" (114). See also Hudson, *Premature Reformation*, 247–64, and Spencer, *English Preaching*, 191–95.

47. Certainly, the absence of exempla should not surprise anyone, given the Wycliffite hostility toward nonscriptural narratives. But one may well ask why the pastoral formulas are also missing. For example, the Wycliffite cycle does not spend much time on the Ten Commandments, although these were central to pastoral instruction; that many did not know this pastoral formula was a common complaint among both Wycliffites and non-Wycliffites. After all, the Ten Commandments were supposed to be preached to the laity at regular intervals. Both the *Ignorantia Sacerdotum* (1281) under Archbishop Pecham and the *Lay Folks' Catechism* (1357) under Archbishop Thoresby included instruction on the Ten Commandments. Mirk's *Festial* and the *MES* contain sermons that detail them. There are also (purportedly) Wycliffite tracts explaining the Pater Noster, such as the tract included in *English Works of Wyclif*, 197–202. The omission of these elements, such as references to the Pater Noster and the Ave, seems to be peculiar to these sermons, since Wycliffites did take up Thoresby's requirements as useful for their position. This lack could be attributed to the sermon authors' focus—providing priests with biblical exposition in the vernacular—and the assumption that that priests could fill in the pastoral details later. See for example, sermons 1, 2, 21 and 46 in the Sunday Gospel Sermons. However, this explanation does not account for the lack of such directions in the majority of the sermons, nor does it account for the Wycliffites' decision to abandon the close connection between narrative and pastoral formulas that is so characteristic of contemporary sermons. When they do provide pastoral instruction, particularly lists of virtues, the instruction is not connected to narratives, either scriptural or nonscriptural, nor is it applied to the future or past stories of those who might be listening.

48. In contrast, the sermons on the Sunday Epistles (set 5) draw their pericopes largely from what was written about how Christians should act, and the sermons refer to sins far more often. For example, the sermons for the second and third Sundays in Lent deal with sins. It is important to note that these sins do not come out of a narrative; they are those named in the epistle. For example, the sermon writer follows Paul in his warning to avoid lechery, pride, and covetousness (E17).

49. In sermon 16, the sermon writer follows the traditional interpretation of the three dead bodies Jesus raised as different states of sin. However, instead of detailing what kind of sins they might be, the writer states, "þus names of offisys, and namus of vertewes also, ben chawnged by ypocrisye, and cursyd men rewlen þe world" (*EWS*, 16/82–84). In other words, the names of virtues have changed, so that we no longer are able to discuss what these sins might be.

50. See, similarly, *EWS*, sermons 10, 14, 16, 19, and 28.

51. This is not to say that the Wycliffites do not have their own ideological investment in the narratives, but what that ideology might mean is more difficult

to discuss in relation to actual practices (the habitus that Althusser describes) because the Wycliffites did not succeed in coming up with an independent church. Their practices were always understood in opposition to those of the established church.

52. Traditionally, this parable has been interpreted to represent the founding of the church. See Stephen L. Wailes's *Medieval Allegories of Jesus' Parables* (Berkeley: University of California Press, 1987). The following explanation is paraphrased from his account (153–59). Starting with Origen, who was then followed by Jerome, Chrysostom, Augustine, and Gregory, this parable figured the founding of the church. In this way, the figuration of the bridal feast differs from that of the Great Supper (Luke 14:16–24), traditionally interpreted as the Day of Judgment. The different groups invited in the parable represent the Jews and Gentiles called to Christianity. The garment represents Christian "precepts and works, the vestment of the new man" according to Jerome or *caritas* according to Augustine (157). The man is tied by his hands and feet in punishment for those sins that he committed in his life.

53. This relationship is made possible because the writer does not invoke this parable for its discussion of the founding of the church. Rather, he conflates it with the parable of the Great Supper in Luke 14:16–24 so that he can warn the audience to prepare themselves for judgment.

54. I have chosen the *Glossa* as a representation of normative exegetical practices; the *Glossa* was a quarry of traditional interpretations for sermon writers (and other authors). Also, glosses from the *Glossa* can be found in Wycliffite translations of the New Testament (Hudson, *Premature Reformation*, 236 and 243).

55. Glosses on Luke 6:41–42: "Quid autem vides festucam" and "Ipocrita" (*Biblia Latina*, 4:163).

56. There is an important exception in the sermon on the Canaanite woman when the author interprets Christ's action in ignoring her: "And here may we lernen to contynewen owr good work, al ȝif God graunte not owre wylle at þe bygynnyng, for God wole haue owre herte deuowt to hym wiþowten eende heere and in heuene" (*EWS*, 41/8–11). This identification works in the traditional manner but is not connected to the woman's sin.

57. The collective terms are meant to create a sense of community among Wycliffite listeners and readers, a community of "initiates." See von Nolcken, "'Certain Sameness,'" and Hudson, "Lollard Sect Vocabulary?"

58. See similarly *EWS*, sermon 16, on the dead raised to life.

59. See *EWS*, 4:291 n. 108 and 4:146–51. I do not mean to suggest that contemporary sermons do not also criticize the status quo; the satire against different estates makes clear that they do. Nevertheless, they do not use scriptural exegesis to expose the foundations of the governing ideology, as do the Wycliffites.

60. The *Glossa* cites Bede on Jesus' fasting in its gloss on Matt. 4:2, "Et cum ieiunasset": "Ieiunat vt tentetur, tentatur quia ieiunat, et exemplum ieiunandi, nobis dat" (He fasts so that he is tempted, he is tempted because he fasts, and he gives us an example of fasting) (*Biblia Latina*, 4:13).

61. In the gloss on Matt. 4:9, "Haec omnia tibi dabo," the three temptations are related to gluttony, avarice, and pride: "In his tribus notantur gula, auaricia, superbia" (*Biblia Latina*, 4:14). These are connected to Adam's sins in the gloss on Matt. 4:10, "Seruies": "Nota dyabolum in his vinci in quibus adam vicit. Quem de gula tentauit: dum de ligno vetito gustare rogauit. De vana gloria: cum dixit: eritis sicut dii, de avaricia cum ait, scientes bonum et malum" (*Biblia Latina*, 4:15). [Note that the Devil is conquered in these things in which he conquered Adam. He tempted him with gluttony while he asked him to taste of the forbidden tree. With vainglory when he said: you will be like gods. With avarice when he said: you will know good and evil.]

62. Of course, the vengeance could also be something more violent. In sermon 22, on the parable about debtors, the writer ends his discussion of mercy with a call for vengeance: "þus schulde þei warly fle to take þer owne veniaunse, but vengen iniurye of God and intenden amendement. þus Crist, mekyst of alle, suffryde his owne iniurye in two temptacionys of þe fend, but in þe þridde he seyde 'Go, Sathan!', and repreuyde hym scharply by auctorite of God. þus Moyses, myldeste man of alle, killide manye þowsande of his folc, for þei worschipoden a calf as þei schulde worschipe God" (*EWS*, 22/66–72).

63. The *Glossa* sees the lesson in terms of the failure of human reason, not the failure of a particular church: "sed nemo debet tentare deum quando habet ex humana ratione quid faciat. . . . Postquam deficit humana ratio: commendet se homo deo non tentando: sed devote confidendo" (gloss on Matt. 4:5, "Mitte," *Biblia Latina*, 4:14). [But no one should tempt God, when he knows from human reason what he might do. . . . After human reason fails, man should commend himself to God, not tempting, but devoutly confessing.]

64. I will return to this aspect in chap. 3, below.

65. For a discussion of these code words, see von Nolcken's "'Certain Sameness'" and Hudson's "Lollard Sect Vocabulary?"

66. Michael Wilks argues that there is no historical evidence to support Wyclif's "steady flow of horror stories about the tribulations of the faithful and the way that their numbers were being cut down" and that "[i]t amounted to one of the most restrained campaigns against heresy in history." "Wyclif and the Great Persecution," *Prophecy and Eschatology*, ed. Michael Wilks, Studies in Church History, Subsidia 10 (Oxford: Blackwell, 1994), 40 and 42. However, we could interpret Wyclif's and the Wycliffites' fear of persecution as an anticipation of what had already happened on the Continent.

67. See also sermons 65, 71, and 96: "And so, as Crist in his ȝougþe was pursuwed of monye men to dispuyse hym and slee hym in his owne persone, so vnto þe day of doom, is he pursuwed in his membrus" (*EWS*, 96/41–44).

68. These formulas are part of the catechism that was supposed to be communicated in English to the laity at least four times per year according to the Lambeth Constitutions. For a discussion of the *pastoralia* in preaching, see Spencer's *English Preaching*, chap. 5.

69. See, for example, *MES*, 190–93.

70. John Mirk, *Instructions for Parish Priests*, ed. Edward Peacock, EETS, o.s., 31 (London: Kegan Paul, Trench, Trübner, 1868), 973–1302 and 1303–1398. Similarly, Jean Gerson insists that both confessors and penitents should know what makes a sin mortal—the "full consent" of the sinner. D. Catherine Brown, *Pastor and Laity in the Theology of Jean Gerson* (Cambridge: Cambridge University Press, 1987), 169. See also her discussion of Gerson on confession, 63–67.

71. This sentiment also appears in a Wycliffite tract, *Nota de Confessione*, in the context of confession rather than preaching: "but begynne we at þe pope, & aske him of dedly synne, & hou men shulden know contricion, & whi siche penaunce shal be enioyned; and it semeþ to many men þat alle þe popes & þere clerkis kunnen not telle on of þise þre" (*English Works of Wyclif*, 338).

72. A derivative of this sermon is discussed by Spencer, *English Preaching*, 224–27; this sermon adds a discussion of the Creed to the exposition.

Chapter Two.   Confession and the Speaking Subject

1. "Sixteen Points on Which the Bishops Accuse Lollards," in *Selections from English Wycliffite Writings*, ed. Anne Hudson (1978; reprint, Toronto: University of Toronto Press, Medieval Academy of America, 1997), 19.

2. *De Pontificum Romanorum Schismate*, in *Select English Works of John Wyclif*, ed. Thomas Arnold, 3 vols. (Oxford: Clarendon Press, 1869–71), 3:252. For a similar view, see the tract "On the Twenty-five Articles," in which a writer asserts that "verrey contricion of hert, þat is never wiþouten special grace of God and charite, does away alle synnes bifore done of þat man þat is verrey contrite, þof alle prestus nowe in erthe were unborne" (*Select English Works of John Wyclif*, 3:461). Anne Hudson gives a useful account of Lollard views on confession in her introduction to *English Wycliffite Sermons* (hereafter *EWS*), ed. Hudson and Pamela Gradon, 5 vols. (New York: Oxford University Press, 1983–96), 4:41–49, and in *The Premature Reformation: Wycliffite Texts and Lollard History* (Oxford: Clarendon Press, 1988), 294–301.

3. It seems to be generally accepted that late medieval England was characterized by an increasing interest in and increasing access to devotional texts on the part of the laity. Recent work that is particularly interested in lay appropriations of clerical material has focused largely on translations and the debates around translation: Rita Copeland, "William Thorpe and His Lollard Community: Intellectual Labor and the Representation of Dissent," in *Bodies and Disciplines: Intersections of Literature and History in Fifteenth Century England*, ed. Barbara Hanawalt and David Wallace (Minneapolis: University of Minnesota Press, 1996), 199–221, "Childhood, Pedagogy, and the Literal Sense: From Late Antiquity to the Lollard Heretical Classroom," in *New Medieval Literatures* 1 (1997): 125–56; and, most recently, *Pedagogy, Intellectuals, and Dissent in the Later Middle Ages: Lollardy and Ideas of Learning* (Cambridge: Cambridge University Press, 2001); Ralph Hanna, "The Difficulty of Ricardian Prose Translation: The Case of the Lollards," *Modern Language Quarterly* 51 (1990): 319–40;

Fiona Somerset, *Clerical Discourse and Lay Audience in Late Medieval England* (Cambridge: Cambridge University Press, 1998); and Nicholas Watson, "Censorship and Cultural Change in Late-Medieval England: Vernacular Theology, the Oxford Translation Debate, and Arundel's Constitutions of 1409," *Speculum* 70 (1995): 822–64. For the lay appropriation of mystical practices, particularly within penitential practice, see Jonathan Hughes, *Pastors and Visionaries: Religion and Secular Life in Late Medieval Yorkshire* (Woodbridge, Suffolk: D. S. Brewer, 1988).

4. Thomas N. Tentler, *Sin and Confession on the Eve of the Reformation* (Princeton: Princeton University Press, 1977), provides a history of confessional practice. See particularly chap. 5 for an account of debates on contrition and absolution. See also John Bossy, "The Social History of Confession in the Age of the Reformation," *Transactions of the Royal Historical Society*, 5th ser., 25 (1975): 21–38.

5. *Decrees of the Ecumenical Councils*, ed. Norman P. Tanner (Washington, DC: Georgetown University Press, 1990), 1:245. The Fourth Lateran Council has been described as a sign of the church's increasing power and influence in the lives of its members; its goals were "to extirpate vices and foster virtues, correct abuses and reform morals, suppress heresy and strengthen the faith, settle disorders and establish peace, encourage princes and Christian peoples to aid and maintain the Holy Land." Innocent III, quoted in Leonard Boyle, "The Fourth Lateran Council and Manuals of Popular Theology," in *The Popular Literature of Medieval England*, ed. Thomas Heffernan (Knoxville: University of Tennessee Press, 1985), 30. In *Sin and Confession*, Tentler writes that the decree "was not the first legal act to require confession to the priest and it can in no sense be said to have invented the necessity of confession. Nevertheless it was momentous; and even if it was originally designed as a disciplinary canon to allow pastors to know their parishioners and watch for heresy; its effects were in fact broader" (22).

6. See Boyle, "Fourth Lateran Council"; W. A. Pantin, *The English Church in the Fourteenth Century* (1955; reprint, Toronto: University of Toronto Press, 1980), chaps. 9 and 10.

7. Mary Flowers Braswell and Jerry Root investigate the language of the self provided by the vernacular penitential tradition in their studies *The Medieval Sinner: Characterization and Confession in the Literature of the English Middle Ages* (East Brunswick, NJ: Fairleigh Dickinson University Press, 1983) and *"Space to Speke": The Confessional Subject in Medieval Literature* (New York: Peter Lang, 1997), respectively. Both Braswell and Root are interested in how this tradition contributed to a "new conception of literary character" (Root, *Medieval Sinner*, 1), or, as Braswell writes, how writers' "understanding of penance enabled them to create characters possessed of a considerable depth and complexity" (*"Space to Speke,"* 16). As will become clear, I am less interested in the representation of the self than in the representation of modes for speaking about the self.

8. *Thomae de Chobham Summa Confessorum*, ed. F. Broomfield (Louvain: Nauwelaerts, 1968), 240, my translation. For a discussion of Chobham's influence, see lxix. William of Pagula's *Oculis Sacerdotis* challenged Chobham's popularity, but it too

relied heavily on Chobham. Leonard Boyle, "The *Oculis Sacerdotis* of William of Pagula," *Transactions of the Royal Historical Society,* 5th ser., 5 (1955): 86.

9. The discussion of sins appears in the Third Article of Chobham's work, in which he considers "quot sunt peccata pro quibus iniungenda est penitentia" (what are the sins for which penitence must be enjoined) (*Thomae de Chobham Summa Confessorum,* 3–4).

10. John Mirk, *Instructions for Parish Priests,* ed. Edward Peacock, EETS, o.s., 31 (London: Kegan Paul, Trench, Trübner, 1868). John Mirk was aware of the Lollards, as his sermon collection, the *Festial,* makes clear. To a certain extent, then, one could argue that Mirk is writing in response to the Lollards and is certainly contemporary with them. The *Festial* has been dated c. 1382–1390 by Alan Fletcher, "John Mirk and the Lollards," *Medium Aevum* 56 (1987): 216–24. See also H. Leith Spencer, *English Preaching in the Late Middle Ages* (Oxford: Clarendon Press, 1993), 311. Mirk's work translates part of William of Pagula and therefore can be placed in the line of influence extending from Chobham (Boyle, "*Oculis Sacerdotis,*" 86).

11. Mirk, *Instructions,* line 973.

12. Tentler, *Sin and Confession,* xv.

13. Allen Frantzen notes this formulaic quality in Anglo-Saxon penitential poetry; one of the uses of this poetry "was to reduce complex situations to clearly formulated generalizations about human behavior and the life to come and to offer examples of individuals whose experience conformed to the general truths maintained by the poetry." *The Literature of Penance in Anglo-Saxon England* (New Brunswick, NJ: Rutgers University Press, 1983), 197. Although Frantzen's texts predate the penitential texts under discussion here, his description is pertinent, since these generalizations were distributed and maintained throughout a long tradition of penitential handbooks as each new book drew on and expanded what had gone before.

14. *The Boke of Penance,* in *Cursor Mundi: A Northumbrian Poem of the Fourteenth Century,* ed. Richard K. Morris, 3 vols., EETS, o.s., 57, 59, 62, 66, 68, 99, 101 (London: K. Paul, Trench, Trübner, 1874–93), vol. 3, pt. 5, lines 27554–55. I quote from the Fairfax manuscript.

15. Of course, this psychological language was not limited to "real" confessions but appears in literary confessions as well, such as that of Thomas Hoccleve in his *Regiment of Princes.* As J. A. Burrow writes, "[The seven sins] provided the moral grid-system most commonly used by men of the period whenever they attempted to map their inner lives. That was how people thought about themselves. Hence if Hoccleve had wanted, for whatever reason, to describe his own experiences as a wild young man, he would most naturally have sorted them out into sin-categories." "Autobiographical Poetry in the Middle Ages: The Case of Thomas Hoccleve," *Proceedings of the British Academy* 68 (1982): 396.

16. Lee Patterson discusses Chaucer's *Parson's Tale* in terms of the theorizing impetus of the penitential scheme in "The *Parson's Tale* and the Quitting of the *Canterbury Tales,*" *Traditio* 34 (1978): 331–80.

17. Tentler, *Sin and Confession,* 134.

18. *Thomae de Chobham Summa Confessorum*, 240–41, my translation. See also the statement "omnis confessio medicinalis est" (14).

19. *Fasciculus Morum: A Fourteenth Century Preacher's Handbook*, ed. and trans. Siegfried Wenzel (University Park: Pennsylvania State University Press, 1989), 466, trans. 467. Similarly, "Precepit enim Dominus homini peccatori illud Luce 5: 'Vade, ostende te sacerdoti'" (For the Lord has given sinful man this command of Luke 5: "Go and show yourself to the priest") (482, trans. 483).

20. Ibid., 492, trans. 493.

21. *Jacob's Well*, ed. Arthur Brandeis, EETS, o.s., 115 (London: Kegan Paul, Trench, Trübner, 1900), 65.

22. Ibid., 68.

23. Ibid., 65.

24. *Boke of Penance*, in *Cursor Mundi*, lines 26092–97, 26110–15.

25. *Handlyng Synne* seems to depart from this approach toward sin by making the reader aware of the privities that cannot be discussed:

> Þe pryuytees wyle y nouȝt name,
> For noun þarfore shuld me blame.
> Leuer ys me þat þey be hydde
> Þan for me oponly were kydde

Robert Mannyng, *Handlyng Synne*, ed. Idelle Sullens (Binghamton, NY: Medieval and Renaissance Texts and Studies, 1983), 31–34. This text does imagine a kind of sin that will not be detailed in the language that the author has provided (and, in this way resembles somewhat the Wycliffite writings). Nevertheless, the author insists that the priest will be able to find a language for that sin when the reader does go to confession: "Noþeles þey mote be shreuyn" (35).

26. *Fasciculus Morum*, 490, trans. 491.

27. Ibid., 474–76, trans. 475–77.

28. *Boke of Penance*, in *Cursor Mundi*, lines 26581–83.

29. *Jacob's Well*, 66–67.

30. *Middle English Sermons*, ed. Woodburn O. Ross, EETS, o.s., 209 (London: Oxford University Press, 1960), 66; hereafter cited as *MES*.

31. Ibid., 116.

32. Ibid., 141. The story of the Pharisee and the publican has the potential to threaten the very message it is trying to convey. In another sermon on the same story, the author contrasts the Pharisee's speech and the publican's lack of speech: "He knew hym-selfe a synnefull man and drewe hym prevely alone and durst not for þe drede of God lifte vp is eyen to-heven-ward, but oonly smote on is breste with is honde and seid no word, but þouthe þis in is herte: 'Now, Lord God, haue mercy on me ȝiff it be þi will, for I am þe synfullest wreche þat euer was born'" (*MES*, 155). This exposition certainly supports the importance of contrition (and sincerity) but works against the directive to confess to a priest. Similarly, another author writes, "[B]y

mans herte is vndirstonde is confession, for þoȝ a man sey is synnes by mowȝthe, but ȝiff he sey hem with herte, þer is no confession" (*MES*, 285). In this passage, the problem with speaking is that of sincerity, and therefore the passage is informed by the same understanding of showing that is found in the manuals discussed above.

    33. *Speculum Sacerdotale*, ed. Edward H. Weatherly, EETS, o.s. 200 (London: Oxford University Press, 1936), 65.

    34. *MES*, 240.

    35. See the Twenty-first Decree of Lateran IV, in which the word is *confiteatur* (*Decrees of the Ecumenical Councils*, 1:245). This word is translated in vernacular handbooks as "shrift," "confession," or "knowlechyng." See the *Middle English Dictionary*, ed. Hans Kurath and Sherman M. Kuhn (Ann Arbor: University of Michigan Press, 1952–).

    36. See Hudson's notes: "[T]he possible uses of oral confession in offering advice and comfort to sinners are admitted, but the abuses outweigh this: *rownyng* is the word, always denigratory, most frequently used for contemporary oral confession" (*EWS*, 4:45).

    37. *EWS*, 63/67–70; my emphasis. See also the sermon for the Feast of St. Matthew: "We schal vndurstonde þat not eche confession is rownyng in an eere of a mannys owne synne, but grawntynge of trewþe wiþ grauntyng of God. And þus spekuþ Crist þat is of more auctorite þan alle þes popis þat ordeynedon confession of rownyng" (*EWS*, 101/10–14). The *Nota* uses the term *rownyng* throughout.

    38. Anne Hudson includes the text of the "Twelve Conclusions" in *Selections*, 24–29. She notes that they were allegedly posted on the doors of St. Paul's and Westminster Abbey during the parliamentary sessions of 1395 (January 27 to February 15 and May) and that they are known only through the record of those who refuted them (150). See Roger Dymmok, *Liber Rogeri Dymmok contra Duodecim Errores*, ed. H. S. Cronin (London: Kegan Paul, 1922), in which he answers each of the Conclusions. The Latin version can also be found in the *Fasciculi Zizaniorum Magistri Johannis Wyclif*, ed. W. W. Shirley (London: Longman, 1858), 360–69.

    39. *Selections from English Wycliffite Writings*, 27.

    40. For the antifraternal views related to confession, see Penn Szittya, *The Antifraternal Tradition in Medieval Literature* (Princeton: Princeton University Press, 1986), 62–63, 85–86, 119, 128, 132, 164, 282–86. Scase sees the attack on confessors in *Piers Plowman* as including priests as well as friars; see Wendy Scase, *Piers Plowman and the New Anticlericalism* (Cambridge: Cambridge University Press, 1989), 38–39.

    41. Geoffrey Chaucer, *The Riverside Chaucer*, gen. ed. Larry D. Benson (Boston: Houghton Mifflin, 1987), I.231–32.

    42. *EWS*, 68/109–10.

    43. *Nota de Confessione*, in *The English Works of Wyclif Hitherto Unprinted*, ed. F. D. Matthew, EETS, o.s., 74 (London: Kegan Paul, Trench, Trübner, 1880), 327.

    44. The term *knowlechyng* seems to occur particularly in late-fourteenth- and fifteenth-century discussions of confessions, according to the evidence collected in the *Middle English Dictionary* (see definitions 6–7).

45. *English Works of Wyclif,* 340.

46. This point is made much more briefly and forcefully in the Wycliffite exposition of the Mary Magdalene episode, which is also traditionally read in terms of confession: "Heere may we see hou pryuey shrifte is autorised of oure Iesu—for but in þis plase alone men shulen not grounde þis onely shrifte. But by þe sentense of þe gospel, ȝif man haue ful sorowe for his synne, ȝif he speke not aftir o word but do wel and leeue to synne, God forȝueþ þis synne, as he forȝaf þis wommanus synne" (*EWS,* 231/27–31). To be sure, orthodox texts also imagine times at which one might not be able to confess verbally: for example, if there is no priest or if a sick person has no power to do so (*Speculum Sacerdotale,* 63). These qualifications do not, however, problematize the larger penitential scheme of contrition and satisfaction.

47. *English Works of Wyclif,* 341.

48. I am here drawing on Larry Scanlon's definition of exempla as "narrative enactment[s] of cultural authority" (*Narrative, Authority,* 34).

49. As Alexander Gelley writes, "But in a rhetorical sense not only does the example picture, it may also induce an imitative reproduction on the part of the receptor or audience. The mimetic effect here is linked not, as is usual, to techniques of representation but to forms of behavior, to a goal of ethical transformation." Introduction to *Unruly Examples: On the Rhetoric of Exemplarity,* ed. Alexander Gelley (Stanford: Stanford University Press, 1995), 3.

50. These texts have received attention most recently from Copeland, *Pedagogy, Intellectuals,* pt. 2, and Somerset, on Thorpe, in *Clerical Discourse,* chap. 6. Both Copeland and Somerset read Thorpe in relation to the university community and the dissemination of academic discourse outside the university community. For Wyche's text, see "The Trial of Richard Wyche," ed. F. D. Matthew, *English Historical Review* 5 (1890): 530–44. See also Christina von Nolcken, "Richard Wyche, a Certain Knight, and the Beginning of the End," in *Lollardy and the Gentry in the Later Middle Ages,* ed. Margaret Aston and Colin Richmond (New York: St. Martin's Press, 1997), 127–54.

51. There are four copies of the text: one medieval manuscript in English, two in Latin, and one printed text in English. *Two Wycliffite Texts,* ed. Anne Hudson, EETS, 301 (Oxford: Oxford University Press, 1993), xxvi–xlv. Hudson argues that the original from which these were derived was written in English (xlii–xlv). There are also a number of sixteenth-century copies (xxxi–xxxvii).

52. *Two Wycliffite Texts,* 29. All citations to Thorpe's testimony are hereafter given parenthetically in the text.

53. See Hudson's introduction, *Two Wycliffite Texts,* lvi–lix. It seems quite fitting for a Lollard hagiography that Thorpe is not a martyr for the cause (in contrast to Sir John Oldcastle, whose examination sometimes circulated with Thorpe's [lvii]). Thorpe's death would certainly draw attention away from his bravery during the examination and might suggest a more "orthodox" kind of sainthood, in which resistance to bodily torture defines sanctity. One could imagine, as an analogous example,

a tale of St. Cecilia that focused on her inquisition and not upon the details of her death.

54. The text appears in John Foxe, *The Acts and Monuments of John Foxe*, ed. Josiah Pratt, 8 vols. (London: Religious Tract Society, 1877), 3:250–85. See Hudson's introduction, *Two Wycliffite Texts*, xxxi–xxxvii.

55. The text has generally been accepted as historically "true," although its veracity is less important for my argument than its modes of address. For a discussion of its historicity, see *Two Wycliffite Texts*, xlv–liii; Peter McNiven, *Heresy and Politics in the Reign of Henry IV: The Burning of John Badby* (Woodbridge, Suffolk: Boydell Press, 1987), 105–14. And, more briefly, see John Fines, "William Thorpe: An Early Lollard," *History Today* 18 (1968): 495–503, and K. B. McFarlane, *John Wycliffe and the Beginnings of English Nonconformity* (New York, Macmillan, 1953), 153–54.

56. To be sure, this text is also an interrogation, and this aspect has been emphasized in Copeland's article, "William Thorpe," in which she sees a blurring of prison and school (207). For this reason, in this article and her later work on Thorpe in *Pedagogy, Intellectuals*, chap. 4, Copeland underlines the violence of representation, the "violent confrontation between the official voice of accusatory interrogation and Thorpe's own violently reactive hermeneutics" (*Pedagogy, Intellectuals*, 194). Although there are certainly similarities between our approaches (in that an interrogation and confession can be seen as analogous), Copeland's approach emphasizes Thorpe's indebtedness to the language of the university (as does Somerset's in *Clerical Discourse*), whereas I see the struggle taking place over the language of pastoral practice.

57. Lee Patterson writes, "[W]hat is most important at the level of form is that in both cases their confessional narratives are preceded by tales that aspire to hagiographical authority: Man of Law-Wife of Bath, Physician-Pardoner." *Chaucer and the Subject of History* (Madison: University of Wisconsin Press, 1991), 367.

58. *Thomae de Chobham Summa Confessorum* has the penitent at the feet of the priest (see citation above), whereas Mirk's *Instructions* advises the penitent to kneel (line 700). Either one of these positions suggests the penitent's supplication and submission.

59. On Wyche, see Copeland, *Pedagogy, Intellectuals*, chap. 3, and von Nolcken, "Richard Wyche."

60. The view of sin as instigated by or corrected through social relations (evil and good company) rather than an individual desire also appears in Sir John Clanvowe's treatise "The Two Ways," in which he describes "euele companie" as "worse þan any of þise ʒre foreseide enemys [the traditional triad of world, flesh, and devil]." In *The Works of Sir John Clanvowe*, ed. V. J. Scattergood (Cambridge: D. S. Brewer, 1965), 71.

61. Elsewhere Thorpe seems completely committed to the traditional language of the church, the *pastoralia*, especially when he is defining the church for Arundel (62). It seems to me that his use of traditional language there is calculated because he is asserting a new, Wycliffite definition of the church (the saved).

62. In Chaucer's *Man of Law's Tale*, when Custance prays to God for help against the knight's false accusations, she also mentions Susannah. The explanatory note points out that "a parallel reference to Susannah's divine rescue from a false charge was also used in rituals associated with ordeals" (*Riverside Chaucer*, 861). Editors of the Middle English alliterative poem *The Pistel of Swete Susan* suggest a Wycliffite connection: see *The Pistel of Swete Susan*, in *Heroic Women from the Old Testament in Middle English Verse*, ed. Russell A. Peck (Kalamazoo, MI: Medieval Institute Publications, 1991), 73; and *Susannah: An Alliterative Poem of the Fourteenth Century*, ed. Alice Miskimin (New Haven: Yale University Press, 1969), which cites the parallels from the Wycliffite Bible. Thorpe's words are, in fact, quite close to those of the Wycliffite Bible, although less so to the poem: "And Susanne inwardly sorewide, and saith, Anguyshis ben to me on eche syde; forsothe ʒif Y do this thing deth is to me; sothely ʒif Y shal not do, Y schal not ascape ʒoure hondis." Daniel 13:22, in *The Holy Bible . . . Made from the Latin Vulgate by John Wycliffe and His Followers*, ed. Josiah Forshall and Frederic Madden, 4 vols. (Oxford: Oxford University Press, 1850), 3:663.

63. For the articulation of this perspective in more definite terms, see the *Nota de Confessione:* "whenne a man is constreyned by bodily peyne to telle his gilte, he confesseþ not; but confession mut be wilful, or ellis it is not medeful to man" (*English Works of Wyclif*, 328).

64. I cite here from Forshall and Madden, *Holy Bible*, 3:664–65 (Dan. 13:42).

65. The phrase "inner man" occurs in the Wycliffite translation of the Epistle to the Ephesians 3:14–16: "For grace of this thing, Y bowe my knees to the fadir of oure Lord Jhesu Crist, of whom ech fadirhod in heuenes and in erthe is named, that he ʒyue to ʒou, aftir the richessis of his glorie, vertu to be strengthid bi his spirit in the ynnere man" (Forshall and Madden, *Holy Bible*, 4:412–13). Von Nolcken has argued that Richard Wyche's letter also shows a concern with the "inner man" ("Richard Wyche," 144).

66. It remains a debate about the power of the priest, but this aspect of it is not new. I refer readers, therefore, to Tentler for the details of this debate (*Sin and Confession*, chap. 5) and, for an overview, to Hudson (*Premature Reformation*, 294–301).

67. Foucault, *History of Sexuality*, 1:59.

68. *MES*, 78.

69. Nicholas Love, *Nicholas Love's Mirror of the Blessed Life of Jesus Christ*, ed. Michael G. Sargent (New York: Garland, 1992). Hereafter all citations are given parenthetically in the text. Sargent's introduction makes clear the way in which Love translated and transformed the pseudo-Bonaventuran text to respond to Lollardy (xxx–lviii). For important discussions of Love's text, see Elizabeth Salter, *Nicholas Love's "Myrrour of the Blessed Lyf of Jesu Christ,"* Analecta Cartusiana 10 (Salzburg: Institut für Englische Sprache und Literatur, Universität Salzburg, 1974); Sarah Beckwith, *Christ's Body: Identity, Culture, and Society in Late Medieval Writings* (London: Routledge, 1993), 63–70; and Kantik Ghosh, *The Wycliffite Heresy: Authority and the Interpretation of Texts* (Cambridge: Cambridge University Press, 2002), chap. 5.

70. The inscription reads in full, "Memorandum quod circa annum domini Millesimum quadringentesimum decimum, originalis copia huius libri, scilicet Speculi vite Christi in Anglicis.' presentabatur Londoniis per compilatorem eiusdem .N. Reuerendissimo in Christo patri & domino, Domino Thome Arundell, Cantuarie Archiepiscopo, ad inspiciendum & debite examinandum antequam fuerat libere communicata. Qui post inspeccionem eiusdem per dies aliquot.' retradens ipsum librum memorato eiusdem auctori.' proprie vocis oraculo ipsum in singulis commendauit & approbauit, necnon & auctoritate sua metropolitica, vt pote catholicum, puplice communicandum fore decreuit & mandauit, ad fidelium edificacionem, & hereticorum siue lollardorum confutacionem" (Love, *Nicholas Love's Mirror*, 7).

71. For a discussion of the importance of Arundel's *Constitutions*, see Watson, "Censorship and Cultural Change," and Spencer, *English Preaching*, 163–88. Hudson writes that Thorpe's testimony and the sermon of William Taylor (printed together with Thorpe's text in *Two Wycliffite Texts*) "provide important information about the events that immediately preceded the drafting of Arundel's *Constitutions*" (*Premature Reformation*, 14). Arundel's encounter with Thorpe might have convinced him of the danger of those who refused to be brought around to orthodoxy. McNiven also agrees that Arundel's encounter with Thorpe revealed that there was a "gap in the Church's defences" against Lollardy and that "[t]here was little purpose in burning even individual miscreants as insolent as Thorpe if the source of the spiritual infection remained unpurged"; hence the *Constitutions* (*Heresy and Politics*, 114).

72. The Wycliffite sermon on this passage is discussed above. Kantik Ghosh understands this episode as one in which Love "turn[s] against the Lollards words which had assumed prominence in the 'Lollard sect vocabulary'" (*Wycliffite Heresy*, 165).

73. See, for example, the exposition in John Mirk's *Festial*, ed. Theodor Erbe, EETS, e.s., 96 (London: K. Paul, Trench, Trübner, 1905), 203–8, which mentions the confession only to continue with far greater detail about her penance (fasting in the desert).

74. As Beckwith writes, "Love's text, though authorized primarily to mitigate anti-clericalism and preference for the vernacular, had conceded the strength of some of its opponents' arguments in the very act of translation and authorization" (*Christ's Body*, 70).

75. See Hudson's discussion of the sects in *EWS*, 4:121–34.

Chapter Three.   Chaucer's Parson and the Language of Self-Definition

1. See the second definition for *lollere* in the *Middle English Dictionary*, ed. Hans Kurath and Sherman M. Kuhn (Ann Arbor: University of Michigan Press, 1952–). For further discussion, see Wendy Scase, *Piers Plowman and the New Anti-clericalism* (Cambridge: Cambridge University Press, 1989), 149–60, and "'Heu!

Quanta desolatio Angliae praestatur': A Wycliffite Libel and the Naming of Here-
tics, Oxford 1382," in *Lollards and Their Influence in Late Medieval England,* ed. Fiona
Somerset, Jill C. Havens, and Derrick G. Pitard (Woodbridge, Suffolk: Boydell
Press, 2003), 19–36; and Andrew Cole, "William Langland and the Invention of
Lollardy," in Somerset, Havens, and Pitard, *Lollards and Their Influence,* 37–58. Al-
though *lollere* can also mean "vagabond" (the first definition in the *Middle English
Dictionary*), for Margery Kempe and Lydgate, it seems pretty clear that *lollere* does in
fact mean "heretic," or "Lollard." And it has these connotations for both Gower and
Chaucer as well, as I shall argue below.

    2. For example, one might ask whether the account of penance in *Piers Plow-
man* is merely traditionally contritionist or influenced by Wycliffite beliefs. See Greta
Hort, *Piers Plowman and Contemporary Religious Thought* (New York: Macmillan,
1938), 148–55; and Pamela Gradon, "Langland and the Ideology of Dissent," *Proceedings of the British Academy* 66 (1980): 179–205.

    3. For arguments on the Parson's relationship to Wycliffism, see Hugo Simon,
"Chaucer a Wicliffite: An Essay on Chaucer's Parson and Parson's Tale," in *Essays on
Chaucer,* pt. 3, ed. Chaucer Society (London: N. Trübner, 1876), 227–92. Simon makes
his argument about interpolations rather haphazardly and impressionistically. Nevertheless, his question "What was Chaucer's relation to the Church?" is still worth
asking, even if his particular answer is guided by farfetched speculations (229). R. S.
Loomis was similarly convinced that the Parson was a Lollard: "It is safe to say that
when Chaucer spoke of the Parson as teaching Christ's lore and that of the apostles,
he left no doubt in the minds of contemporary readers that here was the ideal parish
priest conceived according to the Lollard view." "Was Chaucer a Laodicean?" in
Chaucer Criticism: An Anthology, ed. Richard J. Schoeck and Jerome Taylor (Notre
Dame: University of Notre Dame Press, 1960), 1:303. See also Douglas J. Wurtele,
who takes Simon's charge seriously (although he argues against it), in "The Anti-
Lollardry of Chaucer's Parson," *Mediaevalia* 11 (1985): 151–68. The predominant view
in Chaucer criticism now is that the Parson is orthodox; see below.

    4. *The Riverside Chaucer,* 3d. ed., gen. ed. Larry D. Benson (Boston: Houghton
Mifflin, 1987), II.1173 and 1177. Hereafter, references shall appear in the text. For the
etymology of the word *Lollard,* see 863 n. 1173 and, more fully, Scase, *Piers Plowman,*
and Cole, "William Langland." The association between Lollards and tares (cokkel)
comes from the Latin *lollium.* See n. 1173 and n. 1183 in *Riverside Chaucer.*

    5. There are, of course, textual problems with this passage: it does not appear
in Ellesmere or Hengwrt, and therefore some scholars conclude that it seems to "bear
witness to an early stage in the composition of the *Tales*" (*Riverside Chaucer,* 862). Although the passage may not reflect Chaucer's final order for the tales (862), its relevance to the Parson's characterization should not be dismissed.

    6. Repeated again: "Out of the gospel he tho wordes caughte" and "But Cristes
loore and his apostles twelve/He taughte; but first he folwed it hymselve" (I.498,
I.527–28).

7. As Chaucer's voice, the tale can then demonstrate Chaucer's appropriation of clerical authority, his removal from the world of fiction, a personal penitential manual, or a comment on the rest of the tales (although this last interpretation seems to have long since fallen by the wayside). These views belong to Larry Scanlon, *Narrative, Authority, and Power: The Medieval Exemplum and Chaucerian Tradition* (Cambridge: Cambridge University Press, 1994), chap. 1; Lee Patterson, "The *Parson's Tale* and the Quitting of the *Canterbury Tales*," *Traditio* 34 (1978): 331–80; Albert Hartung, "The *Parson's Tale* and Chaucer's Penance," in *Literature and Religion in the Later Middle Ages: Philological Studies in Honor of Siegried Wenzel*, ed. Richard G. Newhauser and John A. Alford (Binghamton, NY: Center for Medieval and Early Renaissance Studies, 1995), 61–80; and Bernard Huppé, *A Reading of the Canterbury Tales* (Albany: State University of New York Press, 1964), respectively. There are, of course, critics who insist that the Parson's voice is as ironically distanced from Chaucer as the other pilgrims' voices: John Finlayson, "The Satiric Mode and the Parson's Tale," *Chaucer Review* 6 (1971): 94–116, and Judson Boyce Allen, "The Old Way and the Parson's Way: An Ironic Reading of the Parson's Tale," *Journal of Medieval and Renaissance Studies* 3 (1973): 255–71.

8. *Riverside Chaucer*, 863 n. 1173.

9. Both David Aers and Donald Howard note the discrepancy between the "benygne" man of the *General Prologue* and the "vindictive aggression" or "tendency to chide and reprimand" in his later appearances. For the first, see David Aers, *Chaucer, Langland and the Creative Imagination* (London: Routledge, 1980), 110; for the second, see Donald Howard, *The Idea of the Canterbury Tales* (Berkeley: University of California Press, 1976), 378; see further 376–80.

10. Charles A. Owen Jr., "What the Manuscripts Tell Us about the Parson's Tale," *Medium Aevum* 63 (1994): 245. See also Míceál F. Vaughan, "The Invention of the *Parson's Tale*," in *Rewriting Chaucer: Culture, Authority, and the Idea of the Authentic Text, 1400–1602*, ed. Thomas A. Prendergast and Barbara Kline (Columbus: Ohio State University Press, 1999), 45–90.

11. Some scholars have also noted the significance of this contradiction for the Parson's religiosity; see Loomis, "Was Chaucer a Laodicean?" and David Lawton, "Chaucer's Two Ways: The Pilgrimage Frame of the *Canterbury Tales*," *Studies in the Age of Chaucer* 9 (1987): 3–40. Loomis attributes the shift between the *General Prologue* and the *Parson's Tale* to the very different religious and political atmospheres at the times of composition: it was safe to use Wycliffite terms to describe the Parson while Chaucer was writing the *General Prologue* in the 1380s, but by the time Chaucer composed a tale for the Parson (at the end of his life), putative Wycliffite beliefs had become far more dangerous (304–5). Lawton also notices this disjuncture between the tale and "the Parson's portrait in the *General Prologue*, with its recurrent focus not on the Parson's place in the church hierarchy but rather on his personal grounding in 'Cristes gospel'" and states that "we run the risk of underreading them if we overlook their historical context" (Lawton, "Chaucer's Two Ways," 36), a sentiment with which I agree. Perhaps the most recent account of the Parson's religiosity has been offered

by Scanlon, who maintains that the portrait in the *General Prologue* is evidence of Chaucer's anticlericalism but that it is an anticlericalism general to late medieval England (and therefore does not make the Parson unorthodox). See his *Narrative, Authority,* chap. 1.

12. See, for example, Sarah Beckwith, *Christ's Body: Identity, Culture, and Society in Late Medieval Writings* (London: Routledge, 1993); Miri Rubin, *Corpus Christi: The Eucharist in Late Medieval Culture* (Cambridge: Cambridge University Press, 1991); and Nicholas Watson, "Conceptions of the Word: The Mother Tongue and the Incarnation of God," *New Medieval Literatures* 1 (1997): 85–124. This is by no means an exhaustive list of this kind of work.

13. See Paul Strohm's *England's Empty Throne: Usurpation and the Language of Legitimation, 1399–1422* (New Haven: Yale University Press, 1998), chap. 2, in which he argues for a new approach to the study of heresy in England. Rather than see the Lollard as preexisting the category of heretic, we should see that "the Lollard was from the beginning less a real threat to orthodox control than orthodoxy's rhetorical plaything" (34). In her important work on Wycliffism, Anne Hudson emphasizes the ways in which "Wycliffite concerns coincided with the intellectual interests of the time." *The Premature Reformation: Wycliffite Texts and Lollard History* (Oxford: Clarendon Press, 1988), 393. See also Margaret Aston, *Lollards and Reformers: Images and Literacy in Late Medieval Religion* (London: Hambledon Press, 1984), particularly chaps. 1, 4, 5, 6.

14. For recent studies that have put Chaucer's poetry in conversation with contemporary religious debates, see Paul Strohm, "Chaucer's Lollard Joke: History and the Textual Unconscious," *Studies in the Age of Chaucer* 17 (1995): 23–42; David Aers and Lynn Staley, *The Powers of the Holy: Religion, Politics, and Gender in Late Medieval English Culture* (University Park: Pennsylvania State University Press, 1996); Fiona Somerset, "'As Just as Is a Squyre': The Politics of 'Lewed Translacion' in Chaucer's *Summoner's Tale,*" *Studies in the Age of Chaucer* 21 (1999): 187–207; and Glending Olson, "The End of the *Summoner's Tale* and the Uses of Pentecost," *Studies in the Age of Chaucer* 21 (1999): 209–45.

15. Jill Mann points out that "this is no abstract, timeless figure; Chaucer envisages him in a realistic spatial and temporal existence," but she does not link this existence to historical events outside the Prologue itself. *Chaucer and Medieval Estates Satire,* (Cambridge: Cambridge University Press, 1973), 66.

16. Scanlon, *Narrative, Authority,* chap. 1

17. See Scase, *Piers Plowman.* For Scase, the newness of this anticlericalism is its emphasis on poverty and clerical dominion (7).

18. *Confessio Amantis,* in *The English Works of John Gower,* ed. G. C. Macaulay, 2 vols., EETS, e.s., 81 and 82 (London: Kegan Paul, 1900–1901), Prol. 193–97. Hereafter citations are given parenthetically in the text.

19. In the excursus on world religion in book 5, Gower's anticlericalism becomes even more confused. He attacks Lollardy as "newe lore," shifts abruptly to Christ's example, and then returns to attacking "Prelatz." It is important to note that Gower's

anticlericalism in the *Confessio* is markedly different than in the *Vox;* one can assume that his choice of English caused him to consider more carefully his own relationship to Lollardy.

20. *The Book of Vices and Virtues,* ed. W. Nelson Francis, EETS, o.s., 217 (London: Oxford University Press, 1942), 262. Aaron appears in a discussion of priestly chastity—that priests must be clean to consecrate the host: "And ʒit schulde þei be more clene and more holy for þei seruen at Goddis table and seruen hym of his cuppe and of his bred and of his wyne & of his metes" (261). Clearly Gower's discussion is navigating Donatism—the view that priests' sins would undermine the power of the sacraments. Indeed, Gower seems to be echoing the concerns that inform the *Book of Vices and Virtues*—to charge the priest only with providing a good example seems to engage the kind of anticlericalism (and Donatism) of the Wycliffites, so Gower must invoke the sacramental priest.

21. *Book of Vices and Virtues,* 262–63. Gower's note reads: "Qui vocatur a deo tanquam Aaron" (Who is called by God, like Aaron). John Gower, *Confessio Amantis,* ed. Russell A. Peck, trans. Andrew Galloway (Kalamazoo, MI: Medieval Institute Publications, 2000), 1:295. The passage in Hebrews reads: "And therefore he ought, as for the people, so also for himself, to offer for sins. Neither doth any man take the honour to himself, but he that is called by God, as Aaron was." *The Holy Bible, translated from the Latin Vulgate,* Douay-Rheims (Baltimore: John Murphy, 1899), Hebrews 5:3–4.

22. In the early fifteenth century, the established church authorized and circulated a particular model for imitation—the suffering Jesus who appears in Nicholas Love, *Nicholas Love's Mirror of the Blessed Life of Jesus Christ,* ed. Michael G. Sargent (New York: Garland, 1992). This ideal is about as far as one can get from the Parson.

23. Loomis writes, "Now three times Chaucer hammers home the point that the Parson took his doctrine from the gospel" ("Was Chaucer a Laodicean?" 302).

24. Mann, *Chaucer,* 65. See, however, H. Leith Spencer's caveat that "verbal instruction in 'God's word' need not always mean merely instruction in Bible texts, but might signify the formulations of the Church, founded in some sense upon scripture." *English Preaching in the Late Middle Ages* (Oxford: Clarendon Press, 1993), 145. Nevertheless, Chaucer's use of the word *gospel,* which Gower avoids, suggests that he is opposing gospel to other kinds of preaching the Parson might have indulged in (and still be considered moral): saints' lives, exempla, and *pastoralia.*

25. It is important to note that Chaucer uses the phrase to describe his Parson that Gower attributes to Christ. Gower does not, in contrast to Chaucer, apply this ideal directly to priests (only indirectly in his second attack on Lollardy in book 5). Gower writes (in the voice of Genius),

Crist wroghte ferst and after tawhte,
So that the dede his word arawhte;
He yaf ensample in his persone,

And we the wordes have al one,
Lich to the Tree with leves grene,
Upon the which no fruit is sene.
(5.1825–30)

Although this passage is strikingly similar to the portrait of Chaucer's Parson, as noted by Scanlon (*Narrative, Authority,* 9), Gower goes out of his way to avoid relating Christ here to either the Lollards (whom he has just finished discussing) or priests, whom he goes on to attack after an exemplum about Priest Thoas.

26. Lawton, "Chaucer's Two Ways," 36, and Scanlon, *Narrative, Authority,* 10.

27. See David Aers, *Faith, Ethics, and Church: Writing in England, 1360–1409* (Rochester: Boydell and Brewer, 1999), 46–47. Hudson also notes that "what is omitted is, for the date, as significant as what is included: there is no mention of the Parson's administration of the mass, no allusion to his role as confessor" (*Premature Reformation,* 391).

28. See Scanlon, who writes that the Parson's exemplarity "distances clerical authority from the textual" (*Narrative, Authority,* 10), but almost every sentence in the description points to a biblical reference, and the Parson's authority comes from enacting and speaking the words of the gospel.

29. Patterson also finds this understanding of language in the *Tale:* "for the Parson homiletic language remains essentially denotative" ("*Parson's Tale,*" 361). But in the *General Prologue* the denotative nature of language is explicitly linked to the gospels.

30. Very little work has been done on Wycliffite hermeneutics; for an exception, see Kantik Ghosh, *The Wycliffite Heresy: Authority and the Interpretation of Texts* (Cambridge: Cambridge University Press, 2002), chap. 4. Ghosh writes, "The thrust of the sermons seems to be largely in the direction of a certain hermeneutic naiveté (or polemical shrewdness), an attempt to fix and define meaning theoretically while in practice retaining the creative prerogatives of traditional exegesis" (114).

31. See the notes in the *Riverside Chaucer,* 819.

32. *English Wycliffite Sermons,* ed. Pamela Gradon and Anne Hudson, 5 vols. (New York: Oxford University Press, 1983–96), sermon E1, lines 120–22, my emphasis. Hereafter cited as *EWS* with sermon number/line numbers (unless referring to the introductions, which appear as volume number: page numbers).

33. *EWS,* 106/31–33.

34. *EWS,* 48/91–93. The metaphor of the pasture allows the Wycliffites to offer a liberating view of instruction, one in which the laity are promised what they have been denied by the clergy.

35. See Rita Copeland, *Pedagogy, Intellectuals, and Dissent in the Later Middle Ages: Lollardy and Ideas of Learning* (Cambridge: Cambridge University Press, 2001), on "openness," 114–40.

36. *EWS,* 7/1–2. This is, of course, a sentiment repeated across Wycliffite writing. In itself, the sentiment is not heterodox, but the insistence that the "werkys" are

found only in Holy Writ (and not the other teachings of the church) does separate the Wycliffites from less radical contemporaries.

37. Spencer also notes the problematic nature of this sermon, specifically the definition of "God's law" (*English Preaching*, 147 and 194). Interestingly enough, G. R. Owst cites a derivative of this sermon (from MS Royal 18) as evidence for the views of "a simple vernacular homilist" without noting its affiliation with Wycliffism. *Preaching in Medieval England: An Introduction to Sermon Manuscripts of the Period c. 1350–1450* (Cambridge: Cambridge University Press, 1926), 2. The sermon appears as 44 in the collection *Middle English Sermons*, ed. Woodburn O. Ross, EETS, o.s., 209 (London: Oxford University Press, 1960). According to Spencer, it is one of three sermons in this collection that also appear in MS Rylands 109, Sidney Sussex 74, and Bodley 95, which all contain derivatives from the *EWS* (*English Preaching*, 308).

38. *EWS*, 5/49–51 and 5/58–60.

39. *EWS*, 5/63. In both Wyclif's sermon and the *Glossa Ordinaria*, the water Genesareth figures the world. Moreover, neither of these interpretations contains any reference to washing the nets in the water. Wyclif writes, "stagnum Genezareth est turbata fragilitas huius conversacionis lapse, cum mundi confidencia sit labilis et inconstans." *Sermones*, ed. Johann Loserth, 3 vols. (London: Wyclif Society, 1887), 1:246. The *Glossa* cites Bede: "stagnum praesens saeculum designat." *Biblia Latina cum Glossa Ordinaria: Facsimile Reprint of the Editio Princeps, Adolph Rusch of Strassburg, 1480/81*, ed. Karlfried Froehlich and Margaret T. Gibson, 4 vols. (Turnhout: Brepols, 1992), 4:156. Hudson writes in the note to the sermon that "the interpretation of the washing of the nets has probably been developed independently by the English writer" (*EWS*, 4:200).

40. There are, of course, interpretive problems endemic to biblical exegesis, particularly allegorizing. As David Aers writes, "Analysis of exegetical practice has shown the tendency of medieval figuralists to dissolve events and actions, and with these both the text's images and existential dimensions." *Piers Plowman and Christian Allegory* (London: Edward Arnold, 1975), 32. Nevertheless, Wycliffite biblical exegesis closes down the relationship between literal and spiritual meaning in quite notable ways because Wycliffites reject what they see as excessive allegorizing by the established church.

41. The polemic against the preachers of the established church for indulging in the wrong kind of preaching also leads the Wycliffite sermon writers away from detailing what the right kind of preaching would be. See, for example, sermon 48, *EWS*, 1:438–42.

42. The literal sense includes figuration because figuration is also defined as a result of the author's intention. See A. J. Minnis, "'Authorial Intention' and 'Literal Sense' in the Exegetical Theories of Richard Fitzralph and John Wyclif: An Essay in the Medieval History of Biblical Hermeneutics," *Proceedings of the Royal Irish Academy* 75, no. 1 (1975): 1–31.

43. *EWS*, E42/44–46.

44. Here the possibilities for a pedagogy that depends on the literal sense seem rather bleak. In contrast, see Copeland's perspective in *Pedagogy, Intellectuals*, in which she argues that "Lollard teaching and learning redefined pedagogy" (18) and traces the way in which a hermeneutic of the literal sense becomes, under the Wycliffites, a pedagogy, (see chap. 2). Copeland notes that "[t]he marked effects of the policy of openness are not to be found in the content of Lollard biblical exposition, for that is no more 'literalist' in a fundamentalist sense than its counterpart orthodox productions" (127).

45. See chap. 1.

46. Wyclif, *Sermones*, 1:247. Hudson notes that "very little" of the English sermon can be traced to Wyclif's sermon (*EWS*, 4:198).

47. Wyclif, *Sermones*, 1:248.

48. Kantik Ghosh comes to similar conclusions (for different reasons) about Wyclif's writing in "Eliding the Interpreter: John Wyclif and Scriptural Truth," *New Medieval Literatures* 2 (1998): 205–24: "*De Veritate* thus points the way towards a hermeneutic cul-de-sac," and "The baffled idealism of Wyclif's tract and its profound unease with inherited hermeneutics which can neither be accepted nor rejected out of hand, given the nature of Christianity as the evolving religion of a (ceaselessly interpreted) text, arise from an increasingly threatened perception of the extent to which the theoretical source of all transcendent certitude, the Bible, is implicated in rhetoric through institutionalized and variable interpretive practices" (224).

49. Jill Mann also notes the Parson's isolation (along with that of the Ploughman): "The Parson and the Ploughman indeed correspond to the ideal of the estates writer, but Chaucer seems to be showing us that this ideal is inadequate to account for the workings of society. This is the basis on which society *should* be organised; but the isolation of these two figures in the *Prologue* shows us that the actuality is something different. The Parson does not seem to impinge on the other pilgrims, nor does the Ploughman. They exist in a separate sphere which is as exclusive and specialised as those inhabited by the other pilgrims" (*Chaucer*, 73).

50. For the identification of the penitential genre of this tale, see Patterson, "*Parson's Tale*," 339.

51. See *Riverside Chaucer*, 863 n. 1173, 1183.

52. Patterson sees the rejection of narrative as a "withdrawal to a higher, more inclusive perspective" ("*Parson's Tale*," 370); see further 370–80.

53. *EWS*, 61/5–7, 61/10–12.

54. Patterson calls the theology "bland" ("*Parson's Tale*," 353 n. 61). While the tale is purposely nonconfrontational on such matters as justification of auricular confession, it seems quite troubled about such matters as contrition; see below.

55. For a discussion of the sources, see Kate O. Petersen, *The Sources of the Parson's Tale* (Boston: Ginn, 1901), and Siegfried Wenzel, "The Sources for the 'Remedia' of the Parson's Tale," *Traditio* 27 (1971): 433–54. Beryl Rowland also notes the different voices: "The essential difference between the penitential treatises and *The Par-*

son's Tale is that the latter contains more than one voice." "Sermon and Penitential in the *Parson's Tale* and Their Effect on Style," *Florilegium* 9 (1987): 132. She identifies these two voices as "that of the instructor addressing the parish priest and that of the latter his parishioners" (134).

56. The first is the view of Mark H. Liddell, "A New Source of the Parson's Tale," in *An English Miscellany Presented to Dr. Furnivall* (Oxford: Clarendon, 1901), 256. The second is Patterson, *"Parson's Tale,"* 340. Liddell writes that "none of the Latin, English, or French treatises on this subject that I have seen (and I have examined a great number in the hope of finding the source of Chaucer's work) are so confused and disproportioned as Chaucer's is" (256–57). Similarly, Rowland states, "[T]he homogeneity of style that they [critics] imply does not exist" ("Sermon and Penitential," 131). But Patterson, who studied the same treatises as Liddell, comes to quite different conclusions: "Chaucer has elected to use just those elements from the paradigms of religious writing that will enforce a sense of theoretical cohesion" (*"Parson's Tale,"* 340); see further 344–51. As will become clear below, I am greatly indebted to Patterson's article, particularly to his view that "Chaucer is introducing an intellectual and theoretical concern into material that is far more commonly treated in a realistic and hortatory fashion" (344).

57. Although this translation would constitute the lay appropriation of "clergie" that Chaucer shares with the Wycliffites (see, for example, Somerset, "'As Just as Is a Squyre'"), Wycliffites were, of course, uninterested in translating penitential manuals, since they opposed confession (and would therefore find confessional manuals unnecessary). Nevertheless, Chaucer's translation of Pennaforte retains the sophistication of Pennaforte's manual and therefore shares with Wycliffism a rejection of the simplicity (at times insulting simplicity) with which vernacular devotional aids addressed their lay readers. In fact, Rita Copeland's statement that Lollard teaching "refuses pastoral formulas that equate laity with puerility; and it does so by rejecting the historical baggage of pastoral condescension," can be nicely appropriated to describe what Chaucer is doing in the section on contrition. "Childhood, Pedagogy, and the Literal Sense: From Late Antiquity to the Lollard Heretical Classroom," in *New Medieval Literatures* 1 (1997): 156.

58. Patterson, *"Parson's Tale,"* 353–56. Patterson notes that two of Pennaforte's degrees are combined, and "a new more generous feeling is added (number five), 'remembrance of the passioun that oure Lord Jhesu Crist suffred for oure synnes'" (354).

59. The *Boke's* view of contrition seems to be representative of vernacular handbooks. *The Book of Vices and Virtues* spends about thirty lines on contrition, which it calls "Repentance" (172–73), and devotes most of its discussion to the six conditions of shrift and the five things that disturb it; see 173–84. See, similarly, *Jacob's Well,* ed. Arthur Brandeis, EETS, o.s., 115 (London: K. Paul, Trench, Trübner, 1900): it does not spend much time on the "watyr of contricyoun" (65), focusing rather on the "þi scope of penauns" (65), and the writer provides *exempla* that illustrate only the second two

stages of penance, confession and satisfaction (see 64–68). *Handlyng Synne* does discuss "sorowe of hert" as the sixth point of shrift but seems to be interested in externalizing the sins rather than providing an inner mapping of sorrow: "Þy self berest þan on þy bak / Þy vyle synne þat makþ þe blak." Robert Mannyng, *Handlyng Synne*, ed. Idelle Sullens (Binghamton, NY: Medieval and Renaissance Texts and Studies, 1983), 11561–62.

60. *The Boke of Penance*, in *Cursor Mundi*, ed. Richard K. Morris, 3 vols., EETS, o.s. 57 (London: K. Paul, Trench, Trübner, 1874–93), 3:26014–18. I quote from the Cotton MS.

61. Ibid., 3:26080–83.

62. The phrase is Patterson's (*"Parson's Tale,"* 344).

63. See similarly, "Now soothly, whoso wel remembreth hym of thise thynges, I gesse that his synne shal nat turne hym into delit" (175); "Now shal a man understonde in which manere shal been his contricioun. I seye that it shal been universal and total" (292); and "Wherfore I seye that many men ne repenten hem nevere of swiche thoghtes and delites" (298).

64. This same quotation appears in *The Book of Vices and Virtues* under confession, not contrition, and this location suggests that this writer puts the emphasis on speaking sorrow to the priest and not examining it, as Chaucer does. See *Book of Vices and Virtues*, 173.

65. Rowland also notes the interjection of this different voice: "the passage [on contrition] concludes with an intrusive 'I' (298, 304, 308) that has more force than the single rhetorical 'I gesse' (175), and it appears, in these instances, to be the writer of the tract, addressing the priest" ("Sermon and Penitential," 134).

66. Raymond of Pennaforte, *Summa Sancti Raymundi de Peniafort* (1603; reprint, Farnsborough, Hants.: Gregg Press, 1967), bk. 3, sec. 10, 649–50. See also Petersen, *Sources*, 15–16.

67. Wenzel's notes in the *Riverside Chaucer* attribute this citation to Jonah 2.8 (958 n. 304).

68. Chaucer seems to be following different sources here. He uses a tract that is similar to Pennaforte's for the discussion of confession, lines 316–86, and Peraldus for "a large part of lines 390–955" (*Riverside Chaucer*, 956; see also 958 nn. 318–979). Petersen describes the first section as "sin in general," lines 321–386, and writes, "Raymund's tract has important correspondences with the *P.T.*, although they are not brought together as in the *P.T.*" (*Sources*, 34).

69. Petersen notes the following: "At section 17, v. 321, where the Parson fails to expound his second topic of Confession, and in connection with this second topic of Confession in Raymund, the subject of Sin is introduced. The treatment of this topic in Raymund is brief, and hardly interrupts the transition to the third topic of Confession. In the *P. T.*, on the contrary, the exposition of Sin is so full as almost to assume the proportions of a separate treatise. Moreover, from its length and elaboration, the digression interrupts the regular course of the argument, and becomes, as it were, an interpolation between the beginning and the main part of Confession" (*Sources*, 34).

70. Patterson writes, "The inclusion of these elements into one work not only is not unusual in penitential manuals but is virtually mandatory," and "It would be hard to conceive of a more orderly development" (*"Parson's Tale,"* 349–50).

71. *Boke of Penance,* in *Cursor Mundi,* 3:25934, 25935, 25936.

72. Ibid., 3:286068–69.

73. Ibid., 3:28077–79.

74. Ibid., 3:28591.

75. In *Handlyng Synne,* the author informs the reader that the purpose of the book is "Synne to shewe, vs to frame, / God to wrshepe, þe fende to shame" (lines 5–6) and puts the Ten Commandments within the context of confession: "Þe co-muandementys of þe olde lawe / Þyse ten were fyrst vs ʒeuyn / And fyrst we welyn of hem be shreuyn" (14–16). After detailing the Ten Commandments, the seven sins, the sin of sacrilege, and the sacraments, the author ends with the twelve points and twelve graces of confession. *The Book of Vices and Virtues* ends its account of the seven sins with a direction to confess: "Here endeþ þe seuene dedly synnes and alle here braunches; and who-so wolde wel studie in þis boke, it myʒt profiten hym, and he myʒt lerne and rekene alle manere of synnes and to schryue hym wel, for þer may no man schryue hym wel ne kepe hym fro synne but he knowe hem. Now schal he þat redeþ in þis boke ententifly, loke ʒif he be gilty of any of þes synnes, and ʒif he be gilty, repente hym and schryue hym and kepe hym to his power fro þe oþere þat he is not gilty of, and biseke mekely Ihesu Crist þat he kepe hym fro alle þo and oþere; and so mote he kepe vs alle, amen" (68). In addition, the author discusses sins in detail (although not always under the rubric of the seven capital sins) in his account of confession: "First schal a man go to þe herte and telle alle his þouʒtes, whiche þei ben, gosteliche or fleschely: gosteliche, as ʒif any þouʒt bi aʒens þe bileue of holy chirche or of veyn glorie . . . or of enuye þat þei haue in herte to oþere goodnesses, or wrappe" (179).

76. For Julian, see, for example, chap. 27 of the long text *The Shewings of Julian of Norwich,* ed. Georgia Ronan Crampton (Kalamazoo, MI: Medieval Institute Publications, 1994).

Chapter Four.   The Retreat from Confession

1. *Thomas Hoccleve: The Regiment of Princes,* ed. Charles R. Blyth (Kalamazoo: Medieval Institute Publications, Western Michigan University, 1999), line 1975. All further citations of this poem will be given parenthetically. For a discussion of the relationship between the *Regiment* and the *Confessio,* see Charles R. Blyth, "Thomas Hoccleve's Other Master," *Mediaevalia* 16 (1993): 349–59. Blyth notes that "we know that Hoccleve read at least part of the *Confessio,* for he served as one of the scribes for Trinity College Cambridge MS R. 3.2," and "Equally certainly, in his longest and

most important poem, the *Regiment of Princes,* Hoccleve contributed to the 'mirror for princes' genre which Gower had introduced (introduced into English vernacular, that is) with the seventh book of the *Confessio*" (350).

2. The relationship between Gower's text and penitential manuals is noted briefly by J. A. Burrow, *Ricardian Poetry: Chaucer, Gower, Langland, and the Gawain Poet* (New Haven: Yale University Press, 1971), 109–10; John H. Fisher, *John Gower: Moral Philosopher and Friend of Chaucer* (New York: New York University Press, 1964), 137–41; Larry Scanlon, *Narrative, Authority, and Power: The Medieval Exemplum and the Chaucerian Tradition* (Cambridge: Cambridge University Press, 1994), 248; Robert F. Yeager, *John Gower's Poetic: The Search for a New Arion* (Cambridge: D. S. Brewer, 1990), 189; and more extensively by Gerald Kinneavy, "Gower's *Confessio Amantis* and the Penitentials," *Chaucer Review* 19 (1984): 144–61. Kinneavy argues for "the confession device as a massive working principle in the poem" (156) but only briefly notes the use of stories in both Gower and penitentials such as *Handlyng Synne* (152). See also Patrick J. Gallacher, *Love, the Word, and Mercury: A Reading of John Gower's Confessio Amantis* (Albuquerque: University of New Mexico Press, 1975), which is less interested in historical sources than in sacramental confession: "The sacrament of confession can be looked upon as an attempt to penetrate inwardly to the principle of a man's being by clearing away the dishonesties and hypocrisies standing in the way of self-knowledge and of achieving the virtue of truth" (12–13; for a fuller discussion, see chap. 5). A foremost critic of the poem, James Simpson, is primarily interested in reading the confession in Ovidian terms; see *Sciences and the Self in Medieval Poetry* (Cambridge: Cambridge University Press, 1995). Hoccleve's poem has received even less attention to the confessional workings of the dialogue; most critics read this dialogue in terms of the complaint. See, for example, Ethan Knapp, *The Bureaucratic Muse: Thomas Hoccleve and the Literature of Late Medieval England* (University Park: Pennsylvania State University Press, 2001), 96–106, although Knapp notes that the Boethian tradition he draws on has informed penitential theologies (95). Nevertheless, a number of critics do mention that the Old Man is a kind of confessor: Antony J. Hasler, "Hoccleve's Unregimented Body," *Paragraph* 13 (1990): 169; Derek Pearsall, "Hoccleve's *Regement of Princes:* The Poetics of Royal Self-Representation," *Speculum* 69 (1994): 409; and Scanlon, *Narrative, Authority,* 304.

3. This line of scholarship is extensive. A list (by no means exhaustive) of critics concentrating on exempla in both poems would include Judith Ferster, *Fictions of Advice: The Literature and Politics of Counsel in Late Medieval England* (Philadelphia: University of Pennsylvania Press, 1996), chaps. 7 and 8, and Scanlon, *Narrative, Authority,* chaps. 9 and 10. For Gower, see Kurt Olsson, "Rhetoric, John Gower, and the Late Medieval Exemplum," *Medievalia et Humanistica* 8 (1977): 185–200; Russell Peck, *Kingship and Common Profit in Gower's Confessio Amantis* (Carbondale: Southern Illinois University Press, 1978); Elizabeth Porter, "Gower's Ethical Microcosm and Political Macrocosm," in *Gower's Confessio Amantis: Responses and Reassessments,* ed. A. J. Minnis (Cambridge: D. S. Brewer, 1983), 135–62; Charles Runacres, "Art and Ethics in the 'Exempla' of 'Confessio Amantis,'" in Minnis, *Gower's Confessio Aman-*

tis, 106–34. For Hoccleve, see Nicholas Perkins, *Hoccleve's Regiment of Princes: Counsel and Constraint* (Cambridge: D. S. Brewer, 2001); and Paul Strohm, *England's Empty Throne: Usurpation and the Language of Legitimation, 1399–1422* (New Haven: Yale University Press, 1998), chaps. 7 and 8.

4. See works cited in n. 2.

5. In his edition of the poem, G. C. Macaulay notes that "the manuscripts of the first recension bear the date 1390" and dates the later version to 1392–93. *The English Works of John Gower*, 2 vols., ed. G. C. Macaulay, EETS, e.s., 81, 82 (London: Kegan Paul, 1900), 1:xxii. Fisher suggests 1385 for the first version and 1392 for the second (*John Gower*, 116, 118).

6. Peter McNiven writes, "It will be evident that while Lollardy was officially condemned in 1382 by the Church, with the prompt blessing of the lay power, the outburst of orthodox zeal in that year was not followed by any determined or concerted campaign to ensure that heretical doctrines and teachings were totally eradicated in England." *Heresy and Politics in the Reign of Henry IV: The Burning of John Badby* (Woodbridge, Suffolk: Boydell Press, 1987), 50. See further his chap. 3.

7. Blyth's edition dates the poem to 1411 (*Thomas Hoccleve*, 4). Pearsall offers evidence that the poem was written between November of 1410 and November of 1411 ("Hoccleve's *Regement of Princes*," 388).

8. *De Heretico Comburendo* is printed in *The Statutes of the Realm*, 11 vols. (1810–28; reprint, London: Dawsons, 1963), 2:125–28. The trial of William Sawtry and Arundel's Constitutions appear in *Concilia Magnae Britanniae et Hiberniae*, ed. David Wilkins, 4 vols. (1737; reprint, Brussels: Culture et Civilisation, 1964), 3:254–63 and 3:314–19. For Thorpe, see my chap. 2. For an account of Purvey's trial, see McNiven, *Heresy and Politics*, 89–92. For discussions of heresy in this time period, see McNiven, *Heresy and Politics*, chaps. 5–12; Strohm, *England's Empty Throne*, chaps. 2 and 5; and Nicholas Watson, "Censorship and Cultural Change in Late Medieval England: Vernacular Theology, the Oxford Translation Debate, and Arundel's Constitutions of 1409," *Speculum* 70 (1995): 822–64.

9. In some respects, my argument parallels that made by Larry Scanlon in his discussion of Gower and Hoccleve, that the poems demonstrate the appropriation of clerical authority in a laicizing movement; see his *Narrative, Authority*, chaps. 9 and 10. He writes that "the transition from the medieval to the humanist might be more fruitfully understood as one from clerical to lay" (54). Nevertheless, I see this aspect of the poems as being as much a response to Lollardy as to kingship.

10. For the poem's negotiation of orthodoxy around the figure of the prince, see Pearsall's "Hoccleve's *Regement of Princes*."

11. See, for example, on Gower, the essays in Minnis, *Gower's Confessio Amantis*; Derek Pearsall, "Gower's Narrative Art," *PMLA* 81 (1966): 475–84; Simpson, *Sciences and the Self;* Winthrop Wetherbee, "Genius and Interpretation in the *Confessio Amantis*," in *Magister Regis: Studies in Honor of Robert Earl Kaske*, ed. Arthur Groos (New York: Fordham University Press, 1986), 241–60; and Yeager, *John Gower's Poetic*. For Hoccleve, see Hasler, "Hoccleve's Unregimented Body"; Knapp, *Bureaucratic Muse*,

chaps. 3–4; Stephen Medcalf, "Inner and Outer," in *The Later Middle Ages* (New York: Holmes and Meier, 1981), 123–40; and Perkins, *Hoccleve's Regiment of Princes.*

12. Here I am indebted to the discussion of form and content in Fredric Jameson's *The Political Unconscious: Narrative as a Socially Symbolic Act* (Ithaca: Cornell University Press, 1981): "History is therefore the experience of Necessity. . . . Necessity is not in that sense a type of content, but rather the inexorable *form* of events" (102). See also, Slavoj Žižek, *The Sublime Object of Ideology* (London: Verso, 1989), chap. 1. My interest in the relationship between form and historical contexts is similar to that articulated by Paul Strohm, "Form and Social Statement in *Confessio Amantis* and *The Canterbury Tales*," *Studies in the Age of Chaucer* 1 (1979): 17–40, who writes, "Even an artistic dimension as seemingly detached from social concerns as the external form of a literary work may be considered not only in aesthetic terms, but also as a statement conditioned by the social experiences of its author" (18). See, similarly, Scanlon, who writes, "Modern literary criticism tends to isolate form as precisely that which resists the cultural materials out of which it is constructed" (*Narrative, Authority,* 26) and argues instead for considering the ideological resonance of form (for him, the exemplum).

13. Whether Gower is more indebted to a homiletic tradition or an Ovidian tradition has been much debated. Although I certainly do not dispute the influence of Ovid, my focus on confession here underlines his interest in the structures and languages offered by the homiletic tradition. The most thorough discussion of the poem's Ovidian nature is in Simpson, *Sciences and Self.*

14. See *The Complete Works of John Gower,* vol. 1, *The French Works,* ed. G. C. Macaulay (Oxford: Clarendon Press, 1899), pp. 172–75, lines 14797–15096; trans. William Burton Wilson, in John Gower, *Mirour de l'Omme* (East Lansing, MI: Colleagues Press, 1992), 202–6.

15. Fisher writes, "Nowhere did Gower treat sacramental confession as a major theme" (*John Gower,* 141). Nevertheless, one critic of the poem, Gallacher, does see the confession as sacramental (*Love, the Word,* 12).

16. *Confessio Amantis,* in *English Works of John Gower,* 1.164. All further citations of the *Confessio* are hereafter given parenthetically in the text.

17. See n. 2.

18. Despite Genius's important relationship to Venus, he is clearly indebted to the office of a Christian priest. See Yeager, *John Gower's Poetic,* 263–64, and Derek Pearsall, who writes, "Genius, therefore, though he is called the Priest of Venus, is much more conscious of his allegiance to his priesthood than of his allegiance to Venus—indeed he repudiates her on at least one occasion (v.1382)—and he becomes something akin to Conscience" ("Gower's Narrative Art," 476). For the history of this figure, see Denise Baker, "The Priesthood of Genius: A Study of the Medieval Tradition," *Speculum* 51 (1976): 277–91.

19. The relationship between the moral frame and the classical and courtly elements it contains is discussed by A. J. Minnis, "Moral Gower and Medieval Literary

Theory," in Minnis, *Gower's Confessio Amantis*," 57–61. See also A. J. Minnis, "John Gower, *Sapiens* in Ethics and Politics," *Medium Aevum* 49 (1980): 207–29.

20. Kinneavy also notes that "the confessor generally tries to make the exempla relevant to the state of the penitent" ("Gower's *Confessio Amantis*," 148).

21. Here I am focusing on the second version, which Gower revised by editing out references to King Richard II.

22. Burrow, Peck, and Yeager also note this circularity (in *Ricardian Poetry*, 66; *Kingship and Common Profit*, 183; and *John Gower's Poetic*, 233, respectively).

23. See, for example, Ferster, *Fictions of Advice*, chap. 7, and Scanlon, *Narrative, Authority*, chap. 9.

24. James Simpson also identifies this lover's confession as a retreat from the political, when he writes that in book 1 the narrator "abandons the matter of politics and history." *The Oxford English Literary History*, vol. 2, *Reform and Cultural Revolution, 1350–1547* (Oxford: Oxford University Press, 2002), 134. Many critics do not see it as a retreat because they look for thematic connections across the generic divide (most notably love). See, for example, Pearsall, "Gower's Narrative Art," 476, and Fisher, *John Gower*, 187.

25. For this perspective, see Terry Eagleton, *Criticism and Ideology: A Study in Marxist Literary Theory* (London: Verso, 1978), 73–74.

26. For a discussion of this passage with an emphasis on Gower's view of reform, see David Aers, "Reflections on Gower as '*Sapiens* in Ethics and Politics,'" in *Re-visioning John Gower*, ed. Robert F. Yeager (Asheville, NC: Pegasus Press, 1998), 197–201.

27. See, for example, his "Remonstrance against Sir John Oldcastle," in *Selections from Hoccleve*, ed. M. Seymour (Oxford: Clarendon Press, 1981), 61–74. The relationship between Hoccleve and Lollardy has not received much attention, despite the fact that his mention of John Badby is much discussed. For some exceptions, see Ethan Knapp's *Bureaucratic Muse*, chap. 5; Ruth Nisse, "'Oure Fadres Olde and Modres': Gender, Heresy, and Hoccleve's Literary Politics," *Studies in the Age of Chaucer* 21 (1999): 275–99; and Pearsall, "Hoccleve's *Regement of Princes*."

28. Pearsall is persuasive in arguing for the importance of Lollardy in understanding the topical references of Hoccleve's poem: "It is not sensible to look for a Lollard under every bed, but it is not sensible either to underestimate the shock that Lollardy administered to English society, secular and ecclesiastical, and the rigor and pervasiveness of the measures that were taken to combat it" ("Hoccleve's *Regement of Princes*," 407).

29. There is another reference to Lollards, more specifically, the image debate, near the end of the poem, lines 5006–10. See the discussion by Pearsall, "Hoccleve's *Regement of Princes*," 405–6. This reference does not explicitly name Lollards, and Hoccleve dismisses those who reject images with "Passe over that" (5010).

30. Lee Patterson links the Pardoner's despair with Lollard criticism of the church in *Chaucer and the Subject of History* (Madison: University of Wisconsin Press, 1991), 420.

31. Confession is often described as vomiting in vernacular sermons. See, for example, sermon 40 in the *Middle English Sermons,* ed. Woodburn O. Ross, EETS, o.s., 209 (London: Oxford University Press, 1960) (hereafter cited as *MES*), in which the cure for sinful "drinks" (envy, lechery, covetousness) is "vomiting."

32. Patterson, *Chaucer,* 379.

33. On this point, see Knapp, *Bureaucratic Muse,* 102.

34. In the *Festial* the narrative appears in sermons for both the first and the second Sunday in Lent (sermons 20 and 21). See John Mirk, *Mirk's Festial,* ed. Theodor Erbe, vol. 1, EETS, e.s., 96 (London: Kegan Paul, Trench, Trübner, 1905). In the *MES,* the narrative appears in the sermon for the fourth Sunday in Lent (sermon 38).

35. Patterson, *Chaucer,* 379.

36. Although both Burrow and Medcalf mention the parallel, they do not seem to see it as a purposeful allusion, nor do they explore it in depth. See J. A. Burrow, "Autobiographical Poetry in the Middle Ages: The Case of Thomas Hoccleve," *Proceedings of the British Academy* 68 (1982): 389–412, in which he writes that the Old Man "is no more than a pale shadow by comparison with the old man in Chaucer's *Pardoner's Tale*" (402). Medcalf also connects the Old Man to *Pardoner's Tale* but says they are "very different" ("Inner and Outer," 138).

37. The echoes are rather startling, and I have mapped the most important here below, citing the *Pardoner's Tale* as *PT,* the *Pardoner's Prologue* as *PP,* and the *Regiment of Princes* as *RP.* All citations from Chaucer taken from *Riverside Chaucer,* gen. ed. Larry D. Benson (Boston: Houghton Mifflin, 1987).

> *PT:* In Flaundres whilom was a compaignye
>   Of yonge folk that haunteden folye,
>   As riot, hazard, stywes, and tavernes.
>   (6.463–65)

> *RP:* Whan I was yong, I was ful rechelees,
>   Prowd, nyce, and riotous for the maistrie,
>   And among othir, consciencelees.
>   By that sette I nat the worth of a flie;
>   And of hem hauntid I the conpaignie
>   That went on pilgrimage to taverne,
>   Which before unthrift berith the lanterne.
>   (610–16)

> *PT:* Hir othes been so grete and so dampnable
>   That it is grisly for to heere hem swere.
>   Oure blessed Lordes body they totere—
>   (6.475–77)

RP: Whan folk wel reuled dressid hem to bedde
In tyme due by reed of nature,
To the taverne qwikly I me spedde
And pleide at dees while the nyght wolde endure.
There the forme of every creature
Dismembred I with oothes grete, and rente
Lym fro lym or that I thennes wente.
(624–30)

PP: By this gaude have I wonne, yeer by yeer,
An hundred mark sith I was pardoner.
(6.389–90)

RP: Tho mighte I spende an hundred mark by yeer.
(645)

PP: What, trowe ye, that whiles I may preche,
And wynne gold and silver for I teche,
That I wol lyve in poverte willfully?
(439–41)

RP: An office also hadde I lucratyf,
And wan ynow, God woot, and mochil more,
But nevere thoghte I in al my yong lyf
What I injustly gat for to restore,
Wherfore I now repente wondir sore;
(659–63)

With povert for my gilt me feffid He
(670)

Finally, the Old Man mentions covetousness: "And ofte it fals was that I swoor or spak, / For the desir fervent of covetyse" (6.631–32). Scanlon notes the indebtedness of lines 624–30 (*Narrative, Authority*, 305).

38. The relationship between the Old Man and despair has been discussed extensively by both Patterson, *Chaucer*, chap. 9, and H. Marshall Leicester, "'Synne Horrible': The Pardoner's Exegesis of His Tale, and Chaucer's," in *Acts of Interpretation: The Text in Its Contexts, 700–1600: Essays on Medieval and Renaissance Literature in Honor of E. Talbot Donaldson*, ed. Mary Carruthers and Elizabeth D. Kirk (Norman, OK: Pilgrim Books, 1982), 25–50.

39. I was struck by the oddity of this term until I read McNiven's account of Badby's trial, in which Badby mentions a John Rakyer: Badby "expressly declared that he would never in life believe that this [transubstantiation] was possible unless

he were to see Christ's body handled 'in corporeal form' by the priest at the altar. He then added that John Rakyer of Bristol had the same power and the same authority to make the body of Christ as any priest" (McNiven, *Heresy and Politics*, 200). Perhaps Hoccleve's "raker" is a pun on the name Rakyer and therefore mocks Badby's belief that Rakyer had as much power as a priest.

40. *De Pontificum Romanorum Schismate*, in *Select English Works of John Wyclif*, 3 vols., ed. Thomas Arnold (Oxford: Clarendon Press, 1869–71), 3:252. See also the discussion in Anne Hudson, *The Premature Reformation: Wycliffite Texts and Lollard History* (Oxford: Clarendon Press, 1988), 294–301.

41. Innocent III describes the goals of Lateran IV, which instituted annual auricular confession, as the following: "to extirpate vices and foster virtues, correct abuses and reform morals, suppress heresy and strengthen the faith, settle disorders and establish peace, encourage princes and Christian peoples to aid and maintain the Holy Land." Innocent III, quoted in Leonard Boyle, "The Fourth Lateran Council and Manuals of Popular Theology," in *Popular Literature of Medieval England*, ed. Thomas Heffernan (Knoxville: University of Tennessee Press, 1985), 30. In *Formation of a Persecuting Society* (Oxford: Blackwell, 1987), R. I. Moore discusses Constitution 3, *De haereticis*, which was concerned with heretics.

42. Hasler reads the exaggerated nature of the discussion of marriage as calling penitential discourse into question ("Hoccleve's Unregimented Body," 172).

43. My argument here parallels that of Scanlon in *Narrative, Authority*, 299–322, in that I see the Old Man as having "the independent moral authority beggars can possess" (308), although I think it is important that the Old Man is not a beggar. Rather, he has the moral authority a poor and virtuous man can possess, and that authority is one in which the Lollards were very interested.

44. Scanlon writes that both Hoccleve and Lydgate "largely abandon the anticlericalism that so marks the work of the earlier ones" (*Narrative, Authority*, 298). I am not so sure this is true for Hoccleve, as I shall demonstrate. For the Wycliffite views on poverty, see Margaret Aston, "'Caim's Castles': Poverty, Politics, and Disendowment," in *The Church, Politics, and Patronage in the Fifteenth Century*, ed. R. B. Dobson (Gloucester: A. Sutton, 1984). Wendy Scase mentions the Wycliffite connotations of russet robes in *Piers Plowman and the New Anticlericalism* (Cambridge: Cambridge University Press, 1989), 168.

45. Scase notes that renunciation "is also part of an anticlerical poverty polemic, against clerical possession also" (*Piers Plowman*, 58–59), and "the new anticlerical interpretation [of evangelical poverty] asserted the interests not of clerics at all, but of the involuntary lay poor" (62). It is important to note that the Old Man's situation is one of involuntary poverty, and he is definitely not a beggar, as Furnivall calls him in his edition.

46. The Old Man describes his submission to "Holy Chirche" as that of a layperson rather than a cleric:

But see how that the worthy prelacie,
And undir hem the souffisant clergie,

Endowid of profounde intelligence,
Of al this land werreyen thy [presumption's] sentence.

———

That selve same to me were a brydil
By which wolde I governed been and gyed,
And elles al my labour were in ydil.
By Holy Chirche I wole be justified;
To that al hoolly is myn herte applied,
And evere shal. I truste in Goddes grace;
Swich surquidrie in me shal have no place.

(361–71)

47. Patterson, *Chaucer*, 402.

48. Both Leicester, "'Synne Horrible,'" and Patterson, *Chaucer*, chap. 9, read the Pardoner's despair in light of the failure of the church.

49. Pearsall, "Hoccleve's *Regement of Princes*," 407.

50. See, for example, Leicester, "'Synne Horrible,'" 37–41.

51. For the tradition, see Baker, "Priesthood of Genius."

52. Scanlon notes that "the beggar's antecedent is Gower's Genius" and that he both "acts for much of the dialogue like a confessor" and offers his own confession (*Narrative, Authority*, 304).

53. The exemplum tradition and "mirrors for princes" more specifically do not necessarily draw on or converge with confessional genres. Consider, the *Gesta Romanorum* or John of Salisbury's *Policraticus*, both of which are available in translation: *Gesta Romanorum: Or Entertaining Moral Stories*, trans. Rev. Charles Swan, rev. Wynnard Hooper (1894; New York: AMS Press, 1970), and John of Salisbury, *Policraticus: Of the Frivolities of Courtiers and the Footprints of Philosophers*, ed. and trans. Cary J. Nederman (Cambridge: Cambridge University Press, 1990). But both Gower and Hoccleve follow sermon writers and authors of penitential manuals in linking these stories within a confessional frame or relating them to confessional practice instead of following John of Salisbury or the writer of the *Gesta*, who do not. Clearly, both Gower and Hoccleve understand these traditions as importantly connected.

54. On Hoccleve's indebtedness to Gower, see Blyth, "Thomas Hoccleve's Other Master," and Scanlon, *Narrative, Authority*, 314.

55. Although scholars have long debated the digressive nature of Gower's "mirror" in book 7 of the *Confessio*—whether it does or does not fit in the confession—perhaps it is worth turning the question around to ask why it is that both Gower and Hoccleve link confessions and "mirrors for princes," whereas Lydgate, writing in the same tradition, most clearly does not.

56. "Testimony of William Thorpe," in *Two Wycliffite Texts*, ed. Anne Hudson, EETS, o.s., 301 (Oxford: Oxford University Press, 1993), 81–82.

57. Hoccleve's sources do not include these direct addresses to the reader that echo sermons and penitential manuals. See the list of translated passages in Friedrich

Aster, *Das Verhältniss des Altenglischen Gedichtes "De Regimine Principum" von Thomas Hoccleve zu seinen Quellen* (Leipzig: Oskar Peters, 1888), and Perkins, *Hoccleve's Regiment of Princes,* 122–25.

58. Knapp also notes this aspect of despair: the poem is "quite un-Boethian in its conclusion that philosophical consolation is an interminable and insufficient project" (*Bureaucratic Muse,* 94).

59. See *Middle English Dictionary,* ed. Hans Kurath and Sherman M. Kuhn (Ann Arbor: University of Michigan Press, 1952–): the third meaning of *thennes* is "in that place, there."

60. The first meaning of *thennes* is "from that place" *(Middle English Dictionary).*

Afterword

1. This term is Nicholas Watson's. See his "Censorship and Cultural Change in Late-Medieval England: Vernacular Theology, the Oxford Translation Debate, and Arundel's Constitutions of 1409," *Speculum* 70 (1995): 822–64.

2. For a discussion of the *Constitutions,* see Watson, "Censorship and Cultural Change," and James Simpson, *The Oxford English Literary History,* vol. 2, 1350–1547: *Reform and Cultural Revolution* (Oxford: Oxford University Press, 2002), 339–40, 476–89.

3. *Concilia Magnae Britanniae et Hiberniae,* ed. David Wilkins, 4 vols. (1737; reprint, Brussels: Culture et Civilisation, 1964), 3:316; trans. in John Foxe, *The Acts and Monuments of John Foxe,* ed. Josiah Pratt, 8 vols. (1843; reprint, New York: AMS Press, 1965), 3:244–45.

4. It is worth noting that Foxe's translation, cited here, does not include the translation for *observet,* perhaps because he was far more concerned with demonstrating the church's censorship than with the effect of these strictures on church members.

5. See David Aers, "A Whisper in the Ear of Early Modernists; or Reflections on Literary Critics Writing the 'History of the Subject,'" in *Culture and History, 1350–1600: Essays on English Communities, Identities, and Writings,* ed. David Aers (Detroit: Wayne State University Press, 1992), 177–202, and Lee Patterson, "On the Margin: Postmodernism, Ironic History, and Medieval Studies," *Speculum* 65 (1990): 87–108.

References

Primary Sources

Biblia Latina cum Glossa Ordinaria: Facsimile Reprint of the Editio Princeps, Adolph Rusch of Strassburg, 1480/81. Ed. Karlfried Froehlich and Margaret T. Gibson. 4 vols. Turnhout: Brepols, 1992.

The Book of Vices and Virtues. Ed. W. Nelson Francis. EETS, o.s., 217. London: Oxford University Press, 1942.

Brinton, Thomas. *The Sermons of Thomas Brinton, Bishop of Rochester (1373–1389).* Ed. Sister Mary Aquinas Devlin. 2 vols. Camden 3rd ser., 85–86. London: Offices of the Royal Historical Society, 1954.

Chaucer, Geoffrey. *The Riverside Chaucer.* 3rd ed. Gen. ed. Larry D. Benson. Boston: Houghton Mifflin, 1987.

Clanvowe, Sir John. *The Works of Sir John Clanvowe.* Ed. V. J. Scattergood. Cambridge: D. S. Brewer, 1965.

Concilia Magnae Britanniae et Hiberniae. Ed. David Wilkins. 4 vols. London, 1737. Reprint, Brussels: Culture et Civilisation, 1964.

Cursor Mundi: A Northumbrian Poem of the Fourteenth Century. Ed. Richard K. Morris. 3 vols. EETS, o.s., 57, 59, 62, 66, 68, 99, 101. London: Kegan Paul, Trench, Trübner, 1874–93.

Decrees of the Ecumenical Councils. Ed. Norman P. Tanner. 2 vols. Washington, DC: Georgetown University Press, 1990.

Dymmok, Roger. *Liber Rogeri Dymmok contra Duodecim Errores.* Ed. H. S. Cronin. London: Kegan Paul, 1922.

The English Works of Wyclif Hitherto Unprinted. Ed. F. D. Matthew. EETS, o.s., 74. London: Trübner, 1880. Reprint, Millwood, NY: Kraus Reprint, 1978.

English Wycliffite Sermons. Ed. Pamela Gradon and Anne Hudson. 5 vols. New York: Oxford University Press, 1983–96.

Fasciculi Zizaniorum Magistri Johannis Wyclif. Ed. W. W. Shirley. London: Longman, 1858.

Fasciculus Morum: A Fourteenth Century Preacher's Handbook. Ed. and trans. Siegfried Wenzel. University Park: Pennsylvania State University Press, 1989.

Foxe, John. *The Acts and Monuments of John Foxe.* Ed. Josiah Pratt. 8 vols. London: Religious Tract Society, 1877.

Gesta Romanorum: Or Entertaining Moral Stories. Trans. Rev. Charles Swan. Rev. Wynnard Hooper. London, 1894. Reprint, New York: AMS Press, 1970.

Gower, John. *The Complete Works of John Gower.* Ed. G. C. Macaulay. 4 vols. Oxford: Clarendon Press, 1899–1902.

———. *The English Works of John Gower.* Ed. G. C. Macaulay. 2 vols. EETS, e.s., 81, 82. London: Kegan Paul, 1900–1901.

———. *Mirour de l'Omme.* Trans. William Burton Wilson. East Lansing, MI: Colleagues Press, 1992.

———. *Confessio Amantis.* Vol. 1. Ed. Russell A. Peck. Trans. Andrew Galloway. Kalamazoo, MI: Medieval Institute Publications, 2000.

Higden, R. *Polychronicon Ranulphi Higden.* Ed. Churchill Babington and Joseph Rawson Lumby. Trans. John Trevisa. 9 vols. London: Longman, 1865–86.

Hoccleve, Thomas. *Selections from Hoccleve.* Ed. M. C. Seymour. Oxford: Clarendon Press, 1981.

———. *Thomas Hoccleve: The Regiment of Princes.* Ed. Charles R. Blyth. Kalamazoo: Medieval Institute Publications, Western Michigan University, 1999.

The Holy Bible . . . Made from the Latin Vulgate by John Wycliffe and His Followers. Ed. Josiah Forshall and Frederic Madden. 4 vols. Oxford: Oxford University Press, 1850.

The Holy Bible, Translated from the Latin Vulgate. Douay-Rheims. Baltimore: John Murphy, 1899.

Jacob's Well. Ed. Arthur Brandeis. EETS, o.s., 115. London: K. Paul, Trench, Trübner, 1900.

John of Salisbury. *Policraticus: Of the Frivolities of Courtiers and the Footprints of Philosophers.* Ed. and trans. Cary J. Nederman. Cambridge: Cambridge University Press, 1990.

Julian of Norwich. *The Shewings of Julian of Norwich.* Ed. Georgia Ronan Crampton. Kalamazoo, MI: Medieval Institute Publications, 1994.

Kempe, Margery. *The Book of Margery Kempe.* Ed. Sanford Brown Meech and Hope Emily Allen. EETS, o.s., 212. London: Oxford University Press, 1940. Reprint, Woodbridge, Suffolk: Boydell and Brewer, 1997.

Langland, William. *Piers Plowman: The B-Version.* Ed. George Kane and E. Talbot Donaldson. London: Athlone Press, 1975.

———. *The Vision of Piers Plowman: The B Text.* Ed. A. V. C. Schmidt. London: Dent, 1978.

———. *Will's Vision of Piers Plowman.* Trans. E. Talbot Donaldson. Ed. Elizabeth D. Kirk and Judith H. Anderson. New York: Norton, 1989.

The Lay Folks' Catechism. Ed. T. F. Simmons and H. E. Nolloth. EETS, o.s., 118. London: Kegan Paul, Trench, Trübner, 1901.

Love, Nicholas. *Nicholas Love's Mirror of the Blessed Life of Jesus Christ.* Ed. Michael G. Sargent. New York: Garland, 1992.

Mannyng, Robert. *Handlyng Synne.* Ed. Idelle Sullens. Binghamton, NY: Medieval and Renaissance Texts and Studies, 1983.

Medieval Literary Theory and Criticism, c. 1100–c. 1375: The Commentary Tradition. Ed. A. J. Minnis and A. B. Scott. Oxford: Clarendon Press, 1988.

Middle English Dictionary. Ed. Hans Kurath and Sherman M. Kuhn. Ann Arbor: University of Michigan Press, 1952–.

Middle English Sermons. Ed. Woodburn O. Ross. EETS, o.s., 209. London: Oxford University Press, 1960.

Mirk, John. *Instructions for Parish Priests.* Ed. Edward Peacock. EETS, o.s., 31. London: K. Paul, Trench, Trübner, 1868.

———. *Mirk's Festial.* Ed. Theodor Erbe. EETS, e.s., 96. London: K. Paul, Trench, Trübner, 1905.

The Pistel of Swete Susan. In *Heroic Women from the Old Testament in Middle English Verse.* Ed. Russell A. Peck. Kalamazoo, MI: Medieval Institute Publications, 1991.

Raymond of Pennaforte. *Summa Sancti Raymundi de Peniafort.* Rome, 1603. Reprint, Farnsborough, Hants.: Gregg Press, 1967.

Select English Works of John Wyclif. Ed. Thomas Arnold. 3 vols. Oxford: Clarendon Press, 1869–71.

Selections from English Wycliffite Writings. Ed. Anne Hudson. Cambridge: Cambridge University Press, 1978. Reprint, Toronto: University of Toronto Press, 1997.

Speculum Sacerdotale. Ed. Edward H. Weatherly. EETS, o.s., 200. London: Oxford University Press, 1936.

The Statutes of the Realm. 11 vols. London, 1810–28. Reprint, London: Dawsons, 1963.

Susannah: An Alliterative Poem of the Fourteenth Century. Ed. Alice Miskimin. New Haven: Yale University Press, 1969.

Thomas of Chobham. *Thomae de Chobham Summa Confessorum.* Ed. F. Broomfield. Louvain: Nauwelaerts, 1968.

Three Middle English Sermons from the Worcester Chapter Manuscript F.10. Ed. D. M. Grisdale. Leeds: Titus Wilson of Kendal, 1939.

"The Trial of Richard Wyche." Ed. F. D. Matthew. *English Historical Review* 5 (1890): 530–44.

Two Wycliffite Texts. Ed. Anne Hudson, EETS, o.s., 301. Oxford: Oxford University Press, 1993.

Wyclif, John. *Sermones.* Ed. Johann Loserth. 4 vols. London: Wyclif Society, 1887–90.

Secondary Sources

Adams, Robert. "Langland's Theology." In *A Companion to Piers Plowman,* ed. John A. Alford, 87–114. Berkeley: University of California Press, 1988.

Aers, David. *Piers Plowman and Christian Allegory.* London: Edward Arnold, 1975.

———. *Chaucer, Langland and the Creative Imagination*. London: Routledge, 1980.

———. "A Whisper in the Ear of Early Modernists; or, Reflections on Literary Critics Writing the 'History of the Subject.'" In *Culture and History, 1350–1600: Essays on English Communities, Identities, and Writing*, ed. David Aers, 177–202. Detroit: Wayne State University Press, 1992.

———. "Reflections on Gower as '*Sapiens* in Ethics and Politics.'" In *Re-visioning John Gower*, ed. Robert F. Yeager, 185–201. Asheville, NC: Pegasus Press, 1998.

———. *Faith, Ethics, and Church: Writing in England, 1360–1409*. Rochester, NY: Boydell and Brewer, 1999.

Aers, David, and Lynn Staley. *Powers of the Holy: Religion, Politics, and Gender in Late Medieval English Culture*. University Park: Pennsylvania State University Press, 1996.

Alford, John A., ed. *A Companion to Piers Plowman*. Berkeley: University of California Press, 1988.

Allen, Judson Boyce. "The Old Way and the Parson's Way: An Ironic Reading of the Parson's Tale." *Journal of Medieval and Renaissance Studies* 3 (1973): 255–71.

Althusser, Louis. "Ideological State Apparatuses." In *Lenin and Philosophy and Other Essays*, 127–86. Trans. Ben Brewster. New York: Monthly Review Press, 1971.

Aster, Friedrich. *Das Verhältniss des Altenglischen Gedichtes "De Regimine Principum" von Thomas Hoccleve zu seinen Quellen*. Leipzig: Oskar Peters, 1888.

Aston, Margaret. "'Caim's Castles': Poverty, Politics, and Disendowment." In *The Church, Politics, and Patronage in the Fifteenth Century*, ed. R. B. Dobson. Gloucester: A. Sutton, 1984.

———. *Lollards and Reformers: Images and Literacy in Late Medieval Religion*. London: Hambledon Press, 1984.

Baker, Denise. "The Priesthood of Genius: A Study of the Medieval Tradition." *Speculum* 51 (1976): 277–91.

Beckwith, Sarah. *Christ's Body: Identity, Culture, and Society in Late Medieval Writings*. London: Routledge, 1993.

Benveniste, Emile. *Problems in General Linguistics*. Trans. Mary Elizabeth Meek. Coral Gables, FL: University of Miami Press, 1971.

Bloomfield, Morton. *The Seven Deadly Sins: An Introduction to the History of a Religious Concept with Special Reference to Medieval English Literature*. East Lansing: Michigan State College Press, 1952.

Blyth, Charles R. "Thomas Hoccleve's Other Master." *Mediaevalia* 16 (1993): 349–59.

Bossy, John. "The Social History of Confession in the Age of the Reformation." *Transactions of the Royal Historical Society*, 5th ser., 25 (1975): 21–38.

Boyle, Leonard. "The *Oculis Sacerdotis* of William of Pagula." *Transactions of the Royal Historical Society*, 5th ser., 5 (1955): 81–110.

———. "The Summa for Confessors as a Genre and Its Religious Intent." In *The Pursuit of Holiness in Late Medieval and Renaissance Religion*, ed. Charles Trinkaus and Heiko Oberman, 126–30. Leiden: Brill, 1974.

————. "The Fourth Lateran Council and Manuals of Popular Theology." In *The Popular Literature of Medieval England*, ed. Thomas Heffernan, 30–43. Knoxville: University of Tennessee Press, 1985.

Braswell, Mary Flowers. *The Medieval Sinner: Characterization and Confession in the Literature of the English Middle Ages.* East Brunswick, NJ: Fairleigh Dickinson University Press, 1983.

Brooks, Peter. *Troubling Confessions: Speaking Guilt in Law and Literature.* Chicago: University of Chicago Press, 2000.

Brown, D. Catherine. *Pastor and Laity in the Theology of Jean Gerson.* Cambridge: Cambridge University Press, 1987.

Burrow, John. "The Action of Langland's Second Vision." *Essays in Criticism* 15 (1965): 247–68.

————. *Ricardian Poetry: Chaucer, Gower, Langland, and the Gawain Poet.* New Haven: Yale University Press, 1971.

————. "Autobiographical Poetry in the Middle Ages: The Case of Thomas Hoccleve." *Proceedings of the British Academy* 68 (1982): 389–412.

Cole, Andrew. "William Langland and the Invention of Lollardy." In *Lollards and Their Influence in Late Medieval England*, ed. Fiona Somerset, Jill C. Havens, and Derrick G. Pitard, 37–58. Woodbridge, Suffolk: Boydell Press, 2003.

Copeland, Rita. *Rhetoric, Hermeneutics, and Translation in the Middle Ages: Academic Traditions and Vernacular Texts.* Cambridge: Cambridge University Press, 1991.

————. "William Thorpe and His Lollard Community: Intellectual Labor and the Representation of Dissent." In *Bodies and Disciplines: Intersections of Literature and History in Fifteenth Century England*, ed. Barbara Hanawalt and David Wallace, 199–221. Minneapolis: University of Minnesota Press, 1996.

————. "Childhood, Pedagogy, and the Literal Sense: From Late Antiquity to the Lollard Heretical Classroom." *New Medieval Literatures* 1 (1997): 125–56.

————. *Pedagogy, Intellectuals, and Dissent in the Later Middle Ages: Lollardy and Ideas of Learning.* Cambridge: Cambridge University Press, 2001.

Dinshaw, Carolyn. *Getting Medieval: Sexualities and Communities Pre and Postmodern.* Durham, NC: Duke University Press, 1999.

Duffy, Eamon. *The Stripping of the Altars: Traditional Religion in England, c. 1400–c. 1580.* New Haven: Yale University Press, 1992.

Eagleton, Terry. *Criticism and Ideology: A Study in Marxist Literary Theory.* London: Verso, 1978.

————. *Ideology: An Introduction.* London: Verso, 1991.

Ferster, Judith. *Fictions of Advice: The Literature and Politics of Counsel in Late Medieval England.* Philadelphia: University of Pennsylvania Press, 1996.

Fines, John. "William Thorpe: An Early Lollard." *History Today* 18 (1968): 495–503.

Finlayson, John. "The Satiric Mode and the Parson's Tale." *Chaucer Review* 6 (1971): 94–116.

Fisher, John. *John Gower: Moral Philosopher and Friend of Chaucer.* New York: New York University Press, 1964.

Fletcher, Alan J. "John Mirk and the Lollards." *Medium Aevum* 56 (1987): 216–24.

Foucault, Michel. *The History of Sexuality.* Vol. 1. Trans. Robert Hurley. New York: Vintage Books, 1978.

———. "Technologies of the Self." In *Ethics: Subjectivity and Truth,* ed. Paul Rabinow, trans. Robert Hurley and others, 223–51, vol. 1 of *The Essential Works of Michel Foucault, 1954–1984.* New York: New Press, 1997.

Frantzen, Allen. *The Literature of Penance in Anglo-Saxon England.* New Brunswick, NJ: Rutgers University Press, 1983.

Frei, Hans. *The Eclipse of Biblical Narrative: A Study of Eighteenth and Nineteenth Century Hermeneutics.* New Haven: Yale University Press, 1974.

Freud, Sigmund. *The Ego and the Id.* Trans. Joan Riviere. Ed. James Strachey. Introd. Peter Gay. London: Hogarth Press, 1962. Reprint, New York: Norton, 1989.

Fuss, Diana. *Identification Papers.* New York: Routledge Press, 1995.

Gallacher, Patrick J. *Love, the Word, and Mercury: A Reading of John Gower's Confessio Amantis.* Albuquerque: University of New Mexico Press, 1975.

Gelley, Alexander, ed. *Unruly Examples: On the Rhetoric of Exemplarity.* Stanford: Stanford University Press, 1995.

Ghosh, Kantik. "Eliding the Interpreter: John Wyclif and Scriptural Truth." *New Medieval Literatures* 2 (1998): 205–24.

———. *The Wycliffite Heresy: Authority and the Interpretation of Texts.* Cambridge: Cambridge University Press, 2002.

Gillespie, Vincent. "Vernacular Books of Religion." In *Book Production and Publishing in Britain, 1375–1475,* ed. Jeremy Griffiths and Derek Pearsall, 317–44. Cambridge: Cambridge University Press, 1989.

Gradon, Pamela. "Langland and the Ideology of Dissent." *Proceedings of the British Academy* 66 (1980): 179–205.

Greenblatt, Stephen. *Renaissance Self-Fashioning: From More to Shakespeare.* Chicago: University of Chicago Press, 1980.

Hanna, Ralph. "The Difficulty of Ricardian Prose Translation: The Case of the Lollards." *Modern Language Quarterly* 51 (1990): 319–40.

Hartung, Albert. "The *Parson's Tale* and Chaucer's Penance." In *Literature and Religion in the Later Middle Ages: Philological Studies in Honor of Siegried Wenzel,* ed. Richard G. Newhauser and John A. Alford, 61–80. Binghamton, NY: Center for Medieval and Early Renaissance Studies, 1995.

Hasler, Antony J. "Hoccleve's Unregimented Body." *Paragraph* 13 (1990): 164–83.

Hauerwas, Stanley, and L. Gregory Jones, eds. *Why Narrative? Readings in Narrative Theology.* Grand Rapids, MI: William B. Eerdmans, 1989.

Hort, Greta. *Piers Plowman and Contemporary Religious Thought.* New York: Macmillan, 1938.

Howard, Donald. *The Idea of the Canterbury Tales.* Berkeley: University of California Press, 1976.

Hudson, Anne. "A Lollard Sect Vocabulary?" In *Lollards and Their Books*, 165–80. London: Hambledon Press, 1985.

———. *The Premature Reformation: Wycliffite Texts and Lollard History*. Oxford: Clarendon Press, 1988.

Hughes, Jonathan. *Pastors and Visionaries: Religion and Secular Life in Late Medieval Yorkshire*. Woodbridge, Suffolk: D. S. Brewer, 1988.

Huppé, Bernard. *A Reading of the Canterbury Tales*. Albany: State University of New York Press, 1964.

Hurley, Michael. "'Scriptura Sola': Wyclif and His Critics." *Traditio* 16 (1960): 275–352.

Jameson, Fredric. "Imaginary and Symbolic in Lacan: Marxism, Psychoanalytic Criticism, and the Problem of the Subject." *Yale French Studies* 55/56 (1977): 338–95.

———. *The Political Unconscious: Narrative as a Socially Symbolic Act*. Ithaca: Cornell University Press, 1981.

Kay, Sarah. *Subjectivity in Troubadour Poetry*. Cambridge: Cambridge University Press, 1990.

Kinneavy, Gerald. "Gower's *Confessio Amantis* and the Penitentials." *Chaucer Review* 19 (1984): 144–61.

Kirk, Elizabeth. *The Dream-Thought of Piers Plowman*. New Haven: Yale University Press, 1972.

Knapp, Ethan. *The Bureaucratic Muse: Thomas Hoccleve and the Literature of Late Medieval England*. University Park: Pennsylvania State University Press, 2001.

Lacan, Jacques. "The Mirror Stage as Formative of the Function of the I as Revealed in Psychoanalytic Experience." In *Écrits: A Selection*, 1–7. Trans. Alan Sheridan. New York: Norton, 1977.

Lawton, David. "Chaucer's Two Ways: The Pilgrimage Frame of the *Canterbury Tales*." *Studies in the Age of Chaucer* 9 (1987): 3–40.

LeGoff, Jacques. *Time, Work, and Culture in the Middle Ages*. Trans. Arthur Goldhammer. Chicago: University of Chicago Press, 1980.

Leicester, H. Marshall. "'Synne Horrible': The Pardoner's Exegesis of His Tale and Chaucer's." In *Acts of Interpretation: The Text in Its Contexts, 700–1600: Essays on Medieval and Renaissance Literature in Honor of E. Talbot Donaldson*, ed. Mary Carruthers and Elizabeth D. Kirk, 25–50. Norman, OK: Pilgrim Books, 1982.

———. *The Disenchanted Self: Representing the Subject in the Canterbury Tales*. Berkeley: University of California Press, 1990.

Liddell, Mark H. "A New Source of the Parson's Tale." In *An English Miscellany Presented to Dr. Furnivall*, 255–77. Oxford: Clarendon, 1901.

Lochrie, Karma. *Covert Operations: The Medieval Uses of Secrecy*. Philadelphia: University of Pennsylvania Press, 1999.

Loomis, R. S. "Was Chaucer a Laodicean?" In *Chaucer Criticism: An Anthology*, 2 vols., ed. Richard J. Schoeck and Jerome Taylor, 1:291–310. Notre Dame, IN: University of Notre Dame Press, 1960.

Lubac, Henri de. *L'éxegése médiéval: Les quatre sens de l'ecriture.* 4 vols. Paris: Aubier, 1959–64.

MacIntyre, Alasdair. *After Virtue: A Study in Moral Theory.* Notre Dame, IN: University of Notre Dame Press, 1981.

Mann, Jill. *Chaucer and Medieval Estates Satire.* Cambridge: Cambridge University Press, 1973.

McFarlane, K. B. *John Wycliffe and the Beginnings of English Nonconformity.* New York, Macmillan, 1953.

———. *Lancastrian Kings and Lollard Knights.* Oxford: Clarendon Press, 1972.

McNiven, Peter. *Heresy and Politics in the Reign of Henry IV: The Burning of John Badby.* Woodbridge, Suffolk: Boydell Press, 1987.

Medcalf, Stephen. "Inner and Outer." In *The Later Middle Ages,* 123–40. New York: Holmes and Meier, 1981.

Minnis, A. J. "'Authorial Intention' and 'Literal Sense' in the Exegetical Theories of Richard Fitzralph and John Wyclif: An Essay in the Medieval History of Biblical Hermeneutics." *Proceedings of the Royal Irish Academy* 75, no. 1 (1975): 1–30.

———. "John Gower, *Sapiens* in Ethics and Politics." *Medium Aevum* 49 (1980): 207–29.

———. "Moral Gower and Medieval Literary Theory." In *Gower's Confessio Amantis: Responses and Reassessments,* ed. A. J. Minnis, 50–78. Cambridge: D. S. Brewer, 1983.

———, ed. *Gower's Confessio Amantis: Responses and Reassessments.* Cambridge: D. S. Brewer, 1983.

Moore, R. I. *The Formation of a Persecuting Society.* Oxford: Blackwell, 1987.

Mosher, J. A. *The Exemplum in the Early Religious and Didactic Literature of England.* New York: Columbia University Press, 1911.

Murphy, John J. *Rhetoric in the Middle Ages: A History of Rhetorical Theory from St. Augustine to the Renaissance.* Berkeley: University of California Press, 1974.

Nisse, Ruth. "Cobham's Daughter: *The Book of Margery Kempe* and the Power of Heterodox Thinking." *Modern Language Quarterly* 56 (1995): 277–304.

———. "Staged Interpretations: Civic Rhetoric and Lollard Politics in the York Plays." *Journal of Medieval and Early Modern Studies* 28 (1998): 427–73.

———. "'Oure Fadres Olde and Modres': Gender, Heresy, and Hoccleve's Literary Politics." *Studies in the Age of Chaucer* 21 (1999): 279–99.

Oberman, Heiko. *The Harvest of Medieval Theology: Gabriel Biel and Late Medieval Nominalism.* Cambridge: Harvard University Press, 1963.

Olson, Glending. "The End of the *Summoner's Tale* and the Uses of Pentecost." *Studies in the Age of Chaucer* 21 (1999): 209–45.

Olsson, Kurt. "Rhetoric, John Gower, and the Late Medieval Exemplum." *Medievalia et Humanistica* 8 (1977): 185–200.

Owen, Charles A., Jr. "What the Manuscripts Tell Us about the Parson's Tale." *Medium Aevum* 63 (1994): 239–49.

Owst, G. R. *Preaching in Medieval England: An Introduction to Sermon Manuscripts of the Period c. 1350–1450*. Cambridge: Cambridge University Press, 1926.

———. *Literature and Pulpit in Medieval England*. Cambridge: Cambridge University Press, 1933.

Pantin, W. A. *The English Church in the Fourteenth Century*. Cambridge: Cambridge University Press, 1955. Reprint, Toronto: University of Toronto Press, 1980.

Patterson, Lee. "Chaucerian Confession: Penitential Literature and the Pardoner." *Medievalia et Humanistica*, n.s., 7 (1976): 153–73.

———. The *Parson's Tale* and the Quitting of the *Canterbury Tales*." *Traditio* 34 (1978): 331–80.

———. "On the Margin: Postmodernism, Ironic History, and Medieval Studies." *Speculum* 65 (1990): 87–108.

———. *Chaucer and the Subject of History*. Madison: University of Wisconsin Press, 1991.

Payer, Pierre. "Foucault and Penance and the Shaping of Sexuality." *Studies in Religion* 14 (1985): 313–20.

Pearsall, Derek. "Gower's Narrative Art." *PMLA* 81 (1966): 475–84.

———. "Hoccleve's *Regement of Princes*: The Poetics of Royal Self-Representation." *Speculum* 69 (1994): 386–410.

Peck, Russell. *Kingship and Common Profit in Gower's Confessio Amantis*. Carbondale: Southern Illinois University Press, 1978.

Perkins, Nicholas. *Hoccleve's Regiment of Princes: Counsel and Constraint*. Cambridge: D. S. Brewer, 2001.

Petersen, Kate O. *The Sources of the Parson's Tale*. Boston: Ginn, 1901.

Porter, Elizabeth. "Gower's Ethical Microcosm and Political Macrocosm." In *Gower's Confessio Amantis: Responses and Reassessments*, ed. A. J. Minnis, 135–62. Cambridge: D. S. Brewer, 1983.

Rex, Richard. *The Lollards*. London: Palgrave, 2002.

Robertson, D. W., Jr. "The Cultural Tradition of *Handlyng Synne*." *Speculum* 22 (1947): 162–85.

Root, Jerry. *"Space to Speke": The Confessional Subject in Medieval Literature*. New York: Peter Lang, 1997.

Rowland, Beryl. "Sermon and Penitential in the *Parson's Tale* and Their Effect on Style." *Florilegium* 9 (1987): 125–45.

Rubin, Miri. *Corpus Christi: The Eucharist in Late Medieval Culture*. Cambridge: Cambridge University Press, 1991.

Runacres, Charles. "Art and Ethics in the 'Exempla' of the *Confessio Amantis*." In *Gower's Confessio Amantis: Responses and Reassessments*, ed. A. J. Minnis, 106–34. Cambridge: D. S. Brewer, 1983.

Russell, George H. "Poet as Reviser: The Metamorphosis of the Confession of the Seven Deadly Sins in *Piers Plowman*." In *Acts of Interpretation: The Text in Its Contexts, 700–1500: Essays on Medieval and Renaissance Literature in Honor of*

E. Talbot Donaldson, ed. Mary Carruthers and Elizabeth Kirk, 53–65. Norman, OK: Pilgrim Books, 1982.

Salter, Elizabeth. *Nicholas Love's "Myrrour of the Blessed Lyf of Jesu Christ."* Analecta Cartusiana 10. Salzburg: Institut für Englische Sprache und Literatur, Universität Salzburg, 1974.

Scanlon, Larry. *Narrative, Authority and Power: The Medieval Exemplum and the Chaucerian Tradition.* Cambridge: Cambridge University Press, 1994.

Scase, Wendy. *Piers Plowman and the New Anticlericalism.* Cambridge: Cambridge University Press, 1989.

———."'Heu! Quanta desolatio Angliae praestatur': A Wycliffite Libel and the Naming of Heretics, Oxford 1382." In *Lollards and Their Influence in Late Medieval England,* ed. Fiona Somerset, Jill C. Havens, and Derrick G. Pitard, 19–36. Woodbridge, Suffolk: Boydell Press, 2003.

Silverman, Kaja. *The Subject of Semiotics.* New York: Oxford University Press, 1983.

Simon, Hugo. "Chaucer a Wicliffite: An Essay on Chaucer's Parson and Parson's Tale." *Essays on Chaucer, His Words and Works,* pt. III, ed. Chaucer Society, 227–92. London: N. Trübner, 1876.

Simpson, James. *Piers Plowman: An Introduction to the B-Text.* London: Longman, 1992.

———. *Sciences and the Self in Medieval Poetry.* Cambridge: Cambridge University Press, 1995.

———. *The Oxford English Literary History.* Vol. 2. *1350–1547: Reform and Cultural Revolution.* Oxford: Oxford University Press, 2002.

Smalley, Beryl. *The Study of the Bible in the Middle Ages.* 2nd ed. Oxford: Basil Blackwell, 1952.

Somerset, Fiona. *Clerical Discourse and Lay Audience in Late Medieval England.* Cambridge: Cambridge University Press, 1998.

———. "'As Just as Is a Squyre': The Politics of 'Lewed Translacion' in Chaucer's *Summoner's Tale.*" *Studies in the Age of Chaucer* 21 (1999): 187–207.

Spearing, A. C. *Criticism and Medieval Poetry.* New York: Barnes and Noble, 1972.

Spencer, H. Leith. *English Preaching in the Late Middle Ages.* Oxford: Clarendon Press, 1993.

Strohm, Paul. "Form and Social Statement in *Confessio Amantis* and *The Canterbury Tales.*" *Studies in the Age of Chaucer* 1 (1979): 17–40.

———. "Chaucer's Lollard Joke: History and the Textual Unconscious." *Studies in the Age of Chaucer* 17 (1995): 23–42.

———. *England's Empty Throne: Usurpation and the Language of Legitimation, 1399–1422.* New Haven: Yale University Press, 1998.

Swanson, R. N. *Religion and Devotion in Europe, c.1215–c.1515.* Cambridge: Cambridge University Press, 1995.

Szittya, Penn R. *The Antifraternal Tradition in Medieval Literature.* Princeton: Princeton University Press, 1986.

Tentler, Thomas N. *Sin and Confession on the Eve of the Reformation*. Princeton: Princeton University Press, 1977.

Vaughan, Míceál F. "The Invention of the *Parson's Tale*." In *Rewriting Chaucer: Culture, Authority, and the Idea of the Authentic Text, 1400–1602*, ed. Thomas A. Prendergast and Barbara Kline, 45–90. Columbus: Ohio State University Press, 1999.

von Nolcken, Christina. "A 'Certain Sameness' and Our Response to It in English Wycliffite Texts." In *Literature and Religion in the Later Middle Ages: Philological Studies in Honor of Siegfried Wenzel*, ed. Richard G. Newhauser and John A. Alford, 191–208. Binghamton, NY: Center for Medieval and Early Renaissance Studies, 1995.

———. "Richard Wyche, a Certain Knight, and the Beginning of the End." In *Lollardy and the Gentry in the Later Middle Ages*, ed. Margaret Aston and Colin Richmond, 127–54. New York: St. Martin's Press, 1997.

Vooght, Paul de. *Les sources de la doctrine chrétienne d'après les théologiens du XIVe siècle et du début du Xve*. Bruges: Desclée, De Brouwer, 1954.

Wailes, Stephen L. *Medieval Allegories of Jesus' Parables*. Berkeley: University of California Press, 1987.

Watson, Nicholas. "Censorship and Cultural Change in Late-Medieval England: Vernacular Theology, the Oxford Translation Debate, and Arundel's Constitutions of 1409." *Speculum* 70 (1995): 822–64.

———. "Conceptions of the Word: The Mother Tongue and the Incarnation of God." *New Medieval Literatures* 1 (1997): 85–124.

Welter, J. T. *L'exemplum dans la littérature religieuse et didactique du moyen âge*. Paris: Occitania, 1927.

Wenzel, Siegfried. "The Sources for the 'Remedia' of the Parson's Tale." *Traditio* 27 (1971): 433–54.

———. "Medieval Sermons." In *A Companion to Piers Plowman*, ed. John A. Alford, 155–72. Berkeley: University of California Press, 1988.

Wetherbee, Winthrop. "Genius and Interpretation in the *Confessio Amantis*." In *Magister Regis: Studies in Honor of Robert Earl Kaske*, ed. Arthur Groos, 241–60. New York: Fordham University Press, 1986.

Wilks, Michael. "Wyclif and the Great Persecution." In *Prophecy and Eschatology*, ed. Michael Wilks, 39–63. Oxford: Blackwell, 1994.

Woods, Marjorie Curry, and Rita Copeland. "Classroom and Confession." In *The Cambridge History of Medieval English Literature*, ed. David Wallace, 376–406. Cambridge: Cambridge University Press, 1999.

Wurtele, Douglas J. "The Anti-Lollardry of Chaucer's Parson." *Mediaevalia* 11 (1985): 151–68.

Yeager, Robert F. *John Gower's Poetic: The Search for a New Arion*. Cambridge: D. S. Brewer, 1990.

Žižek, Slavoj. *The Sublime Object of Ideology*. London: Verso, 1989.

Index

KATHERINE C. LITTLE

is assistant professor of English at Fordham University.